Meditations/Now

Meditations/Now

by
Leslie F. Brandt

with art by
Corita Kent

Publishing House
St. Louis

Originally published as *Meditations on a Loving God: Daily Readings Through the Church Year*, © 1983 Concordia Publishing House, St. Louis, MO.

Unless otherwise noted, the Scripture quotations in this publication are from the Revised Standard Version of the Bible, copyrighted 1946, 1952, © 1971, 1973, by the Division of Christian Education of the National Council of the Churches of Christ in the U.S.A., and are used by permission.

Scripture quotations marked NEB are from THE NEW ENGLISH BIBLE (NEB) © The Delegates of The Oxford University Press and the Syndics of the Cambridge University Press, 1961, 1970, and are used by permission.

Scripture quotations marked TEV are from the Good News Bible, the Bible in TODAY'S ENGLISH VERSION. Copyright © American Bible Society 1966, 1971, 1976. Used by permission.

Copyright © 1983, 1990 Concordia Publishing House
3558 S. Jefferson Avenue, St. Louis, MO 63118-3968
Manufactured in the United States of America

Library of Congress Cataloging-in-Publication Data

Brandt, Leslie F.
     Meditations/now/Leslie F. Brandt.—Rev. ed.
         p.   cm.
     Rev. ed. of: Meditations on a loving God.
     ISBN 0-570-04251-8—ISBN 0-570-04540-1 (pbk.)
     1. Church year meditations: I. Brandt, Leslie F. Meditations on a loving God. II. Title.
     BV30.B66   1990
     242'.2—dc20   89-49186

---

1 2 3 4 5 6 7 8 9 10   99 98 97 96 95 94 93 92 91 90

To my wife, Edith,
who lovingly rounds off some of the rough edges
of both the author and his writings, and with whom
he, enduring and rejoicing,
has shared life for almost half a century.

Preface

The meditations in this volume are designed for Christ's followers, high-school age and above, who sincerely want to be His disciples in our kind of world.

These meditations were previously written and arranged for the three-year lectionary readings which follow the church year. At the request of the publishers, I have now revised and rearranged them according to the calendar. They begin with January 1 and conclude with December 31. In addition, this present volume includes prayers following each day-by-day meditation.

If these daily meditations are to be meaningful, they must be read in conjunction with the reading of the Scripture portion to which each meditation is assigned. Read the Scripture; meditate with me; conclude with prayer (preferably your own); and have a blessed day!

Leslie F. Brandt

We Are God's Children

When the time had fully come, God sent forth His Son. v. 4a

The time has come. The long-promised Messiah has arrived. Redemption has taken place. God's salvation is available. We are now the sons and daughters of God.

It is difficult to believe—to keep on believing—in this astounding intervention and activity of God, but it is true! We have been restored to the family of God. It began with Christmas; it culminated in the cross and the Resurrection. "Beloved, we are God's children now . . .," wrote John (1 John 3:2). And to make this amazing fact an everlasting conviction in the lives of true believers, "God has sent the Spirit of His son into our hearts . . ."

If we had to rely on our worth or status or any ability of ours to make this come to pass, it would never happen. But it is God's doing. He came to us. He adopted us. We have within us the very Spirit of Christ.

God forbid that this incredible restoration to Himself should ever become commonplace or mundane. May it always be exciting, enriching, renewing, and result in a joyful abandonment of all that we are and have to God and His eternal purposes.

It is so profound, and almost unbelievable, the consequences of the Christmas event in my life! But I do believe, O God, by Your grace, and I begin this new year by celebrating this cosmic event and its glorious consequences for my life and the lives of all who embrace and follow You as revealed through the Christ of Christmas. Amen.

The Christmas Aftermath

For mine eyes have seen Thy salvation. v. 30

There should, of course, be a Christmas aftermath, but it should *not* be one of depression, apathy, or inactivity. There was no Christmas letdown for Simeon or a prophetess named Anna. Simeon, on seeing the baby Jesus, exploded in a beautiful song of praise. He knew that something vastly significant happened in the birth of the Christ Child. Anna, the prophetess, turned from praying to praising after seeing this little one who was to be the Redemption of Israel. Armed with new confidence and courage, our visit to the Bethlehem manger should resolve into spiritual progress and growth in our lives. We have once more seen and commemorated the birthday of our King. We heard the thrilling message in word and song, visualized it in symbol and pageantry, felt it in the spirit of Christmas about us. "Lord, now lettest Thou Thy servant depart in peace, according to Thy Word," prayed Simeon, "for mine eyes have seen Thy salvation." This was not a cry of defeat; it was an exuberant song of victory. He had met the Christmas Christ. Now he was ready for the aftermath—whatever it might be.

We may live between a rock and a hard place. The painful circumstances that surround us may at times be more than we can bear. There may be hours of physical pain, of economic need, of loneliness and frustration. There may be deep, hidden weaknesses or conflicts that we must continually confront and cannot always overcome. But whatever the circumstances before us or the uncertainties about us, the designed aftermath of Christmas and the challenge of the New Year is that we, empowered by divine grace, be the children and ministers of God right where we are.

Loving God, because You have come to me through the Christ of Christmas, enable me now to face the New Year with renewed joy and commitment as Your child and servant. Amen.

God's Intervention

Now . . . an angel of the Lord appeared . . . and said, "Rise, take the Child and His mother, and flee to Egypt. . . ." v. 13

It is a beautiful story—God's care and concern for His Son, the Christ Child. It was His miraculous intervention and guidance that spared the child the terrible fate that was not spared scores of other babies that died at the cruel hands of Herod and his reaction to the birth of Jesus.

It raises some agonizing questions. Where was God during the Holocaust when millions of human beings were slaughtered, or when almost a thousand died by their own hands at the command of a demented cult leader in the jungle of Guyana? Where was God when we yielded to temptation and had to suffer the consequences, or when through no fault of our own, we had to traverse the dark corridors of pain and suffering?

It appears at times that God's power is limited in respect to the calamities and atrocities that fall upon our world and affect our lives, that it isn't His policy to intervene and come between His children and the ugly things that often happen to them, that He chose powerlessness in order that He may grant to us the power to choose. And yet He did intervene in the circumstances of the Christ Child—leading His parents to bring Him to Nazareth where He "increased in wisdom and in stature, and in favor with God and man" (Luke 2:52). He did intervene in this world's hell-bent course when He came to this planet through the Christ. And this is what Christmas is all about—God's great and splendid intervention in the lives and affairs of people on this world.

I thank You, O God, that while You do not come between me and all the pains and problems of my life, You are with me and will face with me the difficult and dark days along the journey of faith. Amen.

Response to Christ's Coming

Put on then, as God's chosen ones . . . compassion, kindness, low-liness, meekness, and patience. v. 12

We have been redeemed and adopted as the very children of God; we *are* His beloved children now. In response to His redemption and our adoption and the gift of the Holy Spirit, we are empowered and expected to reflect the qualities and attributes of the family of God.

It doesn't come naturally. The mind and body of mortal man and woman are still earthbound and subject to temptations that are difficult to resist. A total dedication to God and His purposes and a determination to live as He would have us live are necessary in the daily struggle to allow the Spirit to work in and through us the attributes and objectives of the heavenly Father.

Above all is the high goal and challenge of loving. It is because of God's love that we are His children forever. It is by means of His love through us that others about us may be introduced to His saving grace. This, therefore, must be our response to the events of Christmas, Good Friday, and Easter. Having embraced His saving love, we are to love others even as Christ loved us. The word of Christ and the Word who is Christ dwell within us and are revealed through us. We, the children, are to become more and more like the Parent. God provides the grace and enablement to do this. We must provide the fertile field in which His sown seeds may bring forth fruit.

You have taken me into Your family, my loving Father and God. As I strive by Your grace to follow You as You are revealed through the Christmas Christ, grant that I may walk and work as Your child reflecting and communicating Your eternal love to people about me. Amen.

The Matter of Priorities

Did you not know that I must be in My Father's house? v. 49b

We might conjecture whether or not the boy Jesus was fully aware of His divinity as the very Son of God. His parents soon realized that He was someone special. The teachers at the temple were astounded at His youthful wisdom and insights concerning the revered writings of the prophets and the hand of God in the history of His people. When Jesus responded to His parents' inquiry as to the reason for His remaining at the temple when they returned to their home, they were surprised at His reference to the temple as "[His] Father's house." His mother appears to have recognized some significance in this episode in the life of her son.

It is obvious, whatever Jesus' comprehension of His identity and eventual ministry at this point, that God and His purposes were more important to Him than anything else. Even at a very early age, He had His priorities in order. He began even then a life of commitment and dedication to His God and Father, a life that was to be of greater value and significance to His world and our world than that of any other human being from the beginning of time until now.

What are our priorities, our values, our lifestyles? Whatever they are, they will never be what they ought to be unless we begin to see the importance of our "Father's house" and commit ourselves to God and His purposes for our lives.

I resolve at the beginning of this new year, my Lord, to make You and Your purposes my goal and objective. I claim even now Your grace and seek daily Your strength to make this possible. Amen.

He Is Our Brother

I will proclaim Thy name to my brethren. v. 12a

It happened on that first Christmas. We could not come to God, so He came to us through Jesus Christ—identifying Himself with our earthbound natures—in order that He might take upon Himself the consequences of our sins and release us forever from their bondage. This makes us the brothers and sisters of Jesus Christ, God's Son, and therefore the children of the heavenly Father.

I can't comprehend it; I can only accept it and rejoice in it. He is my Lord; He is also my Brother. As my Brother He identifies with me in my human weaknesses, shares with me my sorrows and conflicts, helps me with life's heavy burdens, and through His Spirit, accompanies me through the dry, heat-stricken deserts, as well as over the green hills and snowcapped mountains of my day-by-day existence.

He is with each of us today—Jesus, our Lord, our Brother. Thus we can push forward without fear, knowing that He cares about us and will help us to confront and overcome whatever obstacles lie in the sometimes torturous course that stretches out ahead.

I rejoice, my Lord, that You truly are my Brother, and will accompany me on the journey of faith before me. Keep me from lagging behind or looking back when that road becomes dark and difficult. Amen.

Turn . . . Turn . . . Turn

Turn to Me and be saved . . . for I am God, and there is no other.
v. 22

"Turn to Me and be saved," is God's word through the prophet. "To Me every knee shall bow . . ." Turning toward God, His life and purposes, is what repentance is all about.

I have discovered that such "turning" does not end with my initial embrace of faith that assured me of God's saving grace and His gift of everlasting life. While I need not, and must not, grovel in and struggle with the guilt of past sins and errors from which I have been forgiven, I need again and again to turn from the temptations that harass, from self-centeredness and the self-serving instincts that cause me to stumble, and face up to God's love and purposes.

We are God's children and servants, and yet each day offers the opportunity and very often the necessity of turning toward Him. This includes, as well, renewal and recommitment to what God wants us to be and to do as His beloved and appointed ministers in our world today.

We need not worry about falling from God's grace today—any more than an adopted child of loving parents need worry about his/her daily status in the human family. We do need to place ourselves at God's disposal day-by-day—to "turn" toward His love and grace and His assignments for us in our broken world.

My loving God, while Your grace is unlimited and never-ending, I do need each day the determination and the strength to keep my life and my heart open to Your love and grace. I joyfully lay claim to Your assurance of my salvation as I face this new year before me. Amen.

The Power to Become Persons

To all who received Him . . . He gave power to become children of God. v. 12

By all appearances, the common denominator of life today is not goodness or beauty or truth, but power. Man and woman's primary quest, in spite of our ideals, is not the quest for peace of mind; it is the reach for power—probably with the assumption that this will bring peace of mind.

One of the significant contributions of Christmas is that it celebrates the gift of true power and points the way to its creative, life-giving use in our disjointed world. "He came to His own home," wrote John, "and His own people received Him not. But to all who received Him, who believed in His name, He gave *power* to become children of God." The key to happy, creative, life-giving, authentic power for this life and the life to come is God's gift of power—the power to become the children of God, sons and daughters of the heavenly Father—the power to become persons.

The Christmas event declares once and for all that identity and personhood was restored to the fractured, failure-fraught creatures of this earth by God Himself when He, in the Person of His Son, broke through into our world of sin, our dimension of humanity, by becoming one of us, identifying Himself with our sin-ridden natures, and paying the supreme penalty in our stead, in order that He might restore us to God's life and purposes once more. He thereby offered to His creatures, lost and estranged, the power to become His sons and daughters through faith in Him, the power to be reunited with His family, reconciled to His kingdom. Our great God is the giver of many gifts, but the greatest gift of all is the gift of personhood and identity. This was God's Christmas gift to each of us.

I thank You, gracious Father, for restoring my identity and personhood through the gift of Your Son, Jesus Christ. You have accepted me as Your child and granted me Your righteousness, and I am Yours forever. Amen.

The Wealth of a Christian

*Blessed be the God and Father of our Lord Jesus Christ, who has
blessed us in Christ with every spiritual blessing . . . v. 3*

Truly, we have much to celebrate as the sons and daughters of
God. We have, through this Christ who came at Christmas, become
the recipients of God's whole treasure house of spiritual gifts. Even
before man and woman and the world itself were created, we were
destined to be His children.

Christ's death on the cross set us free from the Law's demands.
All charges against us were blotted out. Our sins were forgiven.
Reconciled to the divine family, we are now an integral part of
God's plan to reconcile the whole world to Himself. It is not
something we can comprehend, but God created us and chose us to
be His people, and this was God's purpose and plan from the very
beginning. It was made known to us and made possible for us
through Jesus Christ. Through this Christ and His indwelling Spirit
the brand of God's ownership was burned indelibly into our hearts.
With the gracious gifts of His Spirit is the guarantee that all of these
gifts, though at present unseen and little understood, are already
ours and will be revealed to us in God's own time.

God grant that His Spirit will break through the numbness of
our small thinking and reveal to us something of who we are and
what we have become through Jesus Christ. He is Lord over all, and
we are His church, His body, the extension of this Christ in this
world to which we are assigned. How immeasurably and infinitely
blessed we are!

Break through the numbness of my small thinking, Lord, and
enable me to see how immeasurably and infinitely blessed I
am. Amen.

They Walked a New Path

They departed to their own country by another way. v. 12

When it is dark enough, one can see the stars. It has been dark enough for us to see the Star again during the Christmas season—a Star pointing to the one remaining hope for ourselves and our faltering world. Wise men from the east were convinced that it would lead to something or someone significant and set out to follow its directing rays.

They met Christ. "And going into the house they saw the child with Mary His mother, and they fell down and worshiped Him." God's Christmas gift to the world, the Lord Jesus Christ, makes available to every person the peace of sin forgiven, the love and acceptance of a righteous God, the promise of life eternal. Whatever the particular star that leads a person to Christ, he or she must individually and personally meet this Christ.

They gave Him gifts. "Then, opening their treasures, they offered Him gifts . . ." We are aware of the high cost of living; we still have much to learn about the high cost of loving. "God so loved the world that He gave His only Son . . ." The meaning of worship—the giving of ourselves to God and to others on God's behalf—ought to be the consequence of Christmas in our lives.

They walked a new path. "They departed to their own country by another way." Their response to this meeting with Christ symbolizes what ought to happen in response to our meeting with Him. If we plunge into the new year continuing to walk in the old paths of selfishness, we indicate that Christmas has done little for us. A new life means a new walk, a new path—and new goals, attitudes, motivations. God grant that we may walk in the paths that Christ sets before us.

Help me, O God, to shun the old paths of shallow and impotent living, and dare to trust and serve You faithfully and obediently as Your child and servant. Amen.

The Baptism of Christ

This is My beloved Son, with whom I am well pleased. v. 17

Jesus, the Sinless One, God's beloved Son, requested and received baptism by water under the hands of John. Whatever it may have meant to Christ, it is most often regarded as His "ordination" into His public ministry. If we had any doubts about the identity of Jesus as God's Son following His manger birth, the event of Christ's baptism accompanied by the special revelation of the Holy Spirit and the voice of God out of heaven should eliminate those doubts once and for all. This is truly the Christ—the Christ who gave Himself unto death for us, the Christ in whose name we were baptized and to whom we have surrendered our lives.

Perhaps the most significant thing about this event is "the Spirit of God descending like a dove" and the voice from heaven saying, "This is My beloved Son, with whom I am well pleased." It is this, along with many further revelations, that ought to assure us that our commitment is valid. He is not simply a remarkable teacher, a radical revolutionary, or a sainted guru to whom we are signing over our lives. He is the Son of God. Other leaders, as gifted and as qualified as they appear to be, may lead us down some primrose path to darkness and emptiness, but not Jesus, God's Son, "with whom [He] is well pleased."

We can follow Christ today, His teachings and example, without fear, and with the conviction that we are thereby within our Creator's design and destiny for our lives.

You have also granted me Your Spirit, my God, and have empowered me for ministry. I pray that I may ever be faithful to that ministry wherever it may take me. Amen.

Jesus Christ—God Revealed

After me comes He who is mightier than I . . . He will baptize you with the Holy Spirit. vv. 7a, 8b

We live in a day of confusion and confoundment. Our world abounds with false shepherds and bizarre cults. There are "messiahs" of all sorts attempting to control the lives of lonely, unhappy people. There are millions of God's human creatures who continue to create God in their own image—or latch on to some false concoction of a divinity that appears to meet their superficial needs. God has come and revealed Himself through Jesus Christ and through this Christ becomes fully incarnate, relating Himself through His Bethlehem birth, and now in His baptism by John the Baptist, with the human family about Him. He did this that men and women might be found by God and restored to His purpose for their lives.

The significance of this event is in its identification of Jesus as the true Messiah—as God revealed. While our baptism in the name and Spirit of Jesus Christ differs considerably from Christ's baptism, it identifies us as the sons and daughters of God-revealed-in-Christ and the very brothers and sisters of this Christ who was baptized by John. Jesus was God's Son before this world was created; He was revealed as such at His baptismal event. It is our baptism into Christ that unites us with and adopts us into the Holy Family and makes us the very children of God.

It is through Christ that we can know the true God. It is in following this Christ that we follow the true Shepherd who embraces us in love and restores us to our Creator and His purposes for our lives.

I truly want to follow You, my Savior and Lord. May I do so with a clear head and a devoted heart whatever I may face along the journey of faith. Amen.

Christ's Baptism and Mine

Jesus also had been baptized . . . and the Holy Spirit descended upon Him . . . vv. 21a, 22a

There is a difference between Christ's baptism and mine. Through His baptism, Jesus Christ, God's beloved Son, was identified and introduced to His human and divine ministry among us sinful beings. My baptism made me God's child, reclaimed me from sin's bondage, and restored me to His eternal kingdom.

My baptism, in some respects, was also similar to Christ's. It was that event in which I was commissioned and empowered to be His servant. I was made to be God's child at my baptism. The Holy Spirit entered my life at my baptism. As God's work in and through Christ began with His baptism, so my baptism unites me with the saving presence of Christ and initiates the work of God and Christ in and through me. As the baptism of Christ identified Him as the Servant and as a part of the servant-people that had been prophesied and promised in the ancient Scriptures, so my baptism makes me a part of that servant-people.

The baptism of Christ ultimately led to the cross and the resurrection. My baptism makes the death and resurrection of Christ applicable to my life. It also sets my feet upon a narrow path that leads through struggle and conflict and that promises a cross for me to carry on behalf of others. It is a life of joy and peace—in the midst of sorrows and strivings. It is a life that I must often reclaim and return to when the siren voices of the world tempt me to go astray. The momentous event of my baptism was the most important event of my life. It united me to God through Christ and identified me as God's child and servant forever.

I am grateful for my baptism, dear Lord, even though I could not comprehend its true value or understand its implications at that time. Now that I realize its meaning for my life, I rejoice and seek always, by Your enabling grace, to joyfully fulfill its demands upon my life. Amen.

God for the World

*God shows no partiality, but in every nation any one who fears Him
. . . is acceptable to Him.* vv. 34–35

The Old Testament prophets occasionally expressed insights
concerning the God of Israel as indeed the God of all people. Elijah
and Elisha performed miracles of healing, in the name of their God,
upon individuals outside of the family of Israel. Jesus certainly gave
evidence that God is a universal God even though His own three-
year mission was directed primarily to ministering among the Jews.

Peter, in his post-resurrection ministry, was beginning to realize
the implications of Jesus' death and resurrection—and his own
response to them—finally acknowledging and timidly obeying the
charge of the Lord to communicate the saving message of God-
incarnate to the Gentiles as well as the Jews.

Christ's first disciples were fallible creatures who had to grow
in the faith as do all Christians. As with us, so their vision—and
their responsibility—had to be enlarged until it embraced the whole
human family.

As children of God, disciples of Christ, and the brothers and
sisters of Peter, we will either grow in our understanding of Christ's
ultimate mission initiated by His baptism or we will stagnate. The
mission of God was and is to all the world. While our immediate
parishes or arenas of service may be very small, our vision must
encircle the world; our love and concern must be available to
every human creature.

Creator and Master of all creation and including all of its
human creatures, and Redeemer through Christ of all who
will recognize and embrace Jesus Christ as Savior and Lord,
while my arena of activity may be very small, may my vision
and compassion encircle this world on which I live. Amen.

He Is Here

I have given you as a covenant to the people, a light to the nations . . . v. 6b

"Behold, My Servant, whom I uphold, My Chosen, in whom My soul delights; I have put My Spirit upon Him . . ."

These glorious, insightful words are a reference to God-incarnate, Jesus Christ. We truly live in the day of prophecy fulfilled. Jesus has come; He was initiated, through John's baptism and the infilling of the Spirit of His Father, into His ministry to and among the human creatures of God on this planet. "This is the One," our God would say to us. "Hear Him, accept Him, follow Him, for I have sent Him."

Now we are the ones, redeemed and reconciled to our Creator by this Christ and filled with His Spirit, who have become the servants of God and are charged with the enormous task of being "a light to the nations, to open the eyes that are blind, to bring out the prisoners from the dungeon, from the prison those who sit in darkness."

Whatever may be our avocation—the things we do to feed and clothe our bodies and support those who are dependent upon us—our primary vocation is to serve God, to be His servants in our fractured world. We are to emulate Jesus Christ and through proclamation and daily demonstration, through witness in word and deed, bring God through Christ to people about us, to communicate His love and grace to those who cross our paths. This ought to be the consequence of our baptism into the Christ who was baptized by John, and this by the grace of that God who has "taken [us] by the hand and kept [us]" and "given [us] as a covenant to the people."

You are indeed the One, O Christ, who has been promised. You have come to restore me and all who will believe in Your coming to the family of God. I will praise and love and serve You forever. Amen.

This Is the One

Behold, the Lamb of God, who takes away the sins of the world!
v. 29

Whatever John the Baptist may have comprehended about the Christ, his proclamations about this Christ were obviously inspired. In two brief, remarkable statements John summarized what Christ's ministry was to be in the following months. These statements declared who this man Jesus Christ was and, at the same time, what He had come to accomplish in His short sojourn on this planet.

"Behold, the Lamb of God, who takes away the sin of the world!" proclaimed John. He may not have fully understood what he said, no more than the prophets before him could have grasped the full significance of these amazing pronouncements. Nevertheless, he said it, and it must have sounded audacious and incredulous to his hearers.

"This is He who baptizes with the Holy Spirit," continued John. The sacrifice of the Lamb for the sins of the world and the baptism of the Holy Spirit—these were the two central truths in John's preaching that day. They are inseparable. And this is precisely what Jesus accomplished in His earthly ministry. He not only bore our sins on the cross, but we were filled with His Spirit. It is this that is granted to us when we embrace Him as our Savior and Lord. Setting us free from sin's guilt and power and eternal consequences through the sacrifice of the Lamb, Jesus Christ, and incorporating us into His divine family, He has also given us His Spirit.

God grant that John's proclamation—and God's eternal truths—may become a perpetual experience in our lives!

Your great gifts, my Lord are beyond comprehension. Yet I can accept them and rejoice in them. My sins *are* forgiven; You, through Your Spirit, are with me along my journey of faith. May my days and nights be filled with praises to You. Amen.

Let Us Give Thanks

I give thanks always for you . . . v. 4

There is no better way to begin this day—or any day. We can do this even if the sun refuses to break through the cloud cover, or if the conflicts we must face in the coming hours appear foreboding and unsolvable. It is our privilege and our need to begin this day with thankfulness.

Our reason for gratitude? It is, of course, "because of the grace of God which was given [us] in Christ Jesus." Because of that grace we are forgiven sinners and God will keep us—guiltless—to the very end of our lives. Because of that grace we are constantly in fellowship with God's Son, Jesus Christ. Because of that grace we are enriched in every way "so that [we] are not lacking in any spiritual gift, as [we] wait for the revealing of our Lord Jesus Christ."

We are equipped to step boldly into the activity of this day as God's children and His ministers, with the assurance that the grace He has given us will enable us to face any circumstances, to confront violence with courage and hatred with love, and to reflect the joy of our relationship with God in the darkest and most difficult hours that come our way.

Let us give thanks!

You are here, O God; You are now! It is time for celebration! Help us, O God, to fill our homes and sanctuaries, halls of learning, offices of government, streets and marketplaces, with the glad, joyful sounds of celebration! Amen.

"Come and See"

We have found Him . . . Jesus of Nazareth. v. 45

"Come and see." Jesus gave this response to the two disciples who inquired as to where He was staying. Philip gave this same response to Nathanael, who listened to his testimony about the discovery of the One "of whom Moses . . . wrote" and asked, "Can anything good come out of Nazareth?"

"Come and see." Most people in our community have heard the message of John the Baptist: "Behold, the Lamb of God, who takes away the sin of the world!" What a message to proclaim to a sin-ridden, broken world! The problem is that the majority of the people in most communities have never accepted this message or submitted to its Christ in repentance and faith.

While there are various reasons for this—pride, self-sufficiency, blindness to true values—we need to consider the possibility that there may be something wrong with or lacking in the methods the church uses to broadcast this message to the world-at-large. Perhaps the key lies in the interpersonal, eyeball-to-eyeball approach of those first followers of Christ, as exemplified by Philip, who invited Nathanael to "come and see." We are all ministers of the Gospel. We all have our little parishes or arenas of service. We can't coerce people to come to Christ. We certainly can't convert people; that is the task of the Holy Spirit. We can, all of us, in one way or another, invite people to "come and see." They ought to be able to see something of God's love and saving power in our lives, in the things we say and do, and if we are authentically loving and concerned about them, we may be able, as was Philip, to lead such people to the Lamb of God "who takes away the sin of the world."

Help me, O Lord, to be Your witness to others on Your behalf, not only by my words, but by my goals and activities. Amen.

Free to Be

You were bought with a price. So glorify God in your body. v. 20

Through the atoning work of Jesus Christ, we are free to be—what God wants us to be, what He has created and destined us to be. We are set free from man-made laws and regulations, traditions and dogmas, free to live, as enabled by God's grace, in accordance with His plan and design for our lives. We are freed from sin and self-idolization, from our assumed need to satiate the desires and demands of the flesh, free to belong to God and to live and move within His purposes for our lives.

True freedom, however, is discovered only in recognition of God's reign over our life and in commitment to His order and will for us. It means that we are no longer captains of our souls or the masters of our fate. We are the children of God, created in and restored to His image, and have become the vessels and vehicles of His indwelling Spirit. Our very beings become the members of Christ and the means through which the invisible Christ carries out His purposes throughout our world.

We are free—free from the man-made moralities of past and present generations, free from the need for material wealth, free from ancient prejudices, free from the need for self assertion through bigotry or racism, or bizarre activities, free from the fear of death, free to risk our reputations and even our lives in pursuit of divine purposes and of justice and equality for every human creature. We are free to be what our Creator and Redeemer wants us to be. May this happen in and through each of us.

My loving God, I truly do want to be what You intend that I be. And You have delivered me from the bondage of sin and self-centeredness for that very purpose. Have Your way in and through me, my Lord. Amen.

Consecrating the Commonplace

This, the first of His signs, Jesus did at Cana in Galilee, and manifested His glory; and His disciples believed in Him. v. 11

In this day when people are so impressed by big things, large numbers, extravaganzas, wealth and power, fame and fortune, and so oppressed by great problems like war, racism, world poverty, and the national economy, it is paradoxically significant and particularly refreshing that Jesus' first demonstration of divine power took place at the rather commonplace, humdrum circumstances of a wedding party. This same Christ who refused to turn stones into bread to satiate His own hunger did not hesitate to convert water into wine to further the enjoyment of a crowd of merrymaking guests.

This happening in the life and ministry of Jesus says some important things to us. For one thing, it reveals that the glory and splendor, the power and might of our Father in heaven is available and applicable within the ordinary, commonplace, mundane circumstances of everyday living. It means that the Christ who came at Christmas has come to manifest His presence and glory in even the commonplace events of daily life. It means, as well, that the commonplace task need no longer be common or mundane. Whether it be within the realm of tedious housework or the equally drab duty of selling merchandise or running an office or working in a factory or teaching a group of rowdy children, the presence of Christ blesses and clothes it with prestige and purpose. He is able and willing to work miracles in our most ordinary circumstances, thereby transforming the day's drudgery and routine into a vehicle of blessing and abundance for us and for others about us.

The Christ who, without pomp or ceremony, created the best wine of the feast after the natural, ordinary supply was consumed, will give to us, if we will but receive it, a fountain of living water or wine which will supply our needs long after our natural and human resources have been exhausted.

May the day before me, dear Lord, be blessed with Your presence and power. Amen.

God-Incarnate—In Us

Now there are varieties of gifts, but the same Spirit. v. 4

Pentecost was a great deal more than wind and fire, or even the utterance of strange languages by uneducated tongues. God, incarnate in Christ, is also incarnate in the body of His church, His sons and daughters commissioned to carry out His purposes upon this planet. With the gift of the Holy Spirit are made available the great spiritual gifts—the equipment we need to accomplish His objectives in those arenas of service in which He has placed us.

The gifts of the Spirit differ. The Spirit, however, is one and the same, and makes every one of us of equal value and importance to God. We are all credentialed and equipped to be and to do what God would have us to be and to do.

Some of the gifts imparted to God's children are more popular than others—gifts of preaching or healing or intelligence or insight, making money or making music. Other gifts, equally important but less visible, may be little recognized or appreciated. The more popular and visible gifts do not indicate a greater measure of spiritual power or the Spirit's presence.

The most important gifts are available to all of us who will allow the Spirit total access to our bodies and beings. Above all is the grace to love one another, to share with one another, and to help one another in the way of our Lord and Savior, Jesus Christ. That gift comes to us by way of God's love. We need daily to exercise it and utilize it as we grow together in our Christian faith.

Thank You, Lord, for coming to me, for the gift of Your Spirit, for redeeming me and commissioning me to be Your child and servant, Your vessel and vehicle in extending Your kingdom in this world about me. Amen.

God's People for God's Purposes

The Lord called me from the womb . . . v. 1b

Some readers may assume that the author was speaking about himself and his task as God's prophet to the people of Israel. Others will insist that Israel, as God's chosen people, was God's servant to the nations. As we read these words in the light of New Testament revelation, we see Christ projected through this remarkable prophecy—an amazing picture of the Messiah whom God was to send to His people.

He truly was sent by God: "The Lord called [Him] from the womb." He experienced periods of great sorrow when His message and ministry were rejected: "I have labored in vain . . ." He revealed to Israel that He was to be "a light to the nations, that [God's] salvation may reach to the end of the earth."

The message of the prophet, as presumptuous as it sounds, could also be applied to each of us. We, too, are called from the womb. We are His servants. We will often meet with defeat in our efforts to carry out God's purposes in our communities and our world, but we are commanded to keep the faith, to keep witnessing to the faith, and to leave the consequences in God's hands.

O Lord, I need Your grace to keep on believing, to hold firmly to the glorious gospel of my salvation, and to dedicate daily my life to thanksgivings and praises even as I serve You in the process of serving Your children about me. Amen.

His Ministry—Our Ministry

Follow Me, and I will make you fishers of men. v. 19

Jesus had been baptized by John the Baptist and was thereby identified with the human race as the human Christ and initiated into His public ministry. He had been tried by fire in the wilderness and had passed every test. Now was the time to begin the task He had been sent to accomplish. He was made responsible for establishing God's kingdom on this planet, a kingdom, beginning with the Israelites, that would spread out over all the world and draw through its portals men and women of every race and generation.

Jesus took off from where John's ministry had concluded: "Repent, for the kingdom of heaven is at hand." The foundation had to be laid; hearts had to be prepared. John's cry for repentance was well-timed, and Jesus confirmed it. There would be no spiritual kingdom apart from repentance.

He began His selection of men who would learn from Him and continue building the announced kingdom after His own ministry on this earth was terminated. "Follow Me, and I will make you fishers of men." Along with His reaching and teaching was His miracle-working ministry of healing "every disease and every infirmity among the people."

Proclamation, gathering together those who will follow the Christ and serve in His kingdom, communicating God's grace and power to the infirmed bodies as well as the impoverished spirits of people—is this not our ministry as God's sons and daughters, ministers and servants in our world today?

> I am grateful, my loving God, for my arena of service, for a place to put my feet, for burdens to carry and lives to touch in the course of my daily labors. Help me, O Lord, to be faithful in carrying out Your purposes along the journey You have set before me. Amen.

Be Aware of Whom You Follow

For Christ did not send me to baptize but to preach the gospel . . .
v. 17a

It is unfortunate how many Christians latch on to powerful and charismatic personalities that impress them as God's very special saints and leaders and structure their faith in accordance with their precepts and pronouncements. Whereas God may speak through such, there is a great risk in this; their fans or followers may end up with some human concoction about God and His will for their lives.

However such leaders may interpret it, God reveals His love and redeeming power through Christ and His cross. When self-appointed interpreters attempt to go beyond proclamation into some rational or human explanation, to subdue or dilute its offensiveness or dissect its mystery, they come off as confusers rather than articulators and confound rather than clarify the purposes of God.

The fact is clear: Christ died for our sins. We are reconciled to our loving God through this Christ. Nonsensical to some, offensive to others, it remains for us proof positive of our relationship to a living God and our perpetual and eternal acceptance as His sons and daughters. It is because of what Christ has done on our behalf that we can meet this day and every day with the utmost confidence that we are encompassed by His love and indwelt with His Spirit.

There is, O God, no way to be reconciled to You except through Your Son, Jesus Christ, and the cross that He bore on my behalf and on behalf of all Your human creatures. I thank You, my loving God, for the promise of life eternal that is offered to each of us through that cross. Amen.

"Follow Me"

Immediately He called them; and they left their father . . . and followed Him. v. 20

"Stop the world; I want to get off!" It is what some of us are saying—audibly or otherwise—as we are bombarded daily by the tragic, complex, violent events that explode all about us. The storm warnings are out, and people, frustrated and fearful, are running for their lives in search of security or serenity that will blot out the disturbing threats to their well-being.

Those of us who are older tend to reach back into some past generation and try to hang on to those forms and traditions with which we once felt secure, to set the clock back—at least to those postdepression or postwar days, that, in spite of our forgotten tragedies and problems, seem in retrospect so happy and secure. There are many who crawl further back into the womb of the church and cling desperately to the "horns of the altar" as a sanctuary from life's vicious storms. Or they may latch on to those movements that feature religious ecstasy, the get-ready-for-heaven gospel or the Christ-is-coming-soon emphasis in response to the convulsions of our world today.

The message of our Lord is not always comfortable, but this is His message to us in this hour: "Follow Me and I will make you become fishers of men." He does not give us permission to "get off" this calamitous ball of clay we call our world; He invites us—commands us—to follow Him into it, to serve Him and our fellow persons within it, knowing full well, as Christ did, the possible consequences of our obedience to Him. The strange and wondrous thing is that it is precisely in such obedience, which results in loving commitment to people about us, that one discovers an out-of-this-world joy and security that cannot be eradicated by those tragic, complex violent events that explode all about us.

I live, my God, in a churning, conflict-ridden, revolutionary world. Grant to me the courage to put my reputation, job, income, even my life on the line toward the accomplishment of Your purposes and enable me to be faithful to You in precisely this kind of world. Amen.

End-time Christianity

The appointed time has grown very short . . . v. 29a

We don't know the year or the day, but we are nearer to the end of this dispensation and the time of Christ's return than we have ever been before. It is time to consider our priorities. While we are not expected to leave our families or our jobs—or even to discontinue making arrangements for our postretirement years—we had better be aware that earthly relationships and matters are not to have priority over the matters of the Spirit, the kingdom matters for which God has made each of us responsible.

Our relationship to God has first priority. Proceeding from this, our relationship, as His children and servants, to our fellow beings is of vital importance. Whether we are happy or sad, rich or poor, prominent or inconsequential in respect to this world, is not ultimately significant. Our primary concern must be our relationship to God, to "seek first His kingdom and His righteousness."

It is admittedly difficult to be what Jesus—and Paul—exhort us to be. It is not even very rational or reasonable in our kind of society and culture. Our faith has not yet reached the pinnacle that looks down over this world as something that has no eternal significance whatsoever. God's gift of eternal life, and our inclusion in His eternal kingdom, is not comprehensible to our earthbound minds. But we had better, by His grace, work at it—ever reaching toward the glorious freedom that enables us to soar over and above the entanglements that hold us so close to this planet. We have been created and redeemed for far better things.

My great God, I am still learning how to walk on this journey of faith before me. Help me, O Lord, to fix my eyes and the desires of my heart "not on what is seen, but on what is unseen." Amen.

Communicating Christ

The Spirit of the Lord is upon Me, because He has anointed Me to preach . . . v. 17

Advent and Christmas introduced us to the glorious truth that man and woman, as fallible as they are, could not do, God in His love for His wayward creatures did do. He found a way to get through to and communicate with us. It is impossible to comprehend and even difficult for us to accept, but God broke through our conflicts and confusion in the person of His Son, Jesus Christ. We could not come to Him, so He came to us.

What methods did the Son of God, this humble figure from Nazareth, use to accomplish this end? They hardly seem very dramatic in our day of space travel and moon-landings. He did not call down legions of angelic hosts to sweep the world clean of its evil and ugliness. He didn't organize and set up a power block or corporation of influential and wealthy men. He never picked up a pen, much less a sword, to assist Him in His purposes. And yet he, more than any person this world has ever known, succeeded in communicating to billions of human creatures the will and purposes of the loving and eternal God.

For one thing, He did it by *proclamation.* "The Spirit of the Lord is upon Me, because He has anointed Me to preach good news to the poor." He preached. He chose disciples and they preached. Reformations and crusades were launched, revivals born, tidal waves of wickedness checked, lands garrisoned with churches, institutions of mercy inaugurated, slaves set free. The good news of God's saving grace was proclaimed!

He did it through *demonstration.* He came "to set at liberty those who were oppressed," to give "release to the captives" and "sight to the blind." This is what evangelism ought to mean to us: proclamation followed by (and often preceded by) demonstration.

God has come to us; may He in His love and grace come to others through us!

Dear Lord, teach me how to communicate Your love to others "not [only] with words or tongue but with actions and in truth." Amen.

Many Members—One Body

Now you are the body of Christ and individually members of it.
v. 17

Whether we refer to the local congregation, the national synod, or to Christians of every denomination and sect scattered over our world, we are all members of one body. Our baptism made us members not only of our particular congregation, but of the church-at-large, the body of Christ. This does not disavow divisions and disagreements, or the necessity to defend the truth of God's Word with its saving gospel, but it emphatically declares God's pattern and design for His children and servants on this planet.

While we, with tongue in cheek, may agree to this, we seldom act as if we really believe it. It is difficult enough to carry out this divine concept in local churches; it isn't likely that, while we need constantly and obediently to reach for it, we will ever attain to Paul's vision of unity and well-being as the Christian church in a broken world.

If the church is to be what it is gifted and designed to be— Christ-incarnate among the inhabitants of this planet—we must begin to recognize and apply this concept within the group with which we are affiliated. We are all members of the same body. For every mouth to proclaim the good news of God's redeeming love, there are two ears to listen to the joys and sorrows of others, two eyes to see the needs of people about them, two feet to take one into the hard places of human existence, two hands to help bear another's burdens.

We are not all mouths to speak or feet to run. All parts are to be honored and respected and encouraged to perform their various functions. And "if one member suffers, all suffer together; if one member is honored, all rejoice together."

I thank You, my God, for drawing me back into Your divine family. I now seek Your grace to fulfill my responsibilities as a member of Your family. Amen.

Hope for All

*The Spirit of the Lord God is upon me, because the Lord has anointed
me to bring good tidings to the afflicted . . . v. 6*

What makes this selection from the prophet Isaiah especially
significant is that it was the text from which Jesus preached in what
is considered to be His very first sermon. He said to those
synagogue listeners that He, Jesus, was the fulfillment of this ancient
prophecy. The Spirit of the Lord was upon Him. He was sent by His
Father-God "to bring good tidings to the afflicted . . . to bind up the
brokenhearted, to proclaim liberty to the captives . . . to comfort all
who mourn."

Those in attendance at that synagogue service listened to Jesus
only to the point in His sermon where He attempted to apply the
tremendous hope expressed in Isaiah's message to God's creatures
outside the confines of God's ancient people.

There is salvation for all, hope for all. Jesus brought it to pass in
the lives He touched in His earthly ministry. And He brings such
hope to the lives He is able to touch through each of us. While
Isaiah was prophesying the eventual restoration of Israel as the
people of God, Jesus makes that restoration a very present and
personal act in the life of every person who embraces His saving
grace. And we, to extrapolate the prophet's words, are "the priests
of the Lord" and "the ministers of our God" assigned to be the
conveyers and communicators of that divine hope to those who
cross our paths.

Help me to know, O Lord, that You really are here and are
working out Your purposes through me today. Strengthen and
sustain my faith, O God, that I may walk my journey in joy.
Amen.

Life Style of a Christian

Rejoice and be glad, for your reward is great in heaven. v. 12

Mahatma Gandhi praised it; Nietzsche cursed it. Many people sentimentalize over it. Most of us just bow politely to its beautiful thoughts and respectfully put it into cold storage. But always it leaps to life again to provoke and disturb us. And well it should, for it is the Sermon on the Mount, a collection of Jesus' most profound and best remembered words.

For non-Christians this sermon is a frustrating, impossible sort of thing, a picture of life totally contrary to everything that is human in our kind of world; yet even they wistfully return to it, half persuaded that somewhere in its hundred-odd verses is the cure for human ills.

For the Christian it is something else again. It is designed to be his/her style of life—not something attained or accomplished, but something to reach for, to aim at, to become the goal of Christian living.

The Sermon on the Mount does not lead to salvation, except to drive a person to the need for God's grace. It is something which, by that grace, ought increasingly to come out of an authentic Christian. It ought to be the portrait of a saint and to result in the kind of life that will communicate God's healing and power to the lives of sick, lonely, oppressed, broken, unhappy people in our world and in our community about us.

This sermon is meant to be a sort of agenda and guide for our daily activities. It won't win us God's favor; that has already been bestowed upon us through Jesus and His cross. It is, however, the life-style of the family of God—a life-style we are empowered and expected to grow into as the adopted members of that family.

Dear Lord, so many of Your pronouncements and proclamations that were remembered and passed on by Your disciples are difficult to understand and virtually impossible to carry out. Grant, O God, the grace and strength that are essential in order to live out Your commission and serve as Your disciple in my home, my place of work, and wherever I am. Amen.

I Am Eligible

He is the source of your lives in Christ Jesus. v. 30a

I certainly am not wise—according to worldly standards. I have no power over the lives of others—and very little in terms of managing my own life. I have not inherited any sort of nobility, even if many of my ancestors were rugged, noble people. I do not possess the charisma that attracts followers or initiates fan clubs.

Perhaps this serves to make me, according to Paul, eligible for servanthood in respect to the kingdom of God. The fact is, while God may use, even speak through the very gifted personalities about me, the powerful and influential, the very bright and talented people who pull down the spotlights around themselves while they occupy the great pulpits and stages of our world, history bears witness that God has more often revealed His purposes through men and women who were rejected, despised, imprisoned, even martyred by the communities in which they lived.

Whatever the world may think about us, or even if few people ever have occasion or reason to think about us at all, God chose us, however weak or foolish or failure-fraught. He has, through Christ, set us free from sin, even from our subjective feelings about ourselves, to be His children and servants forever.

O God, now I know who I am. I am accepted as Your disciple and servant. I thank You God for making me valid and significant as Your very own child and servant forever. Amen.

Jesus and the Heckler

And they were astonished at His teaching. v. 2a

The ministry of Jesus was on its way. It was when He began teaching in the synagogue at Capernaum that some of the listeners realized that this ordinary-appearing young man, the son of a carpenter, was someone quite extraordinary. "They were astonished at His teaching, for He taught them as one who had authority, and not as the scribes." It was a demented heckler, however, who marked Him for who He really was. "I know who You are, the Holy One of God," he shrieked. It was at this point that Jesus revealed something of His true origin and present mission. He rebuked the evil spirit within this man and commanded it to come out of him.

What the synagogue audience witnessed was the touch of God upon a demon-possessed man—through this ordinary looking itinerant preacher. This and the several astounding confrontations Jesus had following this incident indicated that He was indeed someone very special.

Mark, the Gospel writer, was building up a strong case for Christ as that One sent by God to touch with divine, out-of-this-world power the lives of those who crossed His path. It is this One, this Jesus, who now abides in our hearts and lives and who through us seeks to touch with divine power the lives of those who cross our paths.

My loving God, You have through Your Son revealed something of Yourself and Your love and compassion for Your creatures. I pray that this may be revealed through me as I seek to serve You on this planet in which I live. Amen.

The Ethics of a Christian

Take care lest this liberty of yours somehow become a stumbling block to the weak. v. 9

The Christian life is not lived by rules and regulations. Our salvation is a gift of God's grace and is not dependent upon conformity to the traditions of the past. There is, nonetheless, a limit to our freedom. It is revealed in that ancient absolute or principle spelled out by our God in the command to love Him with our whole being and our fellow persons as ourselves. It is further imposed and demonstrated by our Lord, who commanded us to love one another "as I have loved you" (John 15:12).

This injunction formulates our ethics and our agenda in terms of our everyday relationships. It means that, insofar as possible, we must be all things to all persons, that we become servants to our neighbors. Thus freedom becomes the enslavement of love to God and His human creatures—to spread the Gospel of God's saving love in our interpersonal relationships.

Our standards, as the children and servants of God, ought to be determined in each situation by what we understand to be the most loving thing to do, as Christ would. It is often ambiguous, and we must be sensitive to the enlightenment of history as well as the expectations and requirements of our culture, and open always to the promptings of God's Spirit and the guidance of His Word. This is our ultimate course, our inevitable goal, our day-by-day intention. This constitutes our ethics as "little Christs," to use Luther's phrase, in a broken and disjointed world.

Our gracious heavenly Father, we glorify and praise You for Your unlimited and everlasting love. Now grant to us the grace to be the conveyors and communicators of Your love to our sisters and brothers around us today. Amen.

Would I Know Him If I Saw Him?

They were astonished at His teaching, for His word was with authority. v. 32

When Jesus began preaching His first sermon, the congregation was fascinated if not flabbergasted by the sheer audacity of this young man. Even when He announced that He was about to fulfill the ancient prophecy of Isaiah, they accepted His words as those of an enthusiastic young preacher. The moment, however, that He said something provocative—such as challenging their racist attitude by referring to God's concern for foreigners and through Elijah and Elisha ministering to a widow in Zarephath and Naaman the Syrian, "all in the synagogue were filled with wrath."

He was promptly and forceably dispatched from the synagogue and the city. They failed, of course, to recognize that He was Christ, the Son of God.

"If I had lived in His day," I used to think, "if I could have heard and seen and touched Him, how dearly I would have loved Him; how gladly I would have left all to follow Him!" That, of course, is nonsense. If I can't recognize Him in His Word or in the ministry of this century's prophets, or can't see Him in the lives of my mate, children, teachers, friends, parishioners, and pastors, and perhaps even in some fanatics I instinctively dislike because they appear to threaten my comfortable assumptions, I would have been as blind as those synagogue-goers when Jesus preached His first sermon.

Jesus is here—and He is walking with us every day of our lives. He speaks, sometimes through the joys of young Christians caught up in the ecstasy of conversion, but also through the miseries of minority races, the hungry and oppressed crying out in pain, the ill and addicted, the masses who are in bondage, and even our next-door neighbors in deep despair. God grant that we may recognize Christ and obey Him.

Spirit of the living God, may the eyes of my heart be enlightened that I may know and trust Your presence in and about me today. Amen.

The Supreme Gift

So faith, hope, love abide, these three, but the greatest of these is love. v. 13

God's greatest gift to us is His gift of eternal love revealed through Jesus Christ. This includes the gift of His own Spirit, who consequently indwells each of us and is the Giver of many other gifts to the members of Christ's body, the instruments of His purposes in our world. The most important fruit of this relationship to God is the grace to love one another. That grace is also a gift.

It is a fruit or a gift that most of us appear to possess in rather small measure. We have little difficulty in loving those who love us or in showing concern for those who will respond favorably to our investment in them. If the time and place are right, we are even capable of risking our lives and possessions on behalf of a brother or sister who is in trouble.

True lovers, however, are few and far between. Theirs is a selfless, truth-seeking, all-enduring love. They love in the measure that they acknowledge and experience God's love for them—and are empowered and motivated by divine love. They discover that their response to God's love must be demonstrated in their relationship to humanity about them.

Love, authentic love, is eternal and propagates and perpetuates love. This ability to love is truly the supreme gift—the gift to which we all should aspire. It is only as we rest in God's love for us that we will learn how to respond in love to others.

I have discovered, O Lord, that despite my enthusiastic affirmations and proclamations of Your love for human kind, there are some people I do not like very much. Forgive me, O God, and teach me anew the meaning of Your great love. Teach me how to love and accept others as You love and accept me. Amen.

Presumptuous Prophets

*The prophet who presumes to speak a word in My name which I
have not commanded him to speak . . . shall die. v. 20*

There are prophets and there are prophets. There are those who
are raised up by the Lord and impelled by His Spirit to become His
mouthpiece to community, nation, or world. But there are many
who are guided by some other spirit, and who unwittingly or
purposely use God-language for self-aggrandizement and personal
gain. Those who presume "to speak a word in [God's] name which
[He has] not commanded [them] to speak, or who [speak] in the
name of other gods," they shall die, says our God. In the meantime,
they are leading unsuspecting people down paths that divide them
from God's grace and will for their lives. If we listen to them, we do
so at our peril. "Test the spirits [and the prophets] to see whether
they are of God," exhorted John (1 John 4:1a).

There are those in our midst who do speak the Word of God.
We are to listen to them and hear God speaking to us through them.
In a strange and remarkable sense all of God's servants are called
and empowered to prophesy—to proclaim God's Word of love and
healing and salvation to a sin-ridden, broken world. We need to
listen to one another, to speak in love and concern to each other. If
our lives are submerged in God's love and grace, He speaks through
us, for we are His prophets, the vehicles and transmitters of His love
to others about us

I seek, O Lord, the wisdom to discern Your Word and will
for my life through whomever You will speak to my heart—
and the grace and love and humility to convey Your blessed
Word to others I meet along my journey of faith. Amen.

The Christian and the World

Let your light so shine before men, that they may see your good works . . . v. 16a

"You are the salt of the earth," said Jesus. In the midst of a decadent and sin-permeated world, He set up before His disciples the high task His Father had assigned to Him and through Him to those who would follow Him. It was as if He said: "You, a mere handful, are chosen and imbued agents of God who are to keep this world from decadence and self-destruction." Our Lord implies that human society, without God's influence and grace, would become like a disintegrating carcass. The faithful few before Him who would catch a vision of the mission and a measure of His power were to be rubbed like salt into the rotting mass in order to disinfect its wounds, to arrest its decomposition, to give flavor to its insipidity, and to save it from total destruction.

Jesus Himself set the pace when He became salt amid the corrupted religion of the scribes and Pharisees. The disciples-become-apostles became as salt in the degenerate worship of their day. Luther and the other Reformers became salt in the sickness of the church of the Middle Ages. Kai Munk of Denmark and Dietrich Bonhoeffer of Germany acted as salt in the rotting wounds of the 20th-century German dictatorship.

If there ever was a day in which a wild and wanton world needed salt, it is within the society and culture of this present hour. We are "the salt of the earth" and "the light of the world." Even as God and His salvation is our only hope in the dark night before us, so we who have become His children and servants are His only hope for reaching His human creatures in this rapidly dissipating world.

Heal our land, O Lord. Give to us men and women who will courageously seek and speak the truth and who will dedicate their lives and their leadership to the welfare of all the inhabitants of our great country and our world. Amen.

Ministers or Misconstruers?

I decided to know nothing among you except Jesus Christ and Him crucified. v. 2

Whereas some are especially called or gifted to be preachers and proclaimers of God's Word, all of us are ministers of the Gospel. We are all called to bear witness, in word and deed, to God's forgiving and saving love as revealed through the crucified and resurrected Jesus Christ.

We need to be aware, however, that our task is not to impress people with our knowledge and experience. There is the danger of acquiring fans or followers by flaunting our personality or charm or using whatever gifts we have been endowed with to fortify our shaky egos with the plaudits or commendations of those who gather about us. This may very well result in polluting God's simple message of love, or obscuring the blessed Gospel as revealed in Christ, and thereby contributing to the destruction of people to whom we witness.

This frightening possibility should compel us to search our hearts and examine our feelings and our words in order to make sure that we are promulgating God's testimony and not some half-baked concepts of our own.

We are to proclaim Jesus Christ, to bear witness to His eternal love in the things we say and do. We have neither wisdom nor power of our own. We are vehicles of the indwelling Spirit of God. If we are to bear witness to that Reality who is Christ, we must be sure that we are rooted in that Reality. Only then can God bless and work through our witness in our relationship with others about us.

Help me to understand, my Lord, that I am identified and made significant by Your redemption and gift of righteousness. May my ministry, as Your servant, result in drawing people to You and Your purpose for their lives. Amen.

In Touch with God

He came and took her by the hand and lifted her up . . . v. 31a

This Gospel lesson is a graphic picture of the desperate need of the masses of God's creatures that inhabit this world—and of that One who is able to apply healing and fulfillment for those needs. What we continuously need to review and remember is that this same Christ also applies His divine touch to the ailments of the suffering people in and around us today. He knows all about the "demons" that afflict us—whether they take the form of some abominable habit or despicable weakness, or manifest themselves in some compulsion to hate or covet or lust or worry or fear. He knows, and He stands ready to cleanse and cure—if only we will allow and trust Him to do just that.

The key to Christ's great power—and to the supernatural, abounding power of a Stephen or a Paul or all the unseen and unheralded saints of God who truly are the light of the world and the salt of the earth—is suggested in the practice of Jesus, who early in the predawn hours of the day "rose and went out to a lonely place, and there He prayed." Jesus Christ, and the scores who follow Him, are wells of water to the thirsty and life to the dying, because they were constantly in touch with God.

How can we find the power, that inner joy and peace, the spiritual health that will keep us strong and motivated through the blue Mondays, the difficult Tuesdays, the unhappy Wednesdays of our lives? And how can we channel such power and peace and joy to the difficult people and situations all about us? There is only one way: We must keep in touch with God and allow Him to keep in touch with us through Word and Sacrament, the means of grace, and daily communion through prayer and praise. Then God will have His way with us and through us.

I need Your divine touch, my Lord. Only then can I be what You want me to be. Have Your way in me and through me today. Amen.

Blessed Enslavement

I have become all things to all men, that I might by all means save some. v. 22b

I am free to marry or not to marry, to eat and drink, laugh and cry, work and play. I am free from the "dos" and "don'ts" that become so important to many religious people. I am no longer irrevocably bound to the ancient Law. My salvation is a gift of God's grace and not dependent upon conformity to the traditions of the past or the rules and restrictions set up by religious leaders, whatever may be their claim to divine insight.

Nevertheless, I am enslaved—a bondslave of love to a loving God and consequently committed to His plan and purposes for my life. Set free from the bondage of sin and self-will, I, by God's gracious enablement, freely choose this blessed enslavement and soon discover the faith-full life to be the quenching of my thirst, the satisfying of my heart-hunger, and the total answer to my deepest needs.

The practical consequences of this enslavement, this total commitment to God and His will and purposes, is a commitment to the real needs and best interests of my fellow persons. It means that I "become all things to all men" and women—in order that I may be God's instrument or means of channeling to them divine love and that they may become God's children.

While I am saved by Your grace and Your gift of righteousness, my God, I am thereafter Your servant, as well as Your child and am therefore Your "workmanship, created in Christ Jesus to do good works, which [You] prepared in advance for [me]." I praise You, my Lord, for making me Your child and Your servant. Amen.

Stunted Christianity

Put out into the deep and let down your nets. v. 4

"We toiled all night and took nothing." This has often been our response to our Lord's commands—or what we assume to be His commands—as we follow Him. We have honestly tried to serve Him, to work within His purposes, to extend His kingdom within our little arenas of service. More often than not, we fall flat on our faces. We continue to be more like potted plants than forest giants, sort of stunted Christians that live off the surface roots of God's grace. We wonder if we have ever really discovered the profound, powerful depths of God's eternal love. Perhaps, like the disciples in their early relationship with Christ, we are still fishing in shallow waters.

Shallow waters are necessary to our lives and experiences. We are incapable of plunging from shore to ocean depths without first passing through the shallows. But we need not remain within the shallow waters of human effort and ineffectiveness; we don't have to settle for a stunted Christianity. It is in the great, incomprehensible depths of God's love and promises that we will truly meet the supernatural. We must "put out into the deep." We must lay claim to and lay hold of all that God through Christ has done on our behalf—forgiveness, reconciliation to God, our adoption as His sons and daughters, our commission as His servants.

"Put out into the deep and let down your nets," said Jesus. It means that we get unpotted, that we untie the taproots of our lives and send them deep into the grace of God. Only then will we become effective in channeling the power and provision of God into the weakness and want of humanity.

Forgive me, O God, for settling for less than the very best You have given to me. For the accomplishment of Your purposes in our world, help me to cash in on and live by the fullness of Your grace and gifts. Amen.

The Gifts that Build

Brethren, do not be children in your thinking . . . be mature. v. 20

Whereas a sign or symbol of the Spirit's presence and power may well take the form of strange, ecstatic sounds, and may even stimulate God's servants to a more radical obedience, it is far better that I aspire to those gifts that build up the church—that will more emphatically proclaim God's love and reveal His concern for the human family.

While others may revel in the language of ecstasy, I covet the gift of speaking and writing lucidly in the language of my fellow beings. What I desire most of all is the quality of love that goes beyond verbal witness and proclamation to the dedication of my energies and talents, even my very life, to the bodily welfare and spiritual salvation of God's human creatures on this planet. I sincerely want this because when my loving falls short of this, it falls short of Jesus' requirements for obedient and effective discipleship.

God grant that we may mature in our thinking about spiritual matters and our understanding concerning spiritual values. The church needs the more mature gifts if it is to reach men and women with the message of God's love in Christ. While we need not and must not deny or demean the gifts or experience of others, we must concentrate on those things that will be meaningful and significant for our ministry to our fellow beings.

I thank You for the gifts of forgiveness and life everlasting, my Lord. I covet those gifts that will make me more effective as Your servant in this world. Keep me open to such gifts for my daily ministry, and help me to be faithful in using them. Amen.

The Call of God

Here I am, send me. v. 8b

Isaiah had his eyes, ears, and heart attuned to God. He heard his God calling for ministers and servants, and he responded in humble joy and obedience.

This is the blessed risk of being in the presence of God. We sense our own unworthiness. We are smitten with the enormity of our sin—our human condition. We are forgiven and redeemed by God's grace. We are called into ministry.

Our great God may not tap each of us on the shoulder and beckon us to specific tasks or arenas of service. If we are attuned to Him, however, if we abide daily in His presence, we can overhear Him calling out: "Whom shall I send, and who will go for us?" And we can be assured that He waits on us for our individual responses.

It is in response to His call and appointment that we step out into our world today. This is our arena of service, our place in the sun. God grant that we overhear His call and launch out in loving obedience.

"Here am I! Send me!"

I pray, O God, that You will never give up on me, that I will continue to hear clearly and respond gratefully to Your call to loving obedience. Grant, my Savior and Lord, that I be faithful to You. I want to be Your child and servant wherever You may lead me regardless of the trials and tribulations that come my way. Amen.

Discipleship and Discipline

*Unless your righteousness exceeds that of the scribes and Pharisees,
you will never enter the kingdom of heaven. v. 20*

To be a disciple of Jesus demands a discipline which is far
higher and more stringent than was the law of Moses. Such a
discipline is not projected as a means of winning God's favor; it is
or ought to be our joyful response to God's redeeming love.

The key to the discipline of a Christian is the enthronement of
God and His purposes over and above every other loyalty or
responsibility in our lives. Our human relationships—even with our
family, our personal needs or desires, our responsibilities to
government or corporation or employer, even to the laws of the
state or the expectations of society and culture—must be subservient
to our relationship and responsibility to God. Whatever tends to
come between ourselves and God sabotages our claim upon His
grace and His primary claim upon us and makes us ineffective as
His ministers and servants.

Our initial commitment to Him is well-meant, and our daily
profession of faith is probably generous and passionate, but self-
surrender to God as King and Lord of all we are and have is a day-
by-day, lifelong exercise—and a joy-giving experience.

God is patient, but seeks ever to draw us into loving obedience,
challenging us to take the risk and discover the joy of taking up our
cross to follow Jesus. It is a discipleship and a discipline for which
we were created and into which we have been redeemed and out
of which will come the fulfillment of our most intense longings.

I want to be Your disciple, O Lord. But it is an awesome
responsibility. Enable me, by Your grace, to be Your faithful
and effective servant. Amen.

Unworldly Wisdom

We impart this in words not taught by human wisdom but taught by the Spirit. v. 13

It is not surprising that our non-Christian friends and associates are unable to comprehend our apparently unreasonable faith in and loyalty to an unseen God. They have some understanding of what fuels automobiles or energizes machinery. They cannot be expected to understand what fuels the Christian and gives him or her the hope and joy that keeps that person steady even in the midst of the uncertainty and instability of life in this disjointed world.

The faith of a Christian is secured by an unworldly wisdom, a wisdom that is beyond that of the great intellects and talented people who inhabit this planet. It is the "secret and hidden wisdom of God" imparted to His children by way of His Spirit. It means that even the uneducated Christian possesses a wisdom that may be superior to that of the most profound scholars. The Christian may know little about science or history or economics or medicine but, being in touch with the Creator, is in touch with the eternal and the infinite. While he or she may not be able to communicate with more educated people, the Christian possesses a far more profound and important experience and knowledge than anything the earthbound creatures of this world can assimilate.

We will probably not impress our more intellectual and talented peers with our comprehension of worldly activities and events. We may, however, by our attitudes and actions reflect something of God's divine love and power to people in need.

Eternal and everloving God, while I seek to know, experience, and preserve the beauties and mysteries of this world, may my life embrace and reflect Your love and wisdom as revealed through Your Son, Jesus Christ. Amen.

A Very Special Challenge

Moved with pity, He stretched out his hand and touched him, and said to him, "I will; be clean." v. 41

Like a symphony that gently introduces us to a theme of music and gradually builds it up through the first and second movements only to burst forth in glorious, breathtaking beauty and power—with every instrument, melody, and countermelody revealing the full sweep and the culmination of the theme in the final movement—so Christ, the son of a carpenter, a man among men and women, yet God-incarnate and God-revealed, began gradually to bring the divine touch of the almighty and loving God to people in His path. He first spoke and taught with authority; He exorcised a demon from a man possessed; He healed a woman of her sickness. Now He met a very special challenge by curing and cleansing a leper. Thus the symphony of God's grace moves on—still in its first movement.

Mark, in his brief and pertinent Gospel, singled out only those divine acts that had a particular significance for his writing project. The healing of a leper was, no doubt, a very special challenge in that it could not possibly be credited to magic or witchcraft or trickery. Lepers were always accounted as incurable—as the walking dead—and their only hope, if indeed there ever was hope, lay in the special intervention of God. Jesus, God's Son, met that challenge; He was that Intervention.

The great God, who has forgiven us our sins and reconciled us to Himself, abides with us and within us today. He is also the Great Enabler, who can empower us to face up to whatever challenge comes our way as we travel and labor in His course for our lives. We, the very sons and daughters of God, are now His interveners and enablers in the broken lives that cross our path.

I thank You, great God, for Your intervention in our world and for redeeming and reconciling me to Your family and eternal kingdom. Amen.

Lest I Be Disqualified

. . . lest after preaching to others I myself should be disqualified.
v. 27

I am a son of God. I am justified by faith. It is still necessary, however, that I keep the faith. The failures of my life are and will be forgiven, but the failure to rise from defeat and persist in my walk with God may disqualify me for the final reward.

It means that I give priority to the business of being a Christian, that I make whatever sacrifices necessary to keep this first and foremost in my life.

There is a reward for those who keep the faith. It is not some sentimental, harp-playing, cloud-hopping, pearly-gate nonsense. It is eternal reality—and the answer and fulfillment of one's deepest needs and longings. It is the guaranteed result, not of continual success, but of staying close to the Lord and being faithful and persistent in the Christian conflict.

We don't need to be disqualified. We live in an era of divine grace. If we submit ourselves to God's love and to obedient servanthood, we will run the race successfully and are assured of the ultimate prize.

I dare to come before You, my great and gracious God, not because of anything worthy or desirable within me, but because of Your gift of righteousness which You granted to me through Your Son, Jesus Christ. I dare to believe that I will not be disqualified. Amen.

Words that Disconcert

Woe . . . woe . . . woe . . . vv. 24–26

Some of the words that are attributed to Jesus are downright disconcerting. He speaks the consoling words of blessing and promise to the poor and the hungry and to those who weep in sorrow amid their unfortunate circumstances. To those who have everything they want, who enjoy full stomachs and love the life they lead and have won the respect and admiration of their fellow beings, Jesus appears at times to speak the disturbing words of doom. Most of us, comparatively speaking, are rich in the things of this life, reasonably content, and generally respected. We are among the 10 or 15 percent of this world's population that travel first class on this spaceship called earth while the masses of this world travel in steerage. If we take the words of Jesus literally, it appears that we may be among the damned.

Our loving, forgiving God accepts us as we are—even if we are not poor or hungry or persecuted. Nevertheless, the four "woes" of Jesus' sermon that day are destined to keep us restless and deeply disturbed about the inequities of our society and world, and to lead us to a determination to invest whatever we can to help alleviate the tragic differences between the "haves" and "have-nots" on this planet. They commit us, as well, to incorporate repentance and social renewal, along with our primary mission of proclaiming God's saving love through Jesus Christ.

I realize that I am relatively rich when compared to billions of people throughout this world. I pray, O Lord, that my feelings of guilt be transformed into honest and realistic endeavors to share my life and wealth with those in need. Amen.

Life Beyond Death

But in fact Christ has been raised from the dead. v. 20a

The high point, the constantly recurring theme, and the grand climax in the great symphony of the Gospel, is the resurrection of our Lord Jesus Christ. He died for our sins, and He arose from the dead victorious over sin and death. If we subtract this from our message of love and hope, we really have nothing to say. We must be sure of this—Christ's resurrection—and we can be. It was witnessed by many before us. It has or can be experienced within us.

Maybe other people can discover motivation for good works apart from the commands and promises of the Christian faith, but it is the fact that death in this world is followed by everlasting life in the next that gives most of us the courage to go on—even to the point of risking our lives and possessions on behalf of others.

We shall indeed be raised from the dead. Our God has not given to us an explanation as to just how this shall be done. Our three-dimensional insights would not be capable of comprehending it even if He had. But this we know: the perishable shall become imperishable, and the mortal will become immortal on that great day. And this is all we need to know. It provides all the motivation we need to labor committedly and sacrifically in the purposes of our Lord.

I do praise You, O God. As long as I have breath in my body, I will praise You. There is reason for rejoicing, and so I praise You and rejoice in You. I am Yours, O Lord, Yours forever. Grant that my life be a perpetual offering of thanksgiving and praise. Amen.

At a Time of Decision

Therefore, choose life, that you may live . . . v. 19b

The words of this Old Testament lesson are the words of Moses to the people of Israel. Forty years earlier the parents of these Israelites had come to a similar place, the edge of the Promised Land, and were commanded to cross over into the new country. They refused—and lived and died in the wilderness. Now their children faced the same choice. Moses, the leader, rendered a sort of baccalaureate or graduation address on this momentous occasion. "Choose life," He said, "that you and your descendants may live, loving the Lord your God, obeying His voice, and cleaving to Him . . ."

We have already chosen life when we have embraced Jesus Christ as our Savior and Lord. We have crossed the river and entered the new land. As with the Israelies, however, so with us— the new land and the new life are fraught with pitfalls and precipices, with temptations and trials of every sort. Whereas His grace has led us to the ultimate choice and decision, there are rivers to navigate and paths to tread and enemies to confront. Almost every day of our lives involves decisions. We don't have to be afraid, because God goes with us. But we do have to be wise, cautious, and finely attuned to God and His will and purposes for us if we are to remain in harmony with Him.

"Love the Lord your God, obey His voice, and cleave to Him," said Moses. This remains the key to right decisions and effective living and serving as His sons and daughters.

I have chosen You, O my Lord, only because You first chose me and destined my life to be united to You and directed by Your Spirit along the journey before me. Amen.

Outrageous Exhortations

You must be perfect, as your heavenly Father is perfect. v. 48

If there are tests or portions of the New Testament one might wish to extirpate from the Scriptures, this might well be one of them. Jesus says many difficult things, but these are outrageous, inconceivable, incredible. We often get through them with some mushy, sentimental interpretations—or ignore them altogether—but they continue to stand as Christ's declaration of what authentic Christianity is all about.

Because we can't rid ourselves of these outrageous injunctions from our Lord, we must accept the humiliation they lay on us and determine to do something about them. They are obviously not normal or natural to the human spirit; they are utterly impossible. It is only by means of the Spirit of God that these Sermon-on-the-Mount challenges can be applied to our lives. Whereas they reveal our poverty, they reveal, as well, Christ's expectations of His disciples. They are not a vision of what we will be in some heaven or other; they are what God chooses us to be and would have us to become right here on this planet.

We have a long way to go—to "be perfect as [our] heavenly Father is perfect," but the journey begins with our baptism into Christ and continues as His indwelling Spirit increasingly and determinedly accomplishes His purposes in and through us.

It is, of course, impossible to believe that we will ever reach all of these incredible standards Christ set up for us; it is equally unthinkable that we should ever cease to focus on and struggle toward them. And God will forgive us when we fail.

I fail so miserably to measure up to the standards You have set before me, O Lord. Yet may they always serve to push me ever more deeply into Your compassion and grace—and Your loving forgiveness when I fail. Amen.

Bottle-Bursting Christianity

New wine is for fresh skins. v. 22b

As Jesus demonstrated before the religious leaders of His day, so He would to us, that the Gospel and life He brings cannot be confined to our concoctions and formulas; but like new wine bursting old wine-skins, His life and power—true Christianity—will blow sky-high the self-made forms and notions we sometimes parade as Christianity.

What are some of these homemade formulae which might be construed as bottled-up religion today?

One has to do with a *God-in-a-box* concept adopted by many religious people. They bring God down into something or someone who can be comprehended, packaged, boxed-in in such a way as to no longer be a threat to their way of life—someone they can take or tolerate as it suits them.

Another formula is the *big thumb in the sky* concept. When the pressure is severe, the pains intense, many people are quick to find some god to latch on to. When the clouds clear away, the blue skies resolve into broken promises and the true God is left high and dry. There are so-called Christians who are unwittingly attempting to pack Christ's potent truth into the old bags or bottles of their bigoted and self-made notions, or who regard Christianity only as a haven in a time of storm instead of meaning and motivation for day-by-day living.

It is rather risky to allow Jesus to have His way in us. It will result in some bottle-breaking as He embraces, cleanses, redeems, and claims us fully for Himself and His purposes. But when it happens, beauty will be restored where once there was ugliness, forgiveness where once there was sin and guilt, potency where once there was weakness, and our Christianity will become real and joyfully vital.

My gracious Lord, forgive me for using You to make me more successful or content while You have chosen and appointed me to carry out Your program and purposes in and through my life. Amen.

Confident in Christ

As we share abundantly in Christ's sufferings, so through Christ we share abundantly in comfort too. v. 5

Paul didn't say much, if anything, about self-confidence—as important as this is at times—but he repeatedly focused his confidence on Christ and properly credited Him for whatever was accomplished through his life.

While some people seem naturally to possess the courage and confidence to face anything that comes their way, many of us tip-toe through life's corridors—especially when it comes to carrying out our Christian witness among our peers.

I need to be reminded that fear is often a symptom of faithlessness. If I rely on my own knowledge or skill in my day-to-day relationships, I may have good reason to be afraid. If I, however, rely upon the Spirit and power of God, I *am* qualified to be a minister of the "new covenant," and the Spirit will bear witness through my words and deeds related in love to my fellow beings.

We are not assigned to demonstrate a new law or discipline. Nor are we expected to pass out formulas for proper living. We are here to proclaim and manifest Jesus Christ. We cannot do this by peddling the good news as newsboys peddle papers. We are called upon to offer our lives, to give of ourselves to our fellow persons' needs, and let God take care of the consequences.

And this we will do—if our confidence is in Him.

I don't have to be afraid, Jesus, about the problems that I must face today. Your Spirit is within me and before me, and in Him I can be confident. Amen.

It's a Mystery!

Lo, I tell you a mystery. v. 51

We shall not all sleep, but we shall all be changed—in a moment, in the twinkling of an eye—at the last trumpet? And at the sound of the trumpet the dead will be raised imperishable? It's incredible! To most people utterly unbelievable! This was, however, Paul's conviction—and continues to be a conviction that energizes and motivates Christ's disciples today.

Of course it's a mystery, and very foolish to worry about when and just how all this is to transpire. Paul was content and thankful to know that the victory through Jesus Christ is assured.

So let us be awake and aware—always. Even as we rest in what God has done on our behalf, let us be on the tiptoe of expectancy. Let us be working, giving, loving, keeping the faith, and demonstrating that faith to the world of men and women about us. The time will come soon enough when we shall experience together the eternal wonders of the next dimension. As for now, we need to hold on to one another in our love, serve God and our neighbor in our daily vocation, and dedicate ourselves in loving service to God and humanity.

> Words cannot describe it—this incredible event about to take place, but You, Jesus, are coming soon to take us to Yourself. It is indeed time for celebration! Amen.

Valley to Vision—and Back Again

Lord, it is well that we are here. v. 4a

Twelve men had left their jobs, homes, and families to follow Jesus Christ. Maybe they assumed that their sacrifices would resolve in eventual positions of wealth and glory, deluding themselves into believing that Jesus was Israel's future king and they His right-hand men. It wasn't working out that way and, after several months of following Him, they wondered why He was no closer to earthly power and glory than when He was baptized in the Jordan River. They were in need of a vision, and in view of the trials-by-fire they would experience in future months and years, three of the disciples were permitted such a vision.

We, too, become bored with valley-living and occasionally need mountaintop experiences, something that might put a glow into the daily struggle, cast a halo about our perpetual conflicts, renew the meaning and purpose of this continual battle with life. And there are occasions when we get just that—oases along our desert paths that refresh and revitalize our weary spirits. They might come in the form of a Bach chorale or a Beethoven symphony, or during a walk in the woods, a conversation with a dear friend, a Bible class or worship service, or a meeting with a stranger who is an angel unawares.

Then it is back to the valley again, the hours of pain and frustration, our own defeats, our friends' suffering. But through it all there is joy—deep, profound, inexplicable—the joy of knowing that we are God's sons and daughters, His servants and ministers, that all that is His is ours, that we are His forever. From valley to vision and back again—and the living Christ is with us all the way.

My gracious God, grant me the strength to cling tenaciously to the joy and the assurance of Your love in the valleys through which my faith journey will take me. Amen.

A Necessary Experience

This is my beloved Son; listen to Him. v. 7b

We can only guess why just three of the disciples accompanied Jesus up the mountain on this significant day. Perhaps it was because these three would be especially responsible for continuing the ministry of Christ after He left them. *James* would need the recollection of the experience to cool his intolerant spirit, temper his ambition, comfort him in Gethesame, and strengthen his faith as he laid his head on Herod's block. It was probably, in part, this mountaintop vision that kept *John* from fleeing in haste at Jesus' betrayal and crucifixion and enabled him to endure his exile to Patmos. *Peter* would often need the memory of that vision to strengthen his wavering courage and enable him to stand against persecution, comfort other believers amidst their trials, and testify to millions throughout history that he was an eyewitness of Christ's majesty and heard with his own ears the voice borne from heaven, "This is My beloved Son; listen to Him."

It is not surprising that these men, particularly Peter, wanted to settle down with Jesus on that mountaintop for the rest of their lives. It was not meant to be. It was back to the valley for them—to those places between a rock and a hard place where they were to continue, enriched and renewed by what they had just witnessed, to lovingly and faithfully serve in the difficult arenas of this world. The Transfiguration was a necessary experience for them, but it was not the grand finale. It was designed to equip them for service in the new kingdom, to better enable them to face and overcome the hardships and sufferings involved in witnessing concerning that kingdom on this planet.

Lord, I, too, seek some out-of-this-world experience to give wings to my flagging spirit. Forgive me, gracious Father, for such unworthy thoughts. May the crucible and cross-bearing of this life purge me of my lust for self-esteem. Amen.

Mountains and Valleys

And [they] went up on the mountain to pray. v. 28

When they "went up on the mountain to pray"— the three disciples along with Jesus—they received far more than they had bargained for. It was a majestic vision, something clear out of this world. Peter was so flabbergasted that he immediately wanted to set up shelters for three figures within this mountaintop vision. "Master, it is well that we are here," he exclaimed.

There is point and purpose to the Transfiguration event. It provided a prophetic picture of the glory in which Christ and His followers will ultimately appear—a brief glimpse into the dimension of the spiritual and eternal. Though the disciples may not have realized this at the moment, it was designed to alert them to the fact that they were destined for something far better than this earthly sojourn, that Christ's kingdom was not be centered upon this globe nor in this space-time concept we call life, and that eternity and spiritual reality is something that can never be comprehended by the finite faculties of the human creature.

What ought this vision mean to us? Among other things, it means that there is a victorious conclusion to this valley experience that we are part of, this conflict in which we are engaged. It means that we need not put so much emphasis on temporal values; that poverty or lack of success here, though uncomfortable, is not tragic; and that affliction in this life, though painful, does not have to be bitter and incapacitating.

It was a great and grand event, this mountaintop experience. Now it is back to the valley again—and the transfigured and resurrected Christ is with us to transform us and transmit through us His resurrection power.

I pray, O Lord, for those times when, even as I labor in the valley, I may be freed up to soar above the cloud-shrouded, snowcapped peaks that hover over its edges. Amen.

A Valid Faith

We were eyewitnesses of His majesty. v. 16b

We cannot say with Peter that "we were eyewitnesses of [Christ's] majesty," or that "we heard this voice borne from heaven." Peter was beset by human fallibilities as much as any of us, but he would not be conned into following the "cleverly devised myths" that attract many religious people today. He knew his faith in Jesus Christ was valid; he had *seen* and *heard* the grandeur and glory of God.

But how can we possibly swallow this irrational God-stuff in a world of computers and satellites—and suffering, struggling, dying, people?

We know that Christ is real, that God is alive and well and lovingly concerned about each of us, because we have seen Him through the eyes of faith, have witnessed His miracles in our lives or the lives of others around us, and have experienced His forgiving and life-giving love in our own hearts. We know Him; He is real to us, and He is the source of our joy.

It is this grand experience we are dedicated to sharing with others, the experience of loving fellowship with God. It is this ever-growing and enriching experience that confirms our personal worth as God's redeemed children and draws us into a warm and loving relationship with one another.

Dear Lord, it was truly a transforming, if not transfiguring, experience when I first became aware of Your forgiving love and gift of righteousness and my new-found status as Your child and servant. It is in response to this that I joyfully dedicate my life to You and Your blessed will for now and all eternity. Amen.

The Conflict before Us

Then Jesus was led up by the Spirit into the wilderness to be tempted by the devil. v. 1

We have resonated to the glories of the Epiphany season. It was an exciting time. We were witnesses to a series of manifestations of Jesus' majesty—in His baptism, His miracles, His revelation of Himself as the Son of God at the Transfiguration on the Mount. These were some pretty heady experiences.

Now we have to come back to earth—to our three-dimensional world and the sufferings and conflicts that plague us here. The season of Lent is to prepare us for the high festival of Easter. We do have to consider some things of a very serious nature if we are to properly understand the meaning of Christ's resurrection—things like sin, death, temptation, repentance, crucifixion.

We are introduced to our Lord's conflict with the spiritual forces of evil—the same forces we confront daily in our sojourn and service as the children and servants of God. The temptations Jesus confronted are in many ways comparable to those we face. They were, in essence, Satan's attempt to cross out the cross in the ministry of our Lord. Had the devil succeeded in doing so, salvation would not have been offered to us, sin would not have been atoned for, we would never have known the experience of redemption, God's human creatures would die eternally in their sin, and the spiritual forces of evil would be forever victorious.

Whereas Satan failed in his temptations of the Christ, he has and is too often succeeding with many of us, primarily in the temptation to cross out the cross in our relationship with God. As we focus on the cross of Christ during this and every season of the year, may we embrace and faithfully obey our Lord's injunction to take up our cross and follow Him.

I thank you, O God, that when I gaze at the cross of Your Son, Jesus Christ, I can discover in its terrible pain the joy and peace of forgiveness and acceptance as Your child and servant. Amen.

Security in an Insecure World

Seek first His kingdom and His righteousness, and all these things shall be yours as well. v. 33

If we are to find security in a very insecure world, we will obviously have to seek it on a far different level than do most people today. We will have to return to the Christ, whom we have so often ignored or bypassed while clutching our ephemeral material securities, and embrace once more His person and teachings as they are presented in this Gospel portion.

Jesus begins with a word of *warning*: "No one can serve two masters. . ." If we are to experience peace within revolution, security within instability, we must be set free by God to serve God. There mnust be total and irrevocable committal to Him and His purposes.

Jesus follows His warning with a *promise*. "Your primary concern in life," He is saying in contemporary terms, "must not be with those things that keep you alive—job, income, pension, food, clothes, reputation, status. Your citizenship is in the kingdom of God. You can well afford to lose your possessions, even your very lives, as far as this temporal world is concerned, for you are sons and daughters of God, and God your Father will never fail or forsake you."

The final word of Christ in this lesson is one of exhortation, to "seek first His kingdom and His righteousness," to give first place to His kingdom and to do what He requires and let the chips fall where they may. And this injunction is followed by the guarantee that the things we really need in the course of committing ourselves to this kind of relationship and carrying out the terms of this kind of loyalty will be provided.

Dear Lord, lest the things of this world stifle and disrupt my relationship to You, teach me, in response to Your love, how to make them work for You—and how to fashion them into ways and means of enriching the lives of others. Amen.

The Incomparable Experience

My son, your sins are forgiven. v. 5b

Mark attempts to relate those selected incidents in Christ's ministry that increasingly reveal Him to be God-incarnate. Jesus was noted as one who spoke with authority, who cast out demons, who healed the mother-in-law of one of His followers, who cleansed and healed a leper. Thus far, however, these acts could be ascribed, at least by the religious leaders of His day, to some strange magic or witchcraft. After all, healings and exorcising were not entirely unknown at that time.

There was something different about this event, the healing of the paralytic who was brought to Jesus. In this act Jesus went one step further in the gradual revelation of Himself as the Messiah, the Son of God, as well as the son of Mary, God-incarnate in their midst. His first words to this victim of paralysis who was brought before Him was, "My son, your sins are forgiven." This really got a rise out of the scribes who witnessed this happening: "Why does the fellow talk like that? This is blasphemy! Who but God alone can forgive sins?" (NEB). Then Jesus proceeded to heal the cripple, saying, "Rise, take up your pallet and go home."

The scribes were right in stating that only God could forgive sins, but they refused to believe that this Jesus was anything more than some sort of magician. The paralytic who was brought to Christ for healing received far more than he dared to anticipate, the need for which he may not even have recognized. He came face to face with the incomparable experience of his life. By means of the divine touch of God he was delivered not only from the paralysis that bound his body, but from the paralysis that bound his soul. He was reunited, redeemed, restored to his loving God. "My son," said Jesus, "your sins are forgiven."

This, O Lord, is the miracle You perform on my behalf. I praise You, O God, for this incomparable experience, and the daily assurance that my sins are forgiven. Amen.

From Sin to Grace

Where sin increased, grace abounded all the more. v. 20b

We are aware that all God's human creatures are sinners—that disease and death, physical and spiritual, have permeated the whole human race. We know, as well, that the laws of God, and the precepts of men and women who tried to find and follow God, were initiated to bring order and harmony into humanity's chaos. It was these ancient laws that revealed to man and woman their inner sickness and estrangement from their Creator.

God's love, however, is far greater than the evil that brings death and destruction. His grace is more powerful than human wickedness. It was this that was revealed through Jesus Christ, and it is this that grants us eternal life.

What we cannot comprehend we can still celebrate. For it was through the sacrifice of our Lord Jesus Christ, God's act of grace and love, that we have been made the very sons and daughters of God.

You do not, O Lord, accept my sins or my excuses. You only offer me Your grace. Your grace is always available. I claim it anew, dear God. Envelop me in Your care and enable me to truly love others as You continue to love me. May I by Your grace love with the kind of love that will heal the wounds of those who have been hurt by my self-centeredness and sin. Amen.

Temptation

He was in the wilderness forty days, tempted by Satan. v. 13a

Temptation—it often takes the shape of bread that promises to satiate my hunger and slake my thirst. It promises fulfillment and happiness—poking into my dark hours with beckoning fingers of hope, interrupting my drudge-laden routine with moments of tantalizing excitement, relieving my pain with experiences of pleasure and delight.

It never lets up. I have sometimes envied my Lord who had angels to succor Him after His forty-day ordeal in the wilderness. I wonder if it's fair that I, composed of such human stuff, should be so constantly exposed to that which cannot be humanly resisted.

But I am exposed—and I discover very realistically that I cannot win them all. It is said that temptation is necessary to Christian maturity. It can be used by God to develop my dependence on Him. It ought to result in keeping me close to Him. I am supposed to grow stronger in the heat of conflict and even to discover that my weaknesses can become channels of divine power and sustenance.

God doesn't send temptation, but He obviously allows it. And with every temptation He promises the grace to resist it. I must learn how to tie on to that grace.

My loving God, I am often tired and depressed. Trying to follow Your Son, my Lord, is more difficult than I expected it to be, and I am tempted to give up and do what comes naturally. You know, O Lord, that there are siren calls I cannot in my own strength resist. Grant to me the grace to be faithful to You and to Your will for my life. Amen.

We Are Secure

In all these things we are more than conquerors through Him who loved us. v. 37

Nothing, nothing at all, can come between us and our loving God. Our feelings of guilt and depression will rise up to haunt us, but they will in no way alter God's redeeming and accepting love. The tragedies and conflicts of this life will frighten and discourage us, but they cannot change God's attitude or stifle His love for us. Failures and defeats may trip us up, but they do not affect our relationship to God.

Our boat will rock; the earth will tremble. Revolutions will shake up governments and institutions. Our traditions may be nullified, our convictions threatened. Every temporal security may crumble. God's love and reconciling grace are forever, and He will never let us go. If our allegiance is to God and our faith is fixed on Him, the very atrocities that threaten to destroy us become the means by which He carries out His will in us and through us.

Nothing, absolutely nothing can separate us from the love of God as revealed and proclaimed and demonstrated through Jesus Christ. We are the sons and daughters of God, His servants and disciples forever.

Pull me out of this pit into which I have fallen, O God, I do not belong here; I am Your child and servant. Teach me how to accept my status as Your child and servant—and the validity and power that go with it, and to walk and serve in joy. Amen.

Crossing Out the Cross

The devil departed from Him . . . until an opportune time. v. 13

It is probably a gross oversimplification to state that Satan's whole purpose in Christ's temptation was to cross out the cross in the life and experience of our Lord. As far as Jesus was concerned, it was a vain attempt. For Jesus had set His face toward Jerusalem, placing the cross at the very apex of His plan for the salvation of the human race, and nothing would deter Him from that course.

The spiritual conflict before us does, however, reveal the pattern of temptation as it pertains to all of God's children. There is the temptation to use God to meet our human needs and wants rather than allowing Him to use us in the accomplishment of His purposes. There is the incessant quest on the part of some churchgoers for entertaining, consoling, head-patting, peace-giving, get-ready-for heaven, Christ-is-coming-soon sermons, the desperate search for ecstatic experiences, the common concept of God as a sort of dispenser of good things for good people. There is the temptation to be crowd-gatherers, convert-counters, recognition-seekers, to promote our own image under the guise of Christian servanthood. There is always the temptation to compromise—with the state in promoting destructive wars, with the status quo in perpetrating injustice against the powerless, with the middle class in maintaining high living standards at the cost of oppressing the poor.

Even while we cling to the cross Jesus bore on our behalf, and are fairly successful in fighting off less profound temptations such as pilfering and philandering, we all too easily yield to the temptation to avoid the cross our Lord has commanded us to bear on behalf of our fellow beings.

I pray, my loving God, that You who brought the promise of life to all people through the cross of Christ, will turn the small crosses I am chosen to carry into agents of redemption and channels of love to those I may touch on my pilgrimage through this world. Amen.

Authentic Faith

If you confess with your lips that Jesus is Lord and believe in your heart that God raised Him from the dead, you will be saved. v. 9

"For man believes with his heart and so is justified . . ." Let us understand, however, what it means to "believe" and to proclaim and promote such belief through our confessions of faith. We ought to know that it is not accomplished totally through well-formed phrases or impressive liturgies. This could be as phony as a sales pitch. Our pious exercises may be a ridiculous facade that obscures the real condition of our hearts. To "believe" is more than "calling upon the name of the Lord." We tend to do that every time we are plunged into some dire crisis.

To "believe" is to trust in the redemption wrought by Christ, with the result that we surrender and submit all we are and have to God's loving control. This means that God and His purposes become the consuming passion of our lives, and His purposes point directly to a relationship of loving concern for, and to action on behalf of, our fellow persons about us.

If we truly "believe" in Him—in what God has done for us as revealed through Jesus Christ—then we *are* saved, and this is true irrespective of our race, color, ancestry, social status, or church denomination.

I believe, my Lord, but I pray for Your grace to really believe, and to demonstrate such belief in my faithfulness to You and my concern and compassion for my fellow beings about me. Amen.

The Supreme Test

Take your son . . . and go to the land of Moriah, and offer him there as a burnt offering . . . v. 2

This incident in the life of Abraham is certainly one of the more troublesome stories from the Bible. The God of Abraham, in this instance, does not appear to be the same God who is revealed to us through Jesus Christ. Is it possible that Abraham assumed that his commitment to God and His purposes would be tested in this manner?

Assumption or not, the end result is a grand revelation of Abraham's devotion to his God. More important to Abraham than his very son, who was the focal point of God's promises and the seed that would become Israel and culminate in the coming of the Messiah, was Abraham's personal relationship to God. Abraham proved to himself and to us that he was truly a man of God and could therefore be trusted to carry out God's purposes. Abraham was not devoted to mere human convictions, and certainly not to the tradition of child-sacrifice that may have been prevalent among the religions of his day; he was devoted to God. Another sacrifice was provided to express that devotion, and the purposes of God were carried out through Abraham and his seed.

Jesus also said some very difficult things to His disciples— things like hating one's own father and mother and wife and children or cutting off one's hand or plucking out one's eye if these come between a person and God. While we are not about to take this literally, we get the message—from Abraham and from Jesus— that our response to God's love must be total, unconditional, and more important than anything else in this life.

O Lord, I may not fully understand or realize the meaning of genuine commitment to You and Your purposes, but I pray for that understanding and for the determination to make that kind of commitment to You and Your objectives for my life. Amen.

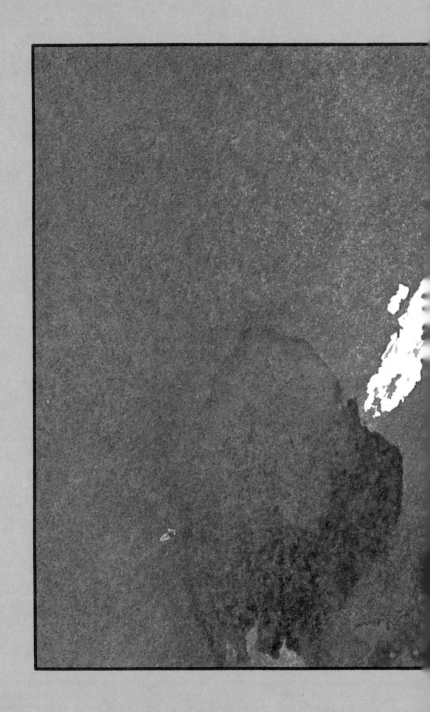

From Futility to Fulfillment

Whosoever drinks of the water that I shall give him, will never thirst.
v. 14a

Back of the glitter and painted scenery out front in our lives there is naked reality—and often disorder, confusion, and excruciating futility. There is the futility of contradiction, conflict, unsatisfied desire, meaninglessness, and purposelessness. We feel something of the strain and stress of Cosette in Victor Hugo's *Les Miserables*, tugging away at her heavy bucket, wishing deeply that she could "fly, fly with all her might, across woods, across fields, to houses, to windows, to lighted candles."

The message of this Gospel lesson is that futility can give way to fulfillment, that our great God has taken upon Himself the heavy load we are so frantically struggling with, that there can be meaning and value, point and purpose in our daily conflicts.

Jesus began His ministry to the Samaritan woman by making her conscious of the futility in her heart and life. He then reached out to offer His fulfillment. She had left home for the purpose of drawing water—expecting, of course, to continue on in the purposeless, vicious futility she had always struggled with. What she found at the well was water of a different sort—a new heart, a new life. She met Jesus and became a new creature.

"My soul thirsts for the living God," said David. Indeed it does. This is the basis of our futility—the thirst in our lives for the living water which Christ offers so freely. We must cease culling our comfort and consolation from an abstract, unknown god and consecrate ourselves to God-revealed, the living Christ—to receive from Him, delight in Him, love and serve Him. Then our futility will give way to fulfillment.

"My soul finds rest in God alone . . . He alone is my rock and my salvation," exclaimed the psalmist. And so it is with me, my Lord. It is from You that I draw the juice of life. It is in You that the deepest longings of my heart are met and my fulfillment is complete. Amen.

Our Salvation—God's Gift

Abraham believed God, and it was reckoned to him as righteousness.
v. 3

From the very beginning of God's dealings with His chosen people, even from the time of Abraham, our great God made it quite clear that His acceptance is not the result of good works on the part of His creatures, but His own incomprehensible, incomparable love. And yet, though it may be very subtle, most of us are still afflicted in some measure with an insidious works-righteousness concept in respect to our relationship to God. Even in our generous proclamations concerning God's grace, we still come down heavy on the side of the Law as well as the assumed "dos" and "don'ts" of the Christian life.

It is so natural to tie our faith to certain acts that we do, to rituals and ceremonies and little sacrifices that we engage in. While these things may be of value, they in no way reconcile us to God.

God's saving love, His eternal righteousness, is a gift, not a reward for good works. We are to embrace that gift, that righteousness as revealed through Jesus Christ, to recognize our obvious inability to measure up to the demands of the Law, to claim our freedom from sin's condemnation with its eternal consequences, and to live and serve as the true sons and daughters of God.

O Jesus, You are full of wonder and splendor! I am dumbfounded that You should care about me. And yet You have called me Your brother and reconciled me to Your heavenly Father, ordained me to be Your priest, chosen me to be Your disciple. What a Savior You are, my Lord! How full of wonder and splendor You are! Amen.

From Salvation to Discipleship

If any man would come after Me, let him deny himself and take up his cross and follow Me. v. 34

It had been a sort of kindergarten experience up to now for these twelve men who had followed Christ. The time had come when they must be prepared for commitment and service. "And He began to teach them that the Son of man must suffer many things . . ."

They were shocked, flabbergasted, bowled over. This was something they could not comprehend—this lovely, gracious, all-powerful Christ who was well on His way to becoming Israel's king was now predicting His own execution.

This is possibly what happens, in some degree, to each of us. As long as our preachers talk about dear old God who condoles and coddles us while allowing us to live pretty much as we please, indulging in our material gifts, using them for our personal aggrandizement while continuing to acquiesce to our sin-ridden desires and instincts, nobody is provoked, and church and religion are accepted as an integral part of our lives. But when religious leaders break through the periphery of Christian teaching and talk about cross-bearing and dying to sin, when they go beyond the "take the love He brought" presentations with which we can readily agree and begin challenging us to "lead the life He taught," then many of us either cop out or crawl more deeply into our kindergarten apprehensions concerning religion and never discover what Christianity is all about.

"Let him deny himself and take up his cross . . .," said Jesus. This is as much a part of Christianity as the cross Jesus bore on our behalf. To "take the love He brought and lead the life He taught!" It is only in Christ, our Savior and Master, that we find the grace and the strength to do both.

Loving Christ, You identified with me in my sins and sicknesses. You adopted me as Your child and commissioned me to be Your servant. You have now entrusted me with an awesome responsibility. Enable me, by Your grace, to be Your faithful and effective servant. Amen.

We Are Accepted

While we were enemies we were reconciled to God by the death of His Son. v. 10a

The truth of the matter is—and this in spite of our foolish efforts to placate God by means of rules and laws and traditions and customs—that we *have been* accepted by God through Jesus Christ. This is where we now stand; this is what we ought to be celebrating. This is no vain hope; it is the Gospel truth. God's love and Spirit *do* abide within us.

It is when we accept and cling to this that God has done for us through Christ, irrespective of our human feelings and frailties, that the very conflicts which beset us, and may even threaten to destroy us, become God's tools to grind and polish and temper our spirits and prepare us for loving and obedient service.

Let this day be filled with praises! We *are* reconciled to God; we are His forever! Now we can lend ourselves to good works on God's behalf and begin to reflect and transmit to others something of our joy as God's children and of God's saving love extended to them.

O God, now I know who I am. You gave me my identity in the moment of my baptism. You touched me with Your cleansing power and filled my heart with Your Spirit. I am accepted as Your disciple and servant. I thank You, God, for making me valid and significant as Your very own child and servant forever. Amen.

The Darkness around Us

You will not see Me until you say, "Blessed be He who comes in the name of the Lord." v. 35

Some of us have wondered, as we follow Christ through His hours of suffering that led to His ultimate sacrifice at Jerusalem, why our paths should be so smooth and our way so easy. Refusing to yield to Satan's temptations to take the easy road to worldly acclaim and power, Jesus chose the painful path of sacrificial service to make possible our salvation. While we claim to follow Him, most of us have found little in our course through life that resembles suffering or sacrifice for the sake of others.

One of the reasons for Jesus' suffering was the hostile reactions of the national and religious leaders to His ministry of redeeming love. In the tradition of the ancient prophets, He courageously spoke out against the oppressive policies of Herod and repeatedly exposed the hypocrisy of Israel's professors and teachers of religion. And it was the "church" of His day that set in motion the machinery that eventually executed Him.

Our Christianity is of little effect unless we begin to live by our Lord's precepts, and this will take us beyond profession into practice, beyond pie-eyed contemplations around spiritual ecstasies into the hard, painful realities of daily living and loving. Along with our brothers and sisters in Christ we have the obligation not only to proclaim God's love but to bring something of that love into our world and to work toward making our society just and equitable. Among other things, this must include the courage to stand up and be counted in respect to our abhorrence of injustices perpetrated by the rich over against the poor or by majorities over against minorities, and the risk of reaching out to correct such inequities wherever they may appear.

Grant to me, O Lord, the courage, the wisdom, and the willingness to risk loving others with whom I come in contact—and to do so regardless of the consequences to my life. Amen.

Keep the Faith!

Our commonwealth is in heaven, and from it we await a Savior, the Lord Jesus Christ. v. 20

"Stand firm thus in the Lord," exhorts the apostle Paul to his friends and co-ministers at Philippi. He even dared to enjoin them to imitate him—"and mark those who so live as you have an example in us." Paul was writing this injunction while in one of the several prisons in which he and his colleagues were often incarcerated. From that time until this, jail sentences have often been the lot of those who have sincerely, if not always wisely, sought to follow in the steps and the teachings of Jesus.

Paul was not suggesting that a jail sentence was inevitable if one is to "obey God rather than men" (Acts 5:29). Man-made laws are supposedly for the benefit of all—pagans and believers alike. Conflicts, adversities, sufferings of one sort or another are inevitable. They are sometimes the consequence of keeping the faith; they are always associated with living in this disjointed world and are as much a part of life as our very environment.

Over and above this life and this world in which we live, however, is the inevitability of life everlasting, the sure hope and assurance that "our commonwealth is in heaven," the guarantee that "the Lord Jesus Christ . . . will change our lowly body to be like His glorious body."

Thus we are enjoined to keep the faith. It will be worth it despite all of the difficult and painful things that happen here. As Paul writes in another of his letters, "The sufferings of this present time are not worth comparing with the glory that is to be revealed to us" (Romans 8:18).

O Lord, I need Your grace to keep on believing, to hold firmly to the glorious gospel of my salvation, and to dedicate daily my life to thanksgivings and praises even as I serve You in the process of serving Your children about me. Amen.

Trust and Obey

Now the Lord said to Abram, 'Go from your country and your kindred and your father's house to the land that I will show you.'
v. 1

"So Abraham went, as the Lord had told him . . ." "By faith Abraham obeyed when he was called to go out to a place . . . and he went out, not knowing where he was to go" (Hebrews 11:8).

Whatever may have been the medium by which God communicated with Abraham—dreams, visions, spoken word, inner conviction—this man was certain that God had spoken and had made His will known. It must have been an exciting, even traumatic experience in the life of Abraham that resulted in his severing all ties with homeland and friends and secure surroundings to launch out into a strange and unknown world. The consequences of his obedience, not totally revealed to Abraham, are known and celebrated by God's children to this very day.

"You are My friends if you do what I command you," said Jesus to His disciples (John 15:14). Our great God continues to reveal Himself and His will through His Son, our Lord. He does not, anymore than He did with Abraham, reveal the immediate consequences or results of doing His will. God commands; our response to His love, His grace, and His commands must be obedience. This is what authentic faith is all about. There are many things which we presently do not know about the will of God. There are other matters in which we do know His will, and all our quibbling and procrastinating only forestalls and inhibits its accomplishment and endangers our relationship to Him.

Let us go, "as the Lord has told *us*," as did Abraham of ancient times, in scorn of cost or unknown consequences. In no other way can God accomplish His purposes in and through our lives.

O Lord, it is not so important that I be successful, but that I be faithful, that I belong to You, that I represent and glorify You, that I allow You to have Your way in and through me. So be it, Lord. Amen.

The Problem of Pain

Rabbi, who sinned, this man or his parents, that he was born blind?
v. 2

The most common malady of humankind is that of suffering. It is so commonplace that it becomes almost routine, and we tend to become hardened and calloused to it—at least in respect to the suffering of others. Every newspaper screams it out in black headlines. The electronic media give form and voice to it in every news broadcast. But until it personally touches us or our loved ones, it is just so much water over the dam, and we continue to nurse our little aches and pains even while we ignore the millions of suffering and pain-ridden souls in the world about us.

Jesus healed the man born blind, but He made no effort to adequately define or explain the sufferings that plagued His world and ours. He accepted them as part of this distorted, sin-permeated planet, confronted them, and brought the power and grace of His loving Father to bear upon its victims. He was revealing the God who is greater than His creatures' sufferings and can cure them of their maladies—or use them in the accomplishment of His loving will and plan for this world's inhabitants.

We will not discover in Jesus Christ any logical answer or explanation for the sufferings of our world or the pain and problems that may come our way. His takeover of our lives, however, will always produce miracles. It may be the miracle of immediate healing or the eradication of the pain—or the supernatural grace of God that enables us to handle our sufferings and even to use them in the accomplishment of God's purposes in and through us.

O God, may Your Word speak to me, and Your promises reassure me, Your Spirit work some miracle within me, that I may remain faithful to You in times of pain and distress. Amen.

Walking in the Light

Try to learn what is pleasing to the Lord. v. 10

Our immediate goal in respect to this day before us is not to be people-pleasing. It is to be God-pleasing. This is God's will for us this day as it is every day. "Try to learn what is pleasing to the Lord," Paul enjoins the Christians at Ephesus. There is no guarantee that we will thereby please the people about us, but it is the only way we can truly serve God and properly communicate to the human family the grace and the power of our loving God. And it is the only way we can bring the divine and eternal light of God into the darkness that confuses and threatens the inhabitants of this planet.

The light that broke into the darkness of our world through Jesus Christ is now to be transmitted through us. This necessitates our walking in the light. Our self-surrender to God is to be reflected in our self-disclosure to His created children about us. We are to walk as Jesus walked, in honesty and openness, and in loving, self-denying concern for others.

It will not always be popular or make us popular—our walking "as children of light." It means that we cannot participate in some of the everybody-does-it, shady, shadowy activities that people consider natural and necessary in their day-by-day existence. It may mean that we will have to make some controversial decisions and support some unpopular causes. It may, on the other hand, compel or encourage others about us to leave the dark paths of fruitless striving to discover Jesus as the Light of the world.

I need Your light, O Lord, to push back the darkness that so often obscures my journey of faith. You are that light. Enable me to be a light to others who cannot find their way. Amen.

A Time for Anger?

And making a whip of cords, He drove them all . . . out of the temple.

v. 15

It is difficult to conceive of Jesus Christ as ever being angry. Perhaps this is because we foolishly assume that there is no room for anger in love or in loving relationships. We can more easily accept anger in a person such as Paul, who told his constituents at Ephesus to "be angry but do not sin" (Ephesians 4:26); and yet the degree of anger demonstrated by Jesus within the circumstance of our Gospel lesson may disturb us at times.

Both the humanity and the divinity of the loving Christ may well have been indicated in the temple incident. We may sincerely question what might be the reaction of Jesus to some of the "temples" we have erected to the glory of God—the Jesus whose concern for the poorest of the poor is far above any multimillion dollar sanctuary that His more affluent children may raise up and support in His name.

There is a time for anger. We ought to be angry about anything that comes between a person and God, about people's misguided focus upon places in which to worship rather than persons to serve, about questionable activities in God's house, about sexual immorality, about drug abuse, about poverty and injustice and war, about the self-centeredness of most of us who put our personal comfort and welfare above the dire needs of millions of God's human creatures that inhabit our planet.

There are times when it may be sinful *not* to be angry in our kind of world. We need to be aware, however, that God-pleasing anger results in the kind of actions that heal those who hurt, succor those who suffer, and bring God's love to bear upon those who are estranged from Him.

Forgive me, O God, for often being acceptive or indifferent to the horrendous things that afflict me and my human family when I should have been angry. Teach me how to righteously hate those things that harm and destroy Your creatures. Amen.

What Foolishness!

Has not God made foolish the wisdom of the world. v. 20b

What foolishness!

—to buy into the nonsense that the crucifixion of a carpenter-turned-preacher could somehow be interpreted as God taking upon Himself the sins of the world. Yet this is what we as Christians hold to, that in which we hope, in which we invest our whole lives—past, present, and future.

What foolishness!

—to believe that a God of love reigns over this fractured, violence-ridden world of ours, that He really cares about the starving millions, the imprisoned, the deprived, the victims of disease and torture, terrorism and warfare, and the natural calamities that almost daily befall the inhabitants of this planet. Yet this is what we claim; this is the proclamation we joyously fling into the teeth of pagans and unbelievers about us. "Cast all your anxieties on Him, for He cares about you" (1 Peter 5:7).

What foolishness!

—to insist that God is in our midst, that He abides within us, that He loves us and cares about us as His own beloved children, that He is personally concerned about each one of us and has a plan for our lives on this world and guarantees life everlasting in the kingdom to come. Yet this is what we believe; it is this that keeps us pushing on through sunshine or rain, highs or lows, whatever the conflicts and calamities that stand in our way.

"For the foolishness of God is wiser than men . . ."

Open my eyes, O God, so I may recognize the difference between You and Your purposes for Your creatures on this world and all the material and finite gifts lavished upon me which I tend to value overmuch. Amen.

The Gospel of Another Chance

Unless you repent you will all likewise perish. v. 5

It is true in most churches; it may be true about our lives. There is a good deal of foliage. There may even be some colorful blooming now and then. But the real test of faith and obedience is in the fruit that is borne as a consequence of our lives and living. This does not mean that evidence of fruit-bearing or productivity is necessarily statistical—or always visible to the naked eye. Fruit-bearing is not always synonymous with good works or service for God. Fruit is what we are; service is what we do. We are required to bear fruit—wherever God has placed us: the shop or the school, the home or the office, main-street or market-place. We are to "live" Christ—not the narrow, severe, critical, unloving Christ as interpreted and reflected by some people, but the Christ of the Gospels, the joyful, loving, compassionate, kind, gentle, selfless Christ of Christmas and Good Friday, Easter and Pentecost. It means that we are to be kind among people who are cruel, tolerant among those who are irritable and complaining, self-controlled among those who live by their appetites, joyful among the unhappy and ungrateful, generous among the poor and needy, and loving and concerned in all situations—even when we have to take a prophetic · stance over against injustice and prejudice and greed.

And this is where all of us have failed—again and again. Let us be grateful for the Gospel of another chance. It is as if Jesus were interceding on our behalf: "Give them another chance, Father. I will stir them, prune them, and allow some hard times to refine and renew them and teach them how to rely on divine grace, but give them another chance . . ."

Our great God is merciful and patient, and He can make us into fruit-bearing Christians."

Forgive me, dear Lord, for my many failures to bear fruit, and thank You for the opportunity to start over again. Amen.

Overconfident?

No temptation has overtaken you that is not common to man.
v. 13a

"With most of them God was not pleased," wrote Paul about the ancestors who followed Moses out of Egypt. We become the unworthy recipients of God's saving grace in our baptism. Paul is alerting us to the fact that a fall from grace is indeed possible, that among the multitudes who call upon His name and faithfully fulfill the requisites and forms of Christian worship and expression are those with whom He is not pleased. "Therefore let anyone who thinks that he stands take heed lest he fall," he warns the Corinthian Christians.

We may disagree with Paul, or misinterpret him, when he says that God "will not let you be tempted beyond your strength . . ." Many of us have indeed been tempted beyond our strength and have fallen on our faces in shame and despair. We celebrate with Paul, however, the conviction that "God is faithful and . . . with the temptation will also provide the way of escape . . ."

There may have been a temptation that we were not "able to endure," and we grieved the Spirit of God and hurt someone we love. We did not fall from grace! God loves us, and He is still faithful, always faithful. There must be confession and repentance, a renewal of our commitment to the grace of God, His forgiveness, and the strength He promises to enable us to resist the temptations that confront us today. Let us be aware that our confidence is to be in the grace of God—not in self-engendered feelings about Him or in some of our works-righteousness attempts to please Him.

Lord, I have failed again. Despite my firm resolutions and determined efforts, I have flopped—fallen on my face. Forgive me, O God. Help me to remember that You accept me fully through Your Son, Jesus Christ. Amen.

Unforsaken

Hear, you deaf; and look, you blind, that you may see! v. 18

"I will turn the darkness before them into light, the rough places into level ground . . . and I will not forsake them." The word of the prophet was proclaimed on behalf of the Israelites and dealt particularly with God's concern for them. It is equally applicable, as revealed through Jesus Christ, to every one of God's human creatures who follow the Christ. We are the people of God, and His word as spoken to the ancient Israelites is His word to us today.

What a precious word and promise it is as we grope fretfully and fearfully through the clouds of darkness that often close in about us! There will be dark clouds and rough paths along our journey, but we have in Jesus Christ a Shepherd to guide us, a Light to beckon us, a Presence to accompany us whatever this day or the coming week may hold for us.

There are, nonetheless, those hours in which we will feel the chill and loneliness of encompassing darkness, and may stumble painfully on unseen obstacles that litter the trail before us. We need not fret nor fear these circumstances or episodes. Darkness will give way to light; rough roads will level off—it's a promise from God Himself. And whatever the obstacles in our path or the blindness that often hampers us, there is the grand assurance in respect to every one of God's children that He "will not forsake them."

O God, sometimes I am frightened by the uncertainties and insecurities about me. I do find peace and joy in Your promise never to forsake me, that even among the difficult circumstances that plague my life, I know that I can find eternal security in You. Amen.

Leadership and Servanthood

Are you able to drink the cup that I am to drink? v. 22

"Whoever would be great among you must be your servant," said Jesus. In the eyes of the world, leadership is usually associated with power and prominence—and is often sought by very egocentric people. This was possibly the feeling of the mother who naturally and proudly wished for it on behalf of her sons. She didn't understand, nor do many of us, that the kingdom of God is to be served and promulgated by those who serve others and that its leaders are those who become the servants of all.

It is certainly true in respect to those who are chosen and gifted to assume positions of leadership in the family of God; their greatness or effectiveness is determined by the quality of their servanthood. As Jesus has been our servant—even to the point of dying on our behalf—so we are made to be His servants, and we carry out that servanthood by serving our brothers and sisters in the human family.

Jesus is not calling us to positions of leadership. He is sending us forth to be servants and to regard such servanthood as more important than our very lives, to carry out that service without concern for consequences and even less concern for accolades or accommodations. It is those who lovingly serve in this manner who, even without official appointment or recognition, become the real leaders in the kingdom of God.

O Lord, there are times when I have little inclination to live for or to love others as You love me and have commanded me to love. Change me, O Lord, from a sponge greedily sopping up all I can get from You into a fruit-bearing branch that exists to serve others. Amen.

The Matter of Mind-Set

There is therefore now no condemnation for those who are in Christ Jesus. v. 1

It's the truth; it's a fact! We need only to claim it and celebrate it! We are not to be judged under the Law, nor are we to be condemned in our Law-breaking. When we accept what God has done for us through Christ, we are delivered completely and forever from the guilt of sin. This is what Christ did for us some two thousand years ago. In the moment that we lay claim to God's great gift of forgiving love, it is applicable to us—here and now.

There is, however, still the matter of mind-set. While we celebrate what God has done for us through Christ, we need daily to set our minds and focus our energies on living "according to the Spirit" rather than "according to the flesh." While we cannot blot out forever the natural, fleshly thoughts and feelings that haunt us daily—lust, greed, envy, pride, self-centeredness, apathy—we are responsible for crowding out these pernicious thoughts and feelings with a mind-set that embraces the fruits of the Spirit—love, joy, kindness, concern for others, thanksgiving to God. It won't be easy, and we will often meet with failure, but it is a blessed struggle that leads to ultimate victory.

Thank You, Lord, for the sweet assurance that You love me, that I belong to You, that You will never let me go. I will fear neither the night nor the morrow. And even if tomorrow never comes, I rest in the arms of Your forgiving love, for I am Yours forever. Amen.

The High Cost of Loving

God sent His Son into the world . . . that the world might be saved through Him. v. 17

We are aware of the high cost of living. We are not so nearly aware of the high cost of loving. "God so loved the world that He gave His only Son . . ." This is the story of the Incarnation—from the manger birth to the cross on Calvary's hill. This is the ultimate example of love, and it is the pattern and model of the kind of love that we are enjoined to manifest in response to God's love for us.

There are not any of us who can fathom the price of true love as it is demonstrated by Christ's crucifixion and all that it means to us in respect to our relationship to God. "But we see Jesus," said the writer of the Letter to the Hebrews, "who for a little while was made lower than the angels, crowned with glory and honor because of the suffering of death, so that by the grace of God He might taste death for everyone" (Hebrews 2:9). And we see in Jesus the kind of love we are to extend to the human family about us. "This is My commandment," said Jesus, "that you love one another as I have loved you" (John 15:12).

It is going to cost something to love—the addicted and the perverted, the selfish and the corrupted, those of classes and races other than our own, even our neighbors down the block or some of the people we worship with in our own churches. Our great God who gave us His love will now extend that love to others—through us.

O Lord, despite my enthusiastic affirmations and proclamations of Your love for humankind, there are people I do not like very much. Forgive me, God, and teach me anew the meaning of Your great love and enable me to love and accept others even as You love and accept me. Amen.

Made to Be Good

For by grace you have been saved through faith . . . It is the gift of God. v. 8

"For by grace you have been saved through faith . . . it is the gift of God . . . for we are His workmanship, created in Christ Jesus for good works."

Whereas God's saving love is a gift which cannot be merited by human efforts to aspire to divine standards, God's deliverance from sin and self-service sets us free to give our lives to good works, to love God, and communicate love to humanity about us. We were not saved for our welfare alone. We were indeed saved to serve, and in serving God by serving His human creatures we thus fulfill the destiny for which we were created.

It is not meant to be a laborious duty—our serving others—but a glorious response to God's love for us. Whatever our life's vocation—farming, teaching, clerking, mothering, building, nursing, writing—our gifts and efforts are generally expended in the process of service to humankind. The Christian is privileged to do this, and to go far beyond this, in the process of serving people out of God-engendered love. It is this that turns drudgery into joy and gives meaning and purpose to our lives, for today and every day.

I pray, Lord, that being Your servant may always be my primary vocation. Help me to be faithful to You whatever the circumstances that close in about me. I am Yours, dear Lord; never leave my side. Stay with me, Lord, stay with me. Amen.

Only Sinners Are Eligible

My son was dead, and is alive again; he was lost, and is found.

v. 32

A Roman philosopher is recorded as saying: "It is impossible for a man of himself to escape. It must be that someone stretch forth a hand to draw him out." It was said about Jesus—and this by His enemies: "This man receives sinners . . ." We discover in these worth-quoting statements both the dilemma and the deliverance, the latter being personified in the man, God's Son, Jesus Christ.

God knows how we have sought for ways of escape. There were times when some of us have become so filled up and fed up with life's bellyaches that we wanted to go over the hill and "hang one on." Usually we took the route of frenzied activity or, like the Prodigal Son, the road of sensual indulgence. We only discovered how impossible it was to run away from life's conflicts and problems. We discovered, as well, that the basis for such conflicts lies deep within us, that we were born out of orbit with God—at odds with His plan and purpose for our lives—and that our past failures, present conflicts, even our fear of the future are part and parcel of this nature of ours. And then we discovered, and it continues to be a perpetual, ever-new discovery in our lives, that our honest acknowledgment of our condition is not the end but really the beginning of life. It makes us eligible for divine deliverance, for new life, health, and happiness. "This man receives sinners," was the self-righteous murmur of the Pharisees, and they never realized how right they were. It means, praise God, that Jesus receives us, accepts us, loves us, forgives us, reclaims us, and reinstates us as His own, and that we then live out His purposes for our lives.

"He was lost, and is found," said the father of the son who finally "came to himself" and returned to the ranch to be reclaimed and reunited with his family. Isn't this what the Gospel—the good news of salvation—is all about?

Nothing in my hands I bring, dear Jesus, simply to Your cross I cling. Amen.

To God Be the Glory

Let him who boasts, boast of the Lord. v. 31

"He is the source of your life in Christ Jesus . . ."

It is often affirmed that one can't argue with success. When it happens to us—success, that is—it is right that we feel good about it, celebrate it, rejoice in it. When some popular faith-healer, however, insists that the power is God's and he or she is only the instrument, or some preacher responds to a compliment with a "give God the credit" cliché, it sometimes sounds a bit super-pious or something of a put-on.

We are indeed to rejoice in the occasional successes that come our way, but let us be aware lest we revel in them. We are to be encouraged by them without being overwhelmed. They do not make us any more important than anybody else, nor do they increase our worthwhileness in the eyes of God.

May our rejoicing resolve in gratitude, in praise to God rather than praise of self, for "He is the source of your life [and of all your successes] in Christ Jesus . . ."

"Let him who boasts, boast of the Lord."

Gracious Father, I no longer want to build empires, to ascend thrones, or to be number one in my little kingdom. I want to love You and respond to Your love for me by communicating such love to others. Help me to use Your precious gifts of life, freedom, and spiritual power as I relate to people by Your grace to draw them into Your kingdom of light and love. Amen.

What a Day!

With joy you will draw water from the wells of salvation. v. 3

The ancient prophet envisioned an exciting, fantastic event that would come upon the children of God. What a day that would be—the Day of the Lord! On that day the hearts of God's people will be filled with thanksgiving. They will sing songs of joy to the God of their salvation. Their lives will be filled with love, and they will embrace each other as brothers and sisters in the great family of God. Those who claimed their freedom from sin and its guilt through their loving Redeemer will then know that freedom totally, and they will be set free from the evil that tempts, the suffering that inhibits, the fears and doubts that once obscured their God. The encompassing darkness of this world will forever be dispelled, and they shall sing and shout for joy as the beloved children of God.

There is light at the end of the tunnel. Whatever today may bring forth, there is that Day to anticipate. While we cannot evade the trials and burdens of today, we ought to find them lighter and less threatening as we look forward to the Day of the Lord.

O Lord, I do celebrate what I in faith anticipate. It is this hope that keeps me afloat in the tempest that rages about me. It is the promise of total union with You, and the dispersion of all my trials and tears on that great Day, the Day of Your coming, that enables me to face the day before me and whatever it may bring my way. I rejoice in the promise of Your coming! Amen.

We Shall Live Forever

I am the resurrection and the life; he who believes in Me, though he die, yet shall he live. v. 25

It is absolutely true: the sons and daughters of God shall live forever. What Christ has promised has already been granted. It is the abolition of death and the gift of eternal life. The atrocious event of death that threatens and appears to destroy what God has created becomes His very servant that swings open the gates to life everlasting. Jesus has overcome death's evil intent and power by rising from the dead.

We are already citizens of the new kingdom—and this status does not change when we leave behind the known and the familiar of our earthly existence. Thus we need not fear that ultimate event. It only guarantees that we shall hereafter know and experience fully the splendor and beauty of the new kingdom where we can live and serve in supreme joy without the limitations and temptations of mortal life upon this planet.

It is true: because we accept the life Jesus has come to bring, we shall live forever.

I do praise You, O God. As long as I have breath in my body, I will praise You. My name is "written in heaven." You are my hope and salvation, my morning sun and evening star, my shade in the desert heat, my warmth in the cold of night. This is truly reason for rejoicing, for I am Yours, O Lord, Yours forever. Grant that my life be a perpetual offering of praise. Amen.

We Are Identified

For all who are led by the Spirit of God are sons of God. v. 14

"For all who are led by the Spirit of God are sons [and daughters] of God," writes Paul to the church at Rome.

We are identified! We are the very sons and daughters of God. It is this, actualized by the Spirit within us, that enables us to turn from self-service and its resultant estrangement from God to godly service and love for those about us. It is this that makes life significant and gives point and purpose to our living. It is this that puts us back into God's orbit for our lives and welds us to Him in a union that nothing can dissolve.

O God, now I know who I am. You gave me my identity in the moment I was brought to the waters of my baptism. You touched me with Your cleansing power and filled my heart with Your Spirit. I am Your child, fallible and often very foolish. When I stumble in my childish attempts to follow You, You pick me up and dry my tears and heal my wounds and draw me back into Your loving embrace. I am Your servant. I am here to serve my fellow beings, to retain and further comprehend my identity in losing my life on behalf of others. I am Your minister destined to represent Your purposes, to demonstrate Your love, to communicate Your healing touch to the fractured, sin-bound creatures in my path.

I praise You, O God, for creating and redeeming me to be Your child, and for the joy and satisfaction of knowing that I am significant to You despite the judgments and opinions of my peers about me. Thank You, dear Lord, for snatching me out of the pit of self-centeredness and restoring my identity as a member of Your eternal family. Amen.

"We Wish to See Jesus"

*Shall I say, "Father save Me from this hour? No?" No, for this purpose
I have come to this hour.* v. 27

I was rather startled, I remember, when I stepped into the pulpit
of a church in Shanghai, China. Carved on the inside of the pulpit
in such a way that it could be seen only by the preacher were these
words: "Sir, we wish to see Jesus." I never forgot those words, I
honestly tried during that service—and have ever since—to proclaim
the Gospel in such a way that Jesus could be seen or sensed by
those who listened to what I had to say.

There are those times when Jesus is obscured by inadequate
presentations. There are also those times when Jesus is not seen or
His message understood because people are not really seeking
Christ and His Word or they are looking for the kind of Christ that
might fit their preconceived notions and fill their assumed needs.

If we want to see the loving, miracle-working Jesus, the tender,
caring, concerned Christ, the consoling, protecting Shepherd of our
souls, and the answer to our needs and longings, we must also see
Him as the One who died and arose again on our behalf, who
accepts us as His brothers and sisters, and who empowers and
appoints us to be His disciples. If we truly embrace this kind of
Christ and yield ourselves to His will and purposes, we will see
Him—again and again—in His Word to us, in the words and deeds
of our colleagues, in the dire needs of those who suffer around us.

I thank You, Jesus, because You are here in my world. I have
seen You and heard You speak in many places and various
ways—through Your Word, the Sacrament of the Altar, the
words and deeds of Your faithful followers. Now I pray that
others may see and hear You through my daily witness. Amen.

For Those Who Suffer

He became the source of eternal salvation to all who obey Him.
v. 9

"Although He was a Son, He learned obedience through what He suffered . . ." Our loving God does not initiate suffering; it is the consequence of living in this world into which He put us—and often the consequence of our own foolish mistakes. If Jesus suffered, and it was on our behalf and because of our sins even though it was perpetrated by the people who pinned Him on the cross: can we as God's children through Christ's redemption expect anything less?

We may not be able to understand how Jesus learned obedience through suffering, but He was obedient even to His final words while on the cross: "Father, into Thy hands I commit My spirit." He didn't reject His suffering; nor did He rebel against it. He faced it, accepted it, and it became the means of redeeming human, sin-ridden creatures for God.

This, then, must be our answer to the problem of suffering: face it, accept it—and *use* it. Allow it to teach us obedience, to make out of us vessels fit for the Master's use and vehicles of healing and blessing to those who suffer about us.

Teach me, O Lord, how to accept and cope with suffering, how to accept my status as Your beloved child and servant, how to embrace the validity and power that goes with it, and to walk and serve in joy even in the midst of misery. Amen.

The Risk of Loving

And they cast him out of the vineyard and killed him. v. 15a

The parable that Jesus related reveals something of the risk of loving. The owner of the vineyard sent one, two, then a third servant to his tenants. They were beat up and cast out. Then he sent his son—and they killed him. And God's human creatures have thus responded to such love from that time until this.

The God of love refuses to let go or give up; He continues the risk of loving. He keeps loving even those who reject His overtures—even until they break and destroy themselves by their own resistance. He loves men and women at their worst; ". . . while we were yet sinners Christ died for us," wrote Paul (Romans 5:8). "I will send my beloved son," said the owner of the vineyard. "It may be they will respect him."

The God who took such a risk on our behalf has every right to expect that we begin to take some risks on behalf of our fellow beings. We have a position of trust and responsibility in the vineyard of the Master; it is to love our brothers and sisters in the human family. This is our primary vocation in this life, regardless of our various avocations. There is a risk in this kind of loving. There are times when those we love are not able to understand, receive, or assimilate such love. Then we are hurt and frustrated; we pull back and become cautious about extending our love to others.

Loving others does involve pain and suffering, discomfort and inconvenience. At the same time, the very effort to love serves to stretch our souls and enlarge our capacity for enrichment. "He who does not love abides in death," wrote John in his First Letter (3:14b). At least we are truly alive when we reach out in love—whether that love is responded to or not.

I thank You for Your eternal love, O Lord. Now grant to me the courage, the wisdom, and the willingness to risk loving others with whom I come in contact—and to do so without concern for the consequences to my life. Amen.

And So We Press On

> . . . *forgetting what lies behind and straining forward to what lies ahead.* v. 13b

Jesus Christ is sufficient—and so is the righteousness He imparts to us. We don't earn or merit it by following certain rules and rituals; we receive it as the gift of God's love. We possess this righteousness even now by faith in Jesus Christ. We have no need for any other.

This by no means indicates that we have arrived, that we have reached the ultimate in respect to our natural state or being. And so we "press on," in painful yet joyful struggle, to surrender our total beings to God—to let Him have His way with us. This does not come easily. It involves the crucible of conflict—even failure and defeat. But even when we fall, we fall only to rise again, to "press on," acknowledging but never nursing our failures, knowing that our loving God understands and perpetually reaches out to draw us to Himself.

Thus we press on that we "may know Him and the power of His resurrection . . ." We "press on to make it [our] own, because Christ has made [us] His own."

"Let those of us who are mature be thus minded" (v. 15).

You never said it would be easy, Lord, my sojourn in this uncertain, pain-ridden world. I am frightened by the evil forces that contend with me, depressed by my many defeats in trying to carry out Your purposes, dismayed over the obstacles that impede my walk of faith. Grant to me the grace to hold on and press on. Amen.

The Past Is Past

I will make a way in the wilderness and rivers in the desert. v. 19b

"Remember not the former days, nor consider the things of old. Behold, I am doing a new thing."

When the days darken and the times in which we live become unstable, at times even unbearable, we are tempted to look back to those years or episodes in our lives when, we assume, we were happy or more content. Or, on the other hand, we may still be burdened by some failure or sin in the past that continues to rattle its bones or inhibit us in respect to our daily activities or our outlook on the future.

The prophet was singing a song of hope and comfort to his people out of his inspired glimpse of God's plan for the future. This vision of what God was about to do would surpass or overcome the joys or the tragedies of the past. Nevertheless, his message may well be God's word to us at the end of a difficult day or week. "Remember not . . . nor consider the things of old. Behold, I am doing a new thing." We are not really enjoined to forget the negative things of the past, lest we repeat them. And it is often past gifts and blessings that encourage us to boldly face our uncertain future. Hope means that God still reigns and that He loves us and is working out His plan for our lives in this world, that we need not be forever crippled or hampered by past errors or events. A new day or week and new opportunities lie ahead of us, and God will, if our hope is in Him, continue to do "a new thing" in and through us.

You have forgiven me the sins and errors of yesterday, my Lord. Now I am privileged to begin a new day. Help me to be faithful and obedient to Your hope within me and to the voice of Your Spirit within me. Amen.

What Shall We Do with Jesus?

Then what shall I do with Jesus who is called Christ? v. 22

It was initially Pilate's question, and he answered it for himself by symbolically washing his hands of this whole sordid affair that was laid on him by the Jewish religious leaders. Judas betrayed Jesus. Peter, who once said he would risk his life to protect his Master, recoiled in fear and denied any relationship with the Christ when Jesus was indicted. The mob called for Jesus' crucifixion, and most of the disciples looked for someplace to hide.

Perhaps all of us have wondered at times just what would have been our reaction had we been on hand to witness what was happening to the Lord Jesus Christ.

While most of us do respond to the Christ as revealed through His Word by *doing* something with Him—using Him, ignoring Him, running from Him, even trying to run with Him—the question is no longer "What shall [we] do with Jesus?" It is "What has He done and what does He seek to do with us?"

Actually, there is nothing we can *do* to or with Jesus. He is Lord and King, Savior and Master. "I am the way, and the truth, and the life," He said; "no one comes to the Father, but by Me" (John 14:6). God's refusal to violate our personhood allows us to shun Him, to refuse to honor Him, to worship self-concocted gods and idols rather than our Creator and Redeemer, but we have no power to do anything with Him. What we, empowered by His Spirit, are enabled to do is to open our hearts and lives to Him, return to Him, relate to Him as He reveals Himself to us, and embrace Him in faith and obedience.

Forgive me, dear Jesus, for using You for my own concerns. I now want more than anything else in life, to place myself, totally and eternally, into Your blessed hands. So be it, Lord. Amen.

"My God . . . Why?"

He saved others; He cannot save Himself. v. 31b

"My God, my God, why hast Thou forsaken me?" It is the question that each of us, at one time or another, has screamed into cold and gray skies—in the face of the little crosses that have come our way or the heavy crosses laid upon those we love. "My God, why?"

Some people get no further than this agonizing query and live most of their lives under the shadow of that twisted question mark. They make for themselves a veritable hell on earth.

Our Lord also asked "Why?" but before He breathed His last breath on the cross, He turned the apparent tragedy of His crucifixion into a basis for universal blessing with the song of victory: "Father, into Thy hands I commit My Spirit" (Luke 23:46). It is in this act that we discover the key to a proper and beneficial response to our sufferings. It is true that Christ's sufferings were on our behalf, but they also came as a consequence of living in this distorted world.

Our great God does not afflict us with suffering. He does, nonetheless, enable us to bear it and even to discover meaning and often some purpose for our conflicts and afflictions. What is the Christian's answer to suffering? Again it is this: face it, accept it— and *use* it. Allow it to make out of us vessels fit for the Master's use and vehicles of blessing to those about us who suffer. And this becomes possible only by the grace of God.

O God, the vacuum, the agony, the bitterness and pain that afflicts me or those whom I love sometimes flattens me with despair, and I pray that You will fill the vacuum, end the agony, resolve the bitterness, and help me to endure the pain. Amen.

Why Did You Let Us Do It?

There they crucified Him, and the criminals, one on the right and one on the left. v. 33b

I always had a problem with the Passion Story in my childhood readings of the Gospels. In those days of heroes and happy-ending tales, this kind of termination to Christ's life and ministry seemed tragically out of character in respect to the hero I had made Him out to be. Every time I arrived at this final episode in Jesus' ministry I was secretly hoping that my Hero would suddenly turn on His persecuters, those stupid, blind religious and political leaders, and demolish them with a bolt out of the blue. But it never happened that way. He who had set His face toward Jerusalem had now arrived—and His miracle-working ministry of love was to be cruelly terminated in His execution.

I grew up. I gradually began to realize that if I had been living in those days I probably would have been one of that jeering crowd that egged on Jesus' tormentors, or like those disciples who took to the woods in fright when the authorities viciously plotted and carried out their objective to destroy the beloved Master.

"Why, O God, did you let us kill Him?" It's a question that haunts many Christians from time to time. God's answer might go something like this: "How else could I get through to you? How else could I convince you of My love for you? I could not ignore your sin; there was no other way to deal with your selfishness and rebelliousness. I didn't want My Son to suffer and die. In His suffering I suffered; in His dying I died. This is the measure of My love for you. I created humankind with the freedom to believe or to doubt, to obey or disobey, to love or hate, to build or tear down, to give life or to destroy it. You had to have this freedom in order to know the meaning of love. You chose to abuse My love, to ignore My will, to walk a self-chosen course in life. And you do these things even now. If I sent My Son to visibly live on your world today, you would probably crucify Him again."

O God, be merciful to me, a sinner! Amen.

The Mind of Christ

Have this mind among yourselves, which is yours in Christ Jesus.
v. 5

Jesus "emptied Himself, taking the form of a servant . . . He humbled Himself and became obedient unto death . . ." And this is the "mind" that Paul enjoined his constituents to demonstrate "among yourselves."

It is rather far-fetched, to say the least, and bears little resemblance to the "me" philosophy that has pervaded our generation. It is obvious that we need to recognize and joyfully accept our own identities. We would hardly have anything to give if we failed to discover who we are—our individual validity as the sons or daughters of God. That validity, however, tends to diminish if it turns in upon itself. Jesus knew who He was, the very Son of God, and this enabled Him to commit Himself to His Father's will and purposes, to take "the form of a servant" among God's human creatures—even to the extent of dying on their behalf.

The old "saved to serve" cliché, though simplistic, is still true. Our value as individuals, though inherent by way of our creation and redemption, is truly enhanced and fulfilled in our dedication to servanthood. As Jesus came to serve us, and thereby to serve His Father, so we are upon this planet—within the kingdom of this world—for the express purpose of serving our fellow beings. "Have this mind among yourselves, which is yours in Christ Jesus . . ."

You have not only redeemed me and adopted me as Your child, You have chosen and appointed me to be Your servant. You have, O God, entrusted me with great responsibility. Help me to be Your faithful and effective servant. Amen.

"It Is Finished!"

He said, "It is finished"; and He bowed His head and gave up His spirit. v. 30

The agony was over. Jesus no longer felt the terrible pangs of crucifixion nor heard the taunts and insults of a blood-thirsty mob. No longer were felt the thorns upon His brow, the stripes on His back, the nails through His flesh. No longer was felt the soul torture and bitterness of separation from His heavenly Father. His heart had now ceased to beat. "It is finished!"

But there were, in the stifling silence following Jesus' death, other sounds: the sounds of bursting fetters, breaking chains, crumbling prison walls, the rending of veils, the overthrowing of barriers, the opening of gates. Christ's last words were not the words of defeat, but the cry of victory, the shout of triumph, the sounds of a trumpet. "It is finished." "Finished" was the work of redemption, the last payment for the guilt of sinful man and woman. "Finished" was the terrible ban of judgment upon the ages, the power of darkness and desolation, the curse of sin upon humanity.

What Christ finished, however, has scarcely begun for us. He accomplished what we could not. He closed the unbridgeable gulf between God and humankind. Now the work of His visible presence was done and the work of His invisible presence was to continue through the followers He left behind. Forgiven by Christ and empowered by the Spirit of God, we are by His grace qualified and commissioned to be members of that great body of Christ that is elected to carry on and continue that which He made possible when He said, "It is finished."

Dear Jesus, help me to recognize my identity as Your child and my appointment as Your servant and to carry on the task You left for me and all Your disciples to accomplish and fulfill in our world. Amen.

Nothing but a Promise

For the Lord will vindicate His people and have compassion on His servants. v. 36a

The lights had gone out. It appeared in those dismal hours following the burial of Jesus that Christianity died with the Christ and was laid with Him in the sepulcher. There was not a single human being who believed it would be possible ever to see Him again. What remained for the disciples but to return to their homes and their fishing nets as tragically disappointed, disillusioned men and try their best to forget the whole amazing experience? There never were men more utterly depressed and dispirited than were the disciples of Christ in those hours immediately following His crucifixion.

There was nothing left but a promise—a promise that went as far back as Moses, that was reiterated by the prophets, that was clearly ennunciated by Jesus Himself before this tragic event. But the disciples appeared to pay little attention to that promise. For them the lights had gone out.

We live in a day of promise-fulfillment—a fact we shall happily celebrate in the next several weeks. Yet we too are people of a promise—the promise of God's total revelation and our complete enjoyment of Him and His kingdom on the day of our resurrection. There will be those hours of pain and darkness in our daily walk through life, but encompassing us through it all is the promise of God's love and our eternal salvation. And this, on the basis of Christ's crucifixion and resurrection, is enough to enable us joyfully to press on, knowing full well that God's Word can be embraced and trusted and "there is none that can deliver [us] out of [His] hand."

O God, You came to us through Your Son as You promised. Jesus died for our sins and arose from the dead as promised. I am Yours and will be Yours forever as promised. I continue my faith journey believing that Your promises will come to pass. Amen.

Christ Alive—and for Real

He is not here; for He has risen, as He said. v. 6a

Christ has arisen; He is alive and for real! Do we want proof of this amazing event? Then let us consider the consequences of Easter and Pentecost in the lives of His first followers. Their faith, which died when Jesus died, was suddenly revived. They report that Jesus arose and that they saw Him. They tell us about their visits to the empty tomb, and how He appeared to Mary Magdalene, to the other women, to Peter, to the two on the way to Emmaus, to ten of them at once, to eleven of them at once, to James, and to the five hundred.

These were more than the verbal reports of excited, exuberant men and women. The amazing thing is that along with these reports of the resurrection of Christ was the indisputable resurrection of Christianity. After Easter and Pentecost the once defeated and disillusioned disciples became men set on world conquest. They who sought for thrones were now fearlessly expecting persecution and death. These few men—ordinary, fallible, blundering men— were changed from inferior failures into flaming messengers, ready to go boldly into the very city that had crucified their leader and to proclaim Him as the world's Savior. Their faith was no longer a consoling convenience, but a consuming passion. They were electrified with a new power; they proclaimed a new message; they sang a new song. Christ is alive! Christ is for real!

When God's Spirit moves us to faith in the resurrection of Christ, giving us God's power to live and act on the basis that it is so—that it really happened—then we will discover, as millions have before us, that Christ is alive—in us, through us, and forever.

Living Christ, raise us from our graves of defeat and despair and send us forth to reflect and to demonstrate Your resurrection power to others in our world. Amen.

Is It Really True?

If then you have been raised with Christ, seek the things that are above. v. 1a

The resurrection of Christ—is it really true?

"No, it cannot be," say some people. "It simply does not fit my idea of God and the world. I didn't see any resurrection. I can't feel it. It doesn't do anything for me. I can see nothing of a living Christ in this distorted, violent, hate-ridden world of today.

Perhaps most of us have, at one time or another, been under the dark cloud of unbelief in respect to the resurrection of our Lord. Equally serious is the possiblity that we, in our lives and attitudes, may have contributed to the unbelief of our brothers and sisters in the human family—even while sincerely confessing and joyously celebrating the resurrection event. The unbelieving masses about us are not likely to put much stock in some historical event if the followers of the living Christ continue to live primarily for the things of this world or have little concern for the hungry, oppressed, and suffering creatures about them.

When we speak to others about Christ being alive and for real, many will believe this only if it is dramatized here and now— through the lives of His followers through whom He is able to communicate His love and healing power in this very hour.

We will continue to celebrate Christ's resurrection. It is even more important that we "set [our] minds on things that are above, not on things that are on earth." Only then will we be lovingly compelled and enabled to concentrate and act upon our responsibilities as Christ's followers within our world.

Touch others through me with Your resurrection power, O Christ, that they may be raised from the dead to live and serve and praise You forever. Amen.

We Can Prove It for Ourselves

He has risen, He is not here; see the place where they laid Him.
v. 6b

The central core and factor of Christianity is the bodily resurrection of Jesus Christ from the dead. We believe that it really happened—among other reasons, because of the millions before us who believed, and because of the fantastic transformation that took place in the lives of men and women who met the resurrected Christ or who have believed in the risen Christ from that day until this.

Even more pertinent to us today is the witness of men and women in this hour who truly believe in the resurrection of Jesus Christ. Most of us know that something indefinable and incomprehensible happens to people who really entrust themselves to the risen Christ. There are pathetic contradictions and inconsistencies—the scores who verbally claim to believe and yet remain but self-centered blobs on the fringe of genuine Christianity—but there are changes that take place in the lives of those who truly commit themselves to the risen Christ that confound the skeptic and help to assure us that Jesus really did arise from the dead and that it is the risen Christ and the eternally living and loving God whom we worship today.

The grand truth is that we can prove the resurrection of Christ for ourselves. We cannot do this with historical evidence or contemporary analysis—and we may not be able to do it for anybody else—but we can prove it for ourselves. We can enter in to this truth-revealing experience by living and acting on the basis that it is true irrespective of whether or not our feelings and emotions immediately attest to it. It is belief in spite of scientific evidences, but it is also life and living in scorn of consequences. It is the only way to discover for oneself the authenticity of Christ's resurrection and personally to experience His life and power.

I pray, O God, that the power that raised Christ from the dead may raise me out of my fears and failures to celebrate forever Your victory over sin and death. Amen.

It's a Fact

If in this life we who are in Christ have only hope, we are of all men most to be pitied. v. 19

"But in fact Christ has been raised from the dead . . ." Paul never hedged in his proclamation of the living Christ. It was a fact; it was his unfaltering conviction. His Damascus experience—the light from heaven driving him to the ground, the voice identifying Jesus: "I am Jesus, whom you are persecuting," the divine command instructing the blinded Paul to submit to God's will for his life—was enough to convince him that "Christ [had] been raised from the dead." It was an experience Paul never forgot. It became the thesis and basis of his preaching from that time to the hour of his martyrdom.

Through Paul, through the apostles who saw the risen Christ, through the multitudes who have followed this Christ and witnessed to Him, who have preached and written about Him throughout the centuries, God has spoken to us.

The fact of Christ's resurrection resolves into another astounding fact: we shall, indeed, be raised from the dead. "The last enemy to be destroyed is death," wrote Paul. It is not logical or comprehensible to our three-dimensional insights; it is a fact, nonetheless, and a glorious hope that gives us the courage to joyfully march on—and even to risk our lives on behalf of others.

It is a fact, my Savior and Master; You have been raised from the dead. Now help me to daily reflect and demonstrate Your resurrection power to others I meet along the journey of faith. Amen.

If I Really Believed

Why do you seek the living among the dead? v. 5b

"These words seemed to them an idle tale, and they did not believe them," it was said about the disciples when the women brought the news of their shocking experience at the empty tomb.

I say that I believe that Christ has risen. I confess my faith in the living Lord every time I attend my church or pray in His name. But do I really believe? What ought to happen in my life or as a consequence of my living if I really believed?

If I really believed that Christ arose from the dead, I would fling aside my garments of self-righteousness, the camouflage, the window-dressing of my life, and fall on my face before the living Christ in repentance of sin.

If I really believed that Christ arose from the dead, my life would be filled with joy unspeakable, peace incomprehensible. I would not be commiserating over guilt feelings out of the past or be too anxious about the future.

If I really believed that Jesus lives, no problem or difficulty, weakness or sin, insufficiency or inadequacy could destroy me. I would discover that the power which raised Christ from the grave cannot be baffled by my thwarting frailties—that the God who performed this amazing feat of might and glory could certainly handle my small pains and problems.

If I really believed in the risen Christ, I would realize my identity and validity as God's child and servant, take up the cross assigned to me, and dedicate my gifts and energies to the splendid task of proclaiming and demonstrating that Christ is alive and that His saving grace and abundant life are available to every human creature.

If I really believed . . .

Loving God, show me how the power that raised Jesus from the dead can be applied to my life and living. Amen.

Keep on Believing

*By the grace of God I am what I am, and His grace toward me was
not in vain.* v. 10a

The high point, the constantly recurring theme, and the grand
climax in the great symphony of the Gospels, is the resurrection of
our Lord Jesus Christ. He died for our sins; He arose from the dead
victorious over sin and death. If we subtract this from our message
of love and hope, we have nothing to say. We must be sure of
this—His resurrection—and we can be. It was witnessed by many
before us; it has or can be experienced within us.

These are the terms in which Paul preached to the church at
Corinth: "the Gospel, which you received, in which you stand, by
which you are saved, *if you hold firmly to the word.*" Equally
important to our salvation is the necessity of holding fast, of keeping
the faith, the determination, in spite of the pluses and minuses in
our lives, to keep on believing and rejoicing in the Easter event.
This does not eradicate the probability of nagging doubts from time
to time. It necessitates our returning, again and again, to the
resurrection event, to the renewal of our convictions—repeatedly
exposing ourselves and grappling with the consequences of the
resurrection of Christ in the lives of His followers throughout the
centuries and embracing the power and grace of that glorious event
for our own lives.

We need often to prostrate ourselves at the foot of the cross in
confession of our sins. We need, as well, to look into the empty
tomb in order to be reassured that Christ lives and is ever present to
enable us to hold fast the faith amidst the doubts that plague us. We
need to keep on believing—by the grace of God.

O God, I need Your grace to enable me to keep on believing,
to hold firmly to the glorious gospel of my salvation as granted
through the resurrection of Christ. Amen.

It Is Done

This is the Lord . . . let us be glad and rejoice in our salvation.
v. 9b

It is done! What Isaiah, inspired by the Holy Spirit, prophesied, has been accomplished! "The covering that is cast over all peoples, the veil that is spread over all nations" has been removed. Death has been swallowed up, and the Lord God has wiped away all tears.

This is what we have been celebrating in these days and will continue to celebrate in the days to come. "Lo, this is our God; we have waited for Him, that He might save us. This is the Lord . . . let us be glad and rejoice in His salvation."

We are no longer waiting for our salvation; it is ours in this very moment—as is the gift of eternal life. As Christ was raised from the dead, so we are guaranteed such a resurrection. These mortal coils and entanglements can no longer bind us. We have been set free to be perfectly reunited to our loving God and Creator forever.

Even while we shuffle along the corridors of this disjointed, broken world, we do so in victory and joy. Even while we cling to our lives and possessions—and taste the afflictions and sorrows of this earthly journey—we do so with the conviction that we have nothing to lose, "that the sufferings of this present time are not worth comparing with the glory that is to be revealed to us" (Romans 8:18).

"Let us be glad and rejoice in His salvation."

"Praise God from whom all blessings flow!" And so I praise You, my Lord. You created the earth and all that is in it. You can heal the wounds and mend the fractures in the lives of Your creatures. You watch out for Your own and love and care for them. I praise You, O God, for truly You are a great God. Amen.

When Believing Is Seeing

Blessed are those who have not seen and yet believed. v. 29b

Some of us envy Peter and Paul and those other apostles of the first-century church who saw the risen Christ, talked to Him, and were challenged by Him. Had we been in their sandals, we too might have been faithful and courageous—even to the point of martyrdom. But we live in a fractured world. We see so many unsaintly and unsanctified things within us and about us that bear no resemblance whatsoever to the resurrected Christ. There are problems we cannot solve, tragedies we cannot explain, conflicts we cannot handle, and we become "Tremulous Thomases" who pine for more tangible evidences of divine power—that power which was supposed to have been made available through the resurrection of Jesus and the indwelling Spirit of Christ.

As with Thomas, our cry is often, "If I could see, I would believe." The response of Christ is always, "If you would believe, you would soon see. Blessed are those who have not seen and yet believe."

Along with the New Testament proclamations of God's loving and saving grace is offered the faith to embrace that grace. It begins when we really believe—when we stop talking *about* God and walk right into His invisible presence to talk *to* Him, throwing our full weight upon Him, plunging into the ocean of His forgiving and sustaining grace and love. We may not feel anything very significant, or see miracles take place before our eyes, but there will eventually come, in response to our believing and obeying, a sense of added strength, new insights, increased courage, and the dawning realization that we are in touch with divine power, the same power that raised Jesus from the dead, the kind that will make a real difference in our lives.

I cannot see You or touch You, O Lord, but I pray that You will lead me into the intimate, risk-filled depths of an authentic relationship with You so that You may truly be God in me and through me. Amen.

119

Response to Easter

By His great mercy we have been born anew to a living hope through the resurrection of Jesus Christ from the dead. v. 3

"Without having seen Him you love Him; though you do not now see Him You believe in Him and rejoice with unutterable and exalted joy."

This is the Christian response to the Easter event, the resurrection of Christ. It is "as the outcome of [our] faith [that we] obtain the salvation of [our] souls." Jesus died for the sins of the whole human family; He arose from the dead as victor over sin and the death that follows as a consequence of sin. Faith, believing without seeing, "the assurance of things hoped for, the conviction of things not seen" (Hebrews 11:1), is that God-imparted faculty or grace which receives and appropriates God's gift of forgiveness and eternal life.

It is genuine faith, imparted by God, tested in the crucible of suffering, demonstrated in believing without seeing, expressed in rejoicing "with unutterable and exalted joy," that formulates the proper response to Easter. God grant that our faith, tempered by the hot fires of adversity, be enlarged and increased. May our love for God and our brothers and sisters about us be made more honest and generous. And may it result in our do-or-die determination to please God and serve our fellow persons regardless of the cost or consequence to our lives.

In response to Your resurrection from the grave, dear Lord, may I claim from You the courage, wisdom, and willingness to risk loving my fellow persons regardless of the cost or consequences to my life. Amen.

Everyone Who Believes

Who is it that overcomes the world but he who believes that Jesus is the Son of God? v. 5

"Everyone who believes that Jesus is the Christ is a child of God . . ." The word "believe" is often shallow and misappropriated in contemporary use. We who have committed our lives to God as He is revealed through Jesus Christ *are* the children of God. And then John says, in essence, that as children of the same Father we are brothers and sisters, and in loving our divine Parent we also love one another.

It is both a command and the response of genuine belief or commitment—love of God equals love of our fellow persons. John is not reluctant about calling it a commandment. We realize, as well, that such love is a consequence of God's love for us. When we allow something to come between ourselves and each other, that something obscures and may cloud our relationship to God. We demonstrate our love of God—and respond to His love—by loving one another and thereby living in obedience to His commandment. Because we obey as a response to God's love for us, the commandment to love one another is "not burdensome"; we obey joyfully, even when our obedience leads into suffering and sacrifice on behalf of others.

John assures us that it is this kind of response and obedience, loving one another even as we love God as revealed through the resurrected Christ, that will grant us the ultimate victory over the rebellious, anti-God forces of the world and society in which we live.

Teach me, Lord, how to love Your children, whatever their race or creed or station in life, and to love them even as You love me and all Your other creatures. Amen.

On to Victory

Behold, He is coming with the clouds, and every eye will see Him.
v. 7a

"I am John, your brother, and as a follower of Jesus I am your partner in patiently enduring the sufferings that come to those who belong to His Kingdom" (v. 9a TEV).

John speaks with authority, and the recounting of his revelation is a message of encouragement and hope to his peers, as well as to each of us in our tumultuous times. "Hang in there! Keep the faith!" he is saying to us. "These are difficult times for Christians, but the final victory is God's—and ours!"

This is not the time for despair; it is the time for celebration. Jesus has come; He is present with us amid the trials of this tempestuous world. "Fear not, I am the first and the last, and the living one; I died, and behold I am alive for evermore." He is about ready to come again and gather His faithful followers into the fully revealed and eternally reigning kingdom of God. At that time the suffering martyrs, the struggling saints, the priests and prophets, servants and disciples of all the ages shall be united together to sing the praises of the resurrected Christ, their eternal Savior and King.

Let us begin the celebration even now!

There are days when I long intensely for Your return to this planet, dear Lord, and for the consummation of Your purposes and the revelation of Your Kingdom, and for my total deliverance from the problems of this world. Come quickly, my Lord, and while I wait, grant to me the grace to hold on. Amen.

We Are Witnesses

God raised Him up, having loosed the pangs of death. v. 24a

"This Jesus God raised up, and of that we all are witnesses."

This was Peter's first and grandest sermon. At least it had a great effect on a large number of people. He was in the right place at the right time. He was indwelt and empowered by the Spirit of God. He had a good text (Psalm 16:8–11). His bottom line in this lesson is the clincher: "This Jesus God raised up, and of that we all are witnesses." This glorious fact gave Peter's sermon the impact it needed on this unforgetful day.

It isn't likely that any of us can be very effective in our proclamation of the Gospel unless we are witnesses and participants in the Good Friday-Easter events in the life of Christ. "We were buried therefore with Him by baptism into death," wrote Paul, "so that as Christ was raised from the dead by the glory of the Father, we too might walk in newness of life" (Romans 6:4).

In a very wonderful sense the children and servants of God *are* witnesses. The death and resurrection of Jesus Christ became real to us as we embraced Him by faith and dedicated our lives to His service. Very few of us will witness the kind of results Peter did when thousands were converted to Christ as the consequence of his preaching, but when we proclaim and demonstrate the Gospel as witnesses of and participants in the power of God as manifested in the living Christ, there are and will be results, for "we are all witnesses."

I thank You, my glorious and ever-loving God, for making me Your child by raising Jesus from the dead. Now grant me the grace to effectively witness to others concerning that grand event and what it means for their lives. Amen.

The Continuing Witness

Repent therefore, and turn again, that your sins may be blotted out.
v. 19a

This is Peter's second sermon—following an act of healing that turned a group of bystanders into a body of witnesses to the power of the resurrected Christ. What an act to follow! Now Peter could really speak with authority and to an audience that would hang on to his every word. He was quick to take advantage of this remarkable event to credit God publicly for the miracle they had seen and to make it clear to his listeners that the crippled beggar was healed in the name of the risen Christ. The once undependable, half-comprehending, and sometimes compromising Peter was becoming the courageous, responsible apostle that Jesus had chosen and destined him to be. And John and Peter were the first disciples of Jesus to be arrested—partly as a result of Peter's second sermon.

Peter's message on this occasion turns out to be a bold and vigorous proclamation of the Gospel. Building on the recorded words of Moses and the prophets, Peter portrays the resurrected Jesus as that long-promised Servant of God who has come, and will indeed come again, to save and bless His people. Like John the Baptist before him, Peter calls on his listeners to repent and turn to the God of their fathers that their sins may be blotted out.

Peter and John were arrested by the religious leaders, the consequence of their courageous and joyful witness, but hundreds more were added to the fold because of their faithful ministry.

Heavenly Father, I have a living hope through the resurrection of Jesus Christ. I not only may walk my journey in joy, but in response to Your great gift desire to witness to Your grace and power granted to everyone who will commit his or her life to You. Amen.

The Complusion to Obey God

We must obey God rather than men. v. 29

The continuing witness of the apostles rapidly built up the Christian fellowship. It also brought down the wrath of the leaders of Israel, who saw their own prestige and authority wearing thin in the light of the glowing success that followed these preachers and healers. Astounding things were happening among the ever-enlarging crowds that gathered around these men. When the chief priests slapped them into jail in an attempt to stifle their dangerous declarations, even the jail could not hold them, and they were back in the streets again "obey[ing] God rather than men."

The apostles were not living dangerously in order to please or satisfy their heavenly Father or to win some crown or other in some other dimension. They were joyously compelled to risk their lives, to bear beatings and imprisonments, in order that the message of the living Christ might be heard by the people. They were filled with faith and trust in God, and the consequence was the abandonment of all that most mortals hold dear in order to commit their minds and bodies to God and His purposes, as well as to their fellow creatures and their needs.

We obviously don't impress God by suddenly becoming interested and concerned about His purposes in our world. We must first recognize and appropriate His eternal love for us—no matter how wretched or miserable we are—and then allow His gracious Spirit to fill, enervate, and propel us toward obedience and toward a committal of all we are and have to Him and His purposes.

O Lord, embracing You as my Savior results in being lovingly compelled to commit my life to You as my Lord, and that means that I am called and commanded to give myself to others for Your sake. This I want to do—by Your grace. Amen.

The Road to Emmaus

Jesus Himself drew near and went with them. v. 15b

The walk to Emmaus was filled with despair for a couple of Christ's disciples as they reviewed the horrible happening in the city they left behind.

The darkness and depression that enveloped these two men are often reflected in our lives today. Whatever may be the distant goal of our travels, *our* Emmaus, there are days marked by despair. We may be economically strapped; there is little security in the things we have pinned our hopes upon. We are confronted with the fact that the ladder of success we have been climbing doesn't go any higher. The traditions we have so avidly clung to are not as relevant as they appeared to be. The church institutions we assumed were perpetually secure are shifting precariously with the winds of our tempestuous times. We reach back for yesterday because we are uncertain of today and afraid of tomorrow.

A stranger joined the two men on their way to Emmaus. Eventually revealing Himself as the resurrected Christ, He transformed their day of despair into the most glorious experience of their lives. It is this same Christ who accompanies us on our daily walk to our Emmaus. It is He who seeks to transform our darkness and despair into brightness and joy. The ugly and painful things that happen to us are not the end of life. We may have lost a loved one, but we need not lose our faith. We may have little worldly security, but our salvation is still intact. We may be terribly lonely, but we are never alone. The death of Jesus resolved in life eternal; the dying that is a part of our daily walk will give way to resurrection.

Christ has arisen; we shall live forever!

"Though I walk in the midst of trouble, You preserve my life . . . with Your right hand You save me," said the psalmist. And so I trust in You and Your presence with me on my daily walk. Amen.

We Are Ransomed

You know that you were ransomed . . . not with silver or gold, but with the precious blood of Christ. vv. 17, 19

Peter was older and wiser at the time he wrote his letters than he was in those exciting, exhilarating days following the resurrection of Christ and the coming of the Holy Spirit to indwell the lives of God's children and servants. He had, sometimes through trial and error, at other times because of persecution and imprisonment, developed into a mature, sensitive leader of the early church. He had learned—what some Christians apparently never learn—how to balance the theology of suffering with the theology of glory, the cross with the resurrection. He was no longer expecting Christ's imminent reappearance as most of the apostles initially did, but was solemnly alerting his constituents to the probability of much suffering and the possibility of violent death if they persisted in following the teachings of the living Christ.

Peter's proclamations, at least as evidenced by his writings, were not a promise of perpetual ecstasy but a theology of hope. "You were ransomed . . . with the precious blood of Christ," he wrote. "Through Him you have confidence in God, who raised Him from the dead and gave Him glory, so that your faith and hope are in God."

We may never face the kind of conflicts and sufferings the early Christians had to deal with—and that thousands of contemporary saints are struggling with today—but each of us who follow Christ have conflicts of our own. There are times when the pain evoked by the cross we carry obscures the joy of the resurrection. But hope, though severely tested, need never die. Foolish, weak, sinful, unworthy, we are "ransomed . . . with the precious blood of Christ." Nothing can change that; it is our eternal condition.

Lord Jesus, while I cherish the moments of ecstasy that You graciously grant to me, I cling tenaciously to the glorious hope of my redemption won for me on the cross You bore on my behalf. Amen.

"Handle Me and See"

See My hands and My feet, that it is I Myself; handle Me, and see.
v. 39a

The wonder and splendor of our loving God will never cease to astound us—unless, that is, we become insensitive, stupified zombies. Above all, the great resurrection event is beyond all human comprehension. Through Christ-incarnate, God came to us as a baby. He died on the cross at the hands of His own creatures. Now, following His resurrection, He marches right into our dull, sinful, earthbound natures and says, "Handle Me and see." It is utterly impossible to even imagine what more a loving God could do for His created children than what He has already done and is doing to heal them, redeem them, and restore them to His divine family. "Handle Me and see." If God has to come as man and submit to the curious, groping, ever-doubting hands of the very beings He created in order to assure them of His eternal love, even that will be done and was done that humanity might return to Him. "Handle Me and see."

The disciples were ultimately convinced that their Lord and Master had risen from the dead. Jesus, the resurrected Christ and as yet, for most part, the still unrecognized Christ in our world today, still bids us, challenges us to recognize and embrace Him as the living Christ. He has conquered death; He has set us free from sin and its eternal consequences. And we are assured that the same power that raised Him from the dead is available still, not only for our salvation but also for our daily sustenance and the accomplishing of His purposes in and through us. He can meet all our needs. He can satisfy the hunger of our barren souls. He can give us, even in the midst of this bewildering and chaotic age, an eternal peace, a vibrant joy like that experience by those first followers when they finally recognized Christ.

"Handle Me and see."

I adore and praise You, my loving God, for coming to me through Christ-incarnate. I embrace Him in faith and will serve Him forever. Amen.

The Resurrection Made Applicable

And we are writing this that our joy may be complete. v. 4

Easter, as properly understood and accepted, means happy endings and new beginnings. It means that there can be a happy ending to the control and reign of sin in our lives, to the loneliness, the doubts, anxieties, and fears that plague us, even to the fear of death. It means, as well, that there can be new beginnings in our lives in terms of joy and effectiveness and love and service.

John tells us how we can respond to the Easter event in such a way as to make all this happen. He writes as a witness and participant in the great Easter happening and is sharing this experience in order that "our joy may be complete," the out-of-this-world joy of being reconciled to God, of being reunited to His kingdom, His orbit and purpose for our lives. John's message is a glorious outpouring of hope—that we can have fellowship with God, that in the midst of our darkness and despair there is divine light, and that we can live and serve within that light amid the darkness and violence and contradictions of our world that press in upon us. "If we confess our sins," he writes, "He is faithful and just, and will forgive our sins and cleanse us from all unrighteousness."

If this happens—and even this can happen only by the enabling power of God—there is the blessed guarantee of God's forgiveness and of our restoration to His redeeming and reconciling love. It is this that will truly make "our joy . . . complete."

Teach me, O Lord Jesus, how to share in Your glorious resurrection, that I may be raised up out of foolish anxieties and earthbound concerns to celebrate and to demonstrate Your resurrection in this world about me. Amen.

Business As Usual?

Simon Peter said to them, "I am going fishing." They said to him, "We will go with you." v. 3a

Easter was over. It was a great happening—a grand climax to all of the tragic and glorious events that had befallen the disciples. Now that the excitement had subsided and there was nothing better to do, Peter turned to the men he had traveled with for the better part of three years and said bluntly, "I am going fishing." "We will go with you," responded the other disciples, and off they went, boats, nets, and men, to business as usual—a business they had at one time assumed they had left behind forever.

It is a glaring portrayal of so many of our post-Easter activities. Like the disciples, we have experienced something of the excitement and joy of Easter. We believe with all our hearts that Jesus arose from the dead. But on Monday it is business as usual— the same commonplace routine, the same problems, anxieties, defeats, bondages as the week before. Easter has impressed us, as it does year after year, but it somehow fails to empower us with a bit of the divine energy that brought Christ from the grave.

The disciples "caught nothing" in their post-Easter fishing expedition—until they recast their nets in response to the order of a stranger on the beach. Then they caught their fish and came up with a post-Easter recognition of their beloved Master, the Lord Jesus Christ.

If we take the great event of Easter seriously, it will no longer be "business as usual" in the days and weeks and years following Easter. It will be a new life lived in the grace and power of the risen Christ. Then we will discover the real meaning of Christianity and how we may become effective channels and communicators of love and healing to lonely, unhappy, defeated people in the Monday-through-Saturday world about us.

You are alive, my Lord! You are here and now! Now I know that nothing that may confound or perplex me is too great for You. Amen.

The Act of Worship

Worthy is the Lamb who was slain. v. 12a

Worship is, in the words of J. B. Phillips, "a declaration of God's worth." This lesson from John's Revelation is his vision of a gigantic worship service, millions of God's creatures, from elders to angels, saying or singing in a loud voice: "Worthy is the Lamb who was slain, to receive power and wealth and wisdom and might and honor and glory and blessing!" They were declaring God's worth, or more explicity, the worth of His Son, the One who was slain and who lives again.

The dominant note of John's vision is *celebration*—and what a celebration! It is proper, and in some cases long overdue, that this becomes the dominant note of our worship services. Jesus died for our sins; He arose from the dead as Victor over sin and death. Let's celebrate, not only through the Easter season, but throughout the church year.

Worship must take into account other things—such as *relationships,* the need to recognize and celebrate our unity with and our need for one another as God's children. Worship includes *action*—as Paul indicated when he stated that worship is the presentation of our "bodies as a living sacrifice, holy and acceptable to God" (Romans 12:1). If our celebration is genuine, as was that of the creatures in John's vision, it will lead to loving relationships and dedicated activities in respect to God's will and purposes for humankind.

God is indeed worthy of our worship. Let us declare His worth. May our lives be perpetual acts of worship as we seek today and always to do His will.

How delightful it is, our great God, to gather together the frayed ends of our lives and our relationships and focus our attention and concern on Your love and grace, to declare Your worth and celebrate Your presence. Amen.

Under No Other Name

This is the stone which was rejected by you builders . . . v. 11a

One can imagine the consternation, even the anger, that would prevail in any of our congregations should the pastor suddenly announce one Sunday morning that he was informed through some vision or voice from another dimension that the Gospel he had been preaching, and which has been embraced by Christendom for the last twenty centuries, was no longer adequate or relevant.

If we can imagine that, we may be able to understand something of the feelings and reactions of the priests and elders, rulers and scribes, that Peter accosted in his explanation concerning this cripple who was healed as a consequence of their ministry. While Peter was not demeaning the ancient traditions and the sacred Scriptures that these learned leaders lived by and which were the basis for the very existence of Israel, he was proclaiming the name and deeds of One who was far superior and who was the very culmination of everything the prophets had declared. Peter was brazenly and bluntly announcing to these officials that the salvation of Israel could only be realized under the name of Jesus Christ, whom they had crucified. Is it any wonder that Peter and most of the apostles were immediately blacklisted by the leaders of Israel?

We are probably more prudent than Peter—and not nearly so courageous—but this is the message of the New Testament that we profess to hold to: "There is no other name . . . there is salvation in no one else . . . [than] by the name of Jesus Christ . . ." We may not impress or convince our peers from non-Christian religions or cults by blasting it out at them as did Peter, but we are expected to live and serve on the basis that we *do* believe that "there is salvation in no one else." It is clearly the proclamation of the New Testament; it ought to be the issue of our daily lives.

Help me, my Lord, to practice and proclaim Your Word and Your life as the way of salvation for all who will embrace You as their Savior and Lord. Amen.

That They May Have Life

I am the Door; if any one enters by Me, he will be saved. v. 9

If we were to speak of the primary subject of the New Testament, the ultimate purpose of religious organizations and movements about us, the aim of all sermons preached and services conducted, the object of God made incarnate and dwelling among us, the significance of the suffering, death, and resurrection of Jesus Christ, it would add up to one word: LIFE. "I came," said Jesus, "that they may have life, and have it abundantly."

It is this Christ, God-incarnate, who is the authentic Door to Life in respect to the *physical being* of His creatures. The New Testament teaches that God is not simply Lord of a particular aspect of human nature, such as the spiritual or the moral, but is the ultimate ground of all being; He is Lord of all. "Your body is a temple of the Holy Spirit within you," said Paul (1 Corinthians 6:19).

Jesus Christ is the Door to Life in respect to a person's *intellectual faculties.* "Brethren, do not be children in your thinking . . . be mature" (1 Corinthians 14:20).

Jesus Christ is the Door to a person's *moral life and nature.* "The body is not meant for immorality, but for the Lord" (1 Corinthians 6:13b).

Jesus Christ is the Door in respect to a person's *spiritual nature.* ". . . it is the Spirit Himself bearing witness with our spirit that we are children of God" (Romans 8:16).

Truly, the resurrected Christ is the Door to abundant living, to fulfillment and enrichment, meaning and purpose. "I came that they may have life, and have it abundantly."

Thank you, God, for coming to us, for opening the Door to abundant living through Christ, for the gift of Your Holy Spirit, and for redeeming and commissioning us to be Your children and Your servants forever. Amen.

To This You Have Been Called

To this you have been called, because Christ also suffered for you.
v. 21

"Christ also suffered for you, leaving you an example, that you should follow in His steps." Perhaps Peter remembered Jesus' words to His disciples just months before His crucifixion. After He had informed them of His impending death and subsequent resurrection, He said that those who follow Him must deny themselves and carry crosses of their own. Now, several years later, Peter understood the meaning of Jesus' words.

It is doubtful that Peter would go along with much of the positive-thinking, ecstasy-seeking, New Age jargon that attracts and hooks multitudes of "born again" Christ-followers today. Suffering was an integral part of Christian discipleship in Peter's day. He prepared his converts to Christ for it and sought to support them within it. This is no less true today. Most of us will escape the kind of violence that befell so many of those first-century Christians, but few if any of us will escape suffering.

"By His wounds you have been healed." And, of course in a far lesser sense, by our wounds others about us may discover healing and wholeness. While we are not about to seek or cause suffering if it is within our power to evade it, we need to be aware that our suffering, the crosses we bear or share on behalf of our fellow persons, is to be expected, willingly embraced, and may even be necessary for our life and growth as disciples of Jesus Christ.

"For to this you have been called . . ."

I thank You, my loving God, that You who brought the promise of life to all people through the cross of Christ, will turn the small crosses of my life into agents of redemption and channels of love to those I may touch on my pilgrimage through this world. Amen.

Christ Is Our Shepherd

The Father knows Me and I know the Father; and I lay down My life for the sheep. v. 15

"I am the Good Shepherd," said Jesus. Either this Christ is a silly fraud, even a dangerous one, as are scores of self-appointed "Christs" enticing the masses today, or He is truly the Son of God, for this is what He claims to be. Moreover, His claims are stronger and more persuasive than when He first made them, for He now presents Himself as the resurrected, living Christ.

Jesus gives His reasons for declaring Himself the Good Shepherd. He is the *Owner* of the flock. "I know My own and My own know Me." He is not hired to care for them; He is their Owner—they are His possession. He came to possess His possessions, to redeem His sheep, to complete and secure His fold.

He is *Caretaker* of His flock. "Behold, He who keeps Israel will neither slumber nor sleep," said the psalmist. He is never off-duty, but with watchful eye and cocked ear is ever attentive to the needs of His lambs.

He is *Provider* for the flock. "He makes me lie down in green pastures; He leads me beside still waters," sang the psalmist. "Seek first His kingdom . . . and all these things shall be yours as well," Jesus promised His disciples (Matthew 6:33). Truly, "The Lord is my Shepherd; I shall not want."

He is *Defender* of the flock. "They shall never perish, and no one shall snatch them out of My hand," promised Jesus (v. 28).

The Lord is our Shepherd—and we are His. This day and every day our lives and all that we are and have belong absolutely and unconditionally to Him, for the Lord is our Shepherd, and we are His forever.

I thank You, my Savior and Lord, for You made it possible for me to know who I am and to whom I belong. Amen.

We Know Who We Are

See what love the Father has given us, that we should be called children of God. v. 1

.The fact is we are God's children now! This status and relationship is not something we work for or wait for; it is ours here and now. It is the gift and consequence of God's eternal love. We are His children by way of His creation. We are His children by way of His redemption and our adoption into His kingdom. We are His children by way of His indwelling Spirit. We are His forever.

"We are called God's children—and so in fact, we are," writes John. "My dear friends, we are now God's children" (1 John 3:2 TEV). "Those who are led by God's Spirit are God's sons [and daughters] . . . The Spirit makes you His children, and by the Spirit's power we cry out to God, 'Father! my Father!'" (Romans 8:14–15 TEV).

We have discovered our identity and significance. We do not have to be fearful of this world's condemnations nor be dependent upon its accolades. Our response to its enmity is self-sacrificing love. It means that we can abandon ourselves to God's purposes and follow His design and destiny for our lives, an exciting, risk-filled style of living that guarantees freedom and joy in the midst of this world's oppression and pain.

We know who we are and to whom we belong and where ultimately, if not presently, we are going. For we are God's children now.

I am, O Lord, redeemed by Your love, sanctified through Your righteousness, ordained by Your calling, empowered with Your grace. Thank You, my God, for restoring my identity as a member of Your eternal family. Amen.

Profile of a Christian

You do not believe, because you do not belong to My sheep. v. 26

What ought to be some of the characteristics or marks of our lives if we truly believe in Jesus Christ?

For one thing, we must be *belongers*. "You do not believe, because you do not belong . . .," said Jesus. He is stating emphatically that believing is belonging when it comes to a person's relationship with God. There ought to be stamped upon our attitudes, manners, and personalities the brand of God's ownership. We are God's property, God's possession, and we should speak and act as such.

We are *listeners*. "My sheep hear My voice," said Jesus. While the devotees of this materialistic existence cock their ears to the sensuous sounds about them or are taken in the bright promises of socialism or communism or capitalism, we should be listening for the voice of God. He may speak in a "still, small voice," but He can also be heard in the whirlwind, the lightning and thunder, the chaos and catastrophes of these times in which we live. We must be listeners, for how else will we be able to steer our frail crafts through the storm except we be in communication with our God?

We are *followers*. "My sheep hear My voice . . . and they follow Me," said Jesus. Following means serving Him; serving Him means serving our fellow beings on His behalf. We do this, first of all, in our family and in our daily calling. But Jesus also leads us out into fields of battle—the world, the community, even the political and economic and civil-rights struggles of our society. Here, too, Christ is—where the suffering shepherdless children of darkness grope for meaning and purpose. Here is where, as recipients of God's love and grace, we should desire to be—as belongers, listeners, and followers of Jesus Christ.

"Lord, I will follow You wherever You go." This has been and is now my vow, dear Lord. Grant to me the grace, courage, and strength to keep this vow. Amen.

A Time to Celebrate

Salvation belongs to our God who sits upon the throne, and to the Lamb! v. 10

This is not the time for despair; it is a time for celebration! The resurrected Christ is with us. He is present with us amid the trials and tribulations of this tempestuous world. He is about ready to reappear and to gather together His faithful followers into the fully-revealed and eternally-reigning kingdom of God.

This great, long-awaited event is about to take place, and the suffering, celebrating children of God of all nations and generations are invited. Christ will once and for all time reveal Himself as the living, conquering, victorious Lord of heaven and earth. Evil will be eradicated; all stumbling blocks will be removed; those who oppose God and His people will be overcome; the spiritual forces of evil will be bound and destroyed.

Sorrow will turn to joy, night into day. Tears will give way to laughter; ugliness will yield to beauty. "Every knee [will] bow . . . and every tongue confess that Jesus Christ is Lord" (Philippians 2:10–11). On this great day the suffering martyrs, the struggling saints, the priests and prophets, the servants and disciples of all ages will be united together to sing their praises to their eternal Savior and King.

There is a time to celebrate, my Lord and Christ, and I begin to do that now, for this is that time and this is that place. I celebrate Your presence on my journey of faith, no matter how rough and dark the road ahead. Amen.

The Cost of Discipleship

Behold, I see the heavens opened, and the Son of man standing at the right hand of God. v. 56

The apostles paid for their courageous and enthusiastic proclamations with numerous arrests and beatings. It was one of their converts, selected and ordained by the apostles to relieve them of their "lesser" duties so as to enable them to give their full attention to the all-important responsibility of preaching, who became the first Christian to pay the ultimate price of discipleship, the first to be martyred as a consequence of his faithful witness.

His name was Stephen. The same Spirit who indwelt and spoke through the apostles seemed to speak with even more courage and wisdom through this newly converted "deacon" than He did through the men who witnessed the crucifixion and resurrection of Jesus. While most of the converts in the first-century church were avid witnesses to their faith in the risen Christ, Stephen's activity as a proclaimer of Christian truth was outstanding. He went farther than most of the apostles in his proclamations by radically insisting that Christianity was destined to supersede Judaism—and this is probably what brought down upon his head the wrath of the Sanhedrin. Stephen, after turning his defense into an opportunity to undermine the errors and hypocrisy of the religious leaders and lift up the risen Christ as the way of salvation for all, was cast out of the city and stoned to death. Stephen's marytrdom introduced a heroic period of persecution in the early church. The cost of discipleship has been extremely high in every century since the resurrection of Jesus. Although it is not always evidenced in martyrdom, strong opposition is or will be the experience of most genuine followers of Christ, whatever the form it takes.

Grant me, O Lord, the will and the courage, not only to listen to Your Word, but to risk all, in scorn of consequences, to proclaim it and to live it in my life and activities. Amen.

Cure for Heart Trouble

Let not your hearts be troubled; believe in God, believe also in Me.
v. 1

The disciples of Jesus were on the brink of the greatest catastrophe of their lives. The One whom they had left all to follow and to serve was soon to be taken away from them and executed on a cross. They were becoming apprehensive as the enemies of Jesus were rapidly closing in on Him, and Jesus (who knew what His course would be) was preparing them for this tragic event. He prescribed a cure for anxious, troubled hearts. It was to "believe in God, believe also in Me."

It is significant to note that Jesus was not passing out some every-cloud-has-a-silver-lining platitude. Such an admonition, even if it included some vague reference to an unknown, invisible God, would do little to brighten troubled spirits. Referring the troubled in heart to some distant God is like pointing to some opaque blur. Jesus, however, was authorized and able to say, "Believe also in *Me*." The human creature cannot come to God; God in His love found a way whereby He could come to His creatures. Jesus presents Himself as God come to earth, God made visible and available, as "the Way, and the Truth, and the Life," and this is not rosy optimism or sentimental good cheer that He dispenses; it is divine truth.

The cure for heart trouble is heart trust. We are not to trust in some vague concept of divinity, but in Jesus Christ, who is God with us and within us. He plumbed the depths of sorrow and suffering. He conquered over death and darkness. He arose from the grave. He lives—and because He lives, we shall live forever. We need not allow the anxieties of this life to trouble us overmuch. We need to listen and to accept in faith the words of Jesus: "Let not your hearts be troubled; believe in God, believe also in Me."

Thank You, our loving God, for coming to us through Jesus Christ. And thank You because You made it possible for us to know You through Jesus Christ. Amen.

We Are the People of God

Once you were no people but now you are God's people. v. 10a

"You are a chosen race, a royal priesthood, a holy nation, God's own people . . ."

We who have sampled God's grace and know that He accepts us as His children and remembers our sins no more are just beginning to realize the magnitude and immensity of that grace. Now it is time to grow in that grace, to put aside our childishness and become mature, dependable Christians. Like blocks that firm up and reinforce a building, we ought to be the kind of men and women that build up God's kingdom on earth. Our great God has accepted us as His sons and daughters and appointed us to be His ministers. We, with Christ as our Savior and King, *are* the kingdom of God.

There are, however, many other blocks, still unprepared, that need to be shaped and formed to fit into this great temple of God. Our Lord has made us the blocks that hold together other blocks— and the artisans that assist in hewing and shaping others to find their places in this structure that God is building. We are to do this by declaring the love of God for all His human creatures and demonstrating that love in our daily contacts and in our sacrificial deeds of kindness on behalf of God and for the benefit of humanity. It is this profound responsibility that shapes our lives and guides our activities in our remaining years on this planet. We can well afford to lose our material possessions, worldly acclaim, even our physical lives in this splendid task—and yet lose nothing at all because we are the people of God and belong to Him forever.

This is the way of love, our response to the gift of divine grace that drew us into the family of God. Let us walk in it.

Lord Jesus, help me to be what You intended me to be, and to live my part as a child of God. Amen.

How to Be Truly Happy

By this My Father is glorified, that you bear much fruit. v. 8

We may not have the right to be happy. If such happiness is designed to satiate our egos or pacify our self-centered natures, we can hardly, as Christians, claim that right. We do have the right to joy—not because we merit it but because God offers it. Nowhere and at no time does God promise sensual happiness, but His Word is full of promises of joy.

It is only as joyous Christians that we can bear fruit. This Gospel lesson underlines the *necessity of fruitfulness* in our lives. "By this My Father is glorified," said Jesus, "that you bear much fruit, and so prove to be My disciples." Jesus is informing us that we have been cut away from the forest of sin, redeemed from its ugly consequences, and engrafted into the Vine, into Christ, not only to bask in His glow, wonder at His miracles, and anticipate eternal rewards, but in order that we may bear fruit toward the accomplishment of God's purposes.

Jesus reveals, as well, the *key to a happy, joy-filled, fruit-bearing life.* "I am the Vine, you are the branches. He who abides in Me, and I in him, he it is that bears much fruit." We don't have to clutch at Christ like a drowning man to floating debris. We need only to "abide," to remain, to rest in Christ the way a baby rests in the mother's arms. This "abiding" is a state of faith; it is perpetuated by faith. As we entrust ourselves to Him by faith, so we "abide" in Him and will remain with Him forever.

It is when we truly abide in Christ—and we invite and allow Him to abide in us, permitting His Spirit to have His way in and through us—that our lives will be full of joy and will bear the fruit of joy.

Forgive me, my Lord, for allowing the things of this earthbound existence to obscure the joy that I can have in You. Amen.

From Doubt to Assurance to Obedience

By this we shall know that we are of the truth . . . v. 19a

Our confession of faith that we participate in every Sunday morning does not eradicate forever all doubts about our relationship to God. There are blue-Monday doubts and the gray, beclouded skies that often obscure the bright sunshine of God's forgiving, accepting love. They do not stifle or smother His love for us, these doubts that plague and harass us, nor do they change our status as God's beloved children. But they do send us scurrying back to God's blessed Word that assures us of His love and mercy. Even when "our hearts condemn us . . . God is greater than our hearts," and so therefore is His mercy and grace.

It is not enough, however, to make confessions or proclamations concerning our faith. We are indeed saved by faith in God's ever-abundant grace—not by works. Yet a genuine faith in God is marked by obedience. We live in obedience to God when, while believing in Him, we lovingly and actively reach out to meet the needs of our fellow beings.

Apart from this level of obedience, according to John, our faith may be in question—and so our relationship to God. "All who keep His commandments abide in Him, and He in them."

Continue to assure us of Your eternal love, dear Lord! And continue to work out, in and through us, Your purposes in our world today. Amen.

143

Something Old, Something New

By this all men will know that you are My disciples . . . v. 35

"A new commandment I give to you, that you love one another . . ." said Jesus to His disciples. It was actually not a new commandment, but the old one made new by the life and teachings of Jesus Christ. It was more a declaration of the truth than a command, a fact of life rather than a directive. "When you love your neighbor," said Kierkegaard, "then you resemble God." What is new about this commandment is that if we are to follow Christ, to be His disciples, we must, by the grace made available to us through His resurrection, love our brothers and sisters within the human family. Our faith apart from or without this inevitable expression would be little more than blasphemous posturing, a ridiculous facade. Our neighbor, in a very real sense, represents the invisible Christ, and Jesus declares that what we do for our neighbor, we do for Christ.

The standard and quality of love is also made new by the life and teachings, the death and resurrection of Jesus Christ. ". . . Even as I have loved you, that you also love one another," He said. The springs of love are in God, not in us. He must give to us through His Spirit the will and the ability to love. We must somehow see Christ in our neighbor, or we must see him as one whom Christ loves and seeks, as one for whom He died and arose from the dead.

"By this all men will know that you are My disciples, if you have love for one another," said our Lord. It would appear that the sole, sufficing evidence of our Christianity is our love, a genuine, sacrificial, Christ-inculcated love for our fellow beings. It doesn't come naturally, nor all at once, but it is something we must be empowered to do and learn to do. And we had better begin now— right where we are.

When I fail to love, I fail to serve You, gracious Father. Forgive me and teach me anew how to love and accept others as You love and accept me. Amen.

God Is with Us

Behold, the dwelling of God is with men . . . . and they shall be His people. v. 3

John's vision illuminates the great event that will ultimately take place. God's faithful children—clothed in His righteousness—can believe it and hope for it and ready themselves for it, because it will happen. When it does happen, all the pain and suffering that encompassed them in this world will be forgotten in that glorious revelation of Christ as King and God ever-present with His people in the world to come. For "He will dwell with them, and they shall be His people, and God Himself will be with them." What a harbinger of hope and comfort John's Revelation must have been to the suffering, persecuted Christians of his day! It continues to offer comfort and hope to God's children and servants in our day.

There is even greater hope and comfort spelled out by John and the other apostles in the assurance that God is already with us amid the conflicts and trials we encounter today. He is not visibly present in this hour, but through His indwelling Spirit walks and works and worships with us whatever our course through life. Our conviction about this ever-present God is demonstrated in our faith, which accepts the fact of His presence despite the pains and problems of this life. There are ample evidences of that presence—in the words of those who witnessed Christ's resurrection and the coming of His Spirit to indwell them; in the lives of thousands of His children who testify as to His wonder-working power in their experiences; in those times when we have felt His loving interventions in our own lives; in the Service of Holy Communion where He touches us in a very special way through the bread and the wine we receive.

"Behold, the dwelling of God is with [us]!"

You are, O God, my hope and salvation, the Bread of Life, a life-giving spring, the ultimate fulfillment of my deepest longings. May my life be a perpetual offering of praise to You. Amen.

Joy and the Holy Spirit

The word of the Lord spread throughout all the region. v. 49

"And the disciples were filled with joy and with the Holy Spirit." Though we know that the apostles were filled with the Holy Spirit, it doesn't always appear that they had a great deal to be joyful about. They were constantly on the run—proclaiming the blessed Gospel and then leaving behind them an angry mob that drove them out of their city. It happened here; it would happen again in Iconium, the next city where they would minister.

But their joy superseded any fear for their own welfare. They were proclaiming the Gospel of God's saving love as revealed through the risen Christ and, wherever they went, they sowed seeds that would take root and bear fruit unto the great, eternal kingdom of God. Furthermore, such fruit-bearing was not to be limited to the people of Israel but would continue among the Gentiles—unto all the nations of the world. They understood now what the ancient prophet meant when he said that the salvation of God was destined for the Gentiles as well as the Jews, "to the uttermost parts of the earth."

What a ministry they had! And what a commission we have! There may be a price to pay along the way—as there was for the apostles—but we also have a part to play in enlarging God's kingdom. We may not always see much fruit as a consequence of our seed-sowing, but our witness in life and word will bring results. We can indeed be "filled with joy," knowing that the Spirit of God works and speaks through us. Let us be faithful to our ministry, as were those first-century disciples.

You have, O Lord, accepted me as a beggar and turned me into a child of Your eternal kingdom. Now grant to me the grace and wisdom to tell other beggars where they can find the Bread of Life. And may I walk and serve in joy. Amen.

We Are Not Alone

I will pray the Father, and He will give you another Counselor, to be with you for ever. v. 16

"I will not leave you desolate," said Jesus. "He dwells with you and will be in you," He said concerning the Holy Spirit. The church of Jesus Christ is privileged to proclaim the profound truth that we are not alone. It is this message that we are responsible not only to proclaim but essentially to demonstrate to God's creatures who inhabit our community and world. We are to do this, not through ecstatic manifestations or supernatural gifts that attract and amaze people, but through sacrificial acts of love.

Our Lord's words announced the Spirit's indwelling, which was to be the fruit and crown of His redeeming work. It was for this that man and woman had been created. If it were not for Pentecost, the Father's purpose and Christ's own work would never have been accomplished. Christ knew that His disciples would not understand at this point; but He discloses the divine secret that, when He left them, their loss would be compensated for by a greater blessing than that of His bodily presence. Another would come in His place, to abide with them, to dwell in them forever.

Of course we are not alone. It is time that we stop cheating ourselves out of that divine power so needed and so available, and cheating our fellow beings out of the divine touch that can redeem their empty, meaningless lives, and yield ourselves totally, abandon ourselves completely, to the control of the Holy Spirit and allow Pentecost to happen to us. It has happened to us—even from the time of our baptism into Christ. Now let it happen to others through us, and it will become increasingly apparent that we are not desolate.

Thank You, Lord, for coming to us, for the gift of Your Spirit, for redeeming, commissioning, indwelling us by way of Your Spirit that we might be Your children and servants, vessels and vehicles, in extending Your kingdom in this world about us. Amen.

Suffering that Is Honorable

Even if you do suffer for righteousness sake, you will be blessed.
v. 14a

The Christian witness to a rebellious world will involve pain as well as blessing. There will be negative reaction as well as positive response. Whereas there is no call for a martyr complex and we cannot assume, as do some cultists, that the abuse received as a result of witnessing on this planet guarantees special consideration in some future heaven, suffering can be honorable and may result in some maturation in our lives as well as progress in the advancement of God's kingdom. It is far better to bear patiently the hurts that others may inflict upon us than to be the cause of their pain—or to be guilty of not making any effort to alleviate their suffering.

It is not so tragic or unfortunate that we suffer. It is probable that such suffering will enrich our lives and enlarge our faith. Jesus Christ Himself, God's Son, suffered much in the course of His brief life upon this strife-ridden world. How dare we expect any less?

While we will not seek suffering, conflicts and trials come to all of us at one time or another. They cannot be avoided or ignored. They are real—and they hurt. But we need never be ashamed of suffering for Jesus' sake. May God grant to us the kind of love and courage we need to enter into suffering, if such is necessary, in order to declare in witness and good works God's love and salvation for disoriented people in a disjoined world.

O God, fill the vacuum, resolve the bitterness. Turn the ashes of my great loss into something beautiful and useful. I can't do this, dear Lord, but You can. Do it now, Lord; please do it now. Amen.

The Responsible Christian

You are My friends if you do what I command you. v. 14

We continue to affirm that salvation is by faith—the acceptance of God's loving, forgiving, redeeming grace as revealed to us through the crucified and risen Lord Jesus Christ. Salvation—the forgiveness of our sin, eternal life, our adoption into the very family of God—all this is a gift of God. It is not deserved; it cannot be merited or earned; it must be acknowledged and embraced through repentance and by faith.

Yet there is more to the Christian life. There are responsibilities to consider, commands to obey, directives to carry out. "If you keep My commandments, you will abide in My love . . . This is my commandment, that you love one another . . . You did not choose Me, but I chose you and appointed you that you should go and bear fruit . . ."

While it is correctly understood that a total commitment to the saving love of God will resolve in sacrificial discipleship and obedient servanthood, in fruit-bearing, in being a responsible Christian, we realistically insist that the journey from salvation to servanthood is often a long and painful, as well as joyful, experience. Christian growth comes by the grace of God—as does forgiveness and love—but only if we responsibly walk in that grace and in obedience to the commands of our Lord.

What are the commands of Jesus? "Love one another . . . Go and bear fruit." Every one of us is called into full-time service for Jesus Christ, to be His servant and minister in the parish or arena of life and activity in which we find ourselves today.

God, help me to be a responsible Christian, not only in accepting You and living by faith within Your saving grace, but in obeying You, and by Your grace committing myself to the desperate needs of the human family about me. Amen.

The Acid Test

Every spirit which confesses that Jesus Christ has come in the flesh is of God. v. 2

"Do not believe every spirit," writes John. In his day, and in ours, there were and there are other "spiritual" forces seeking the loyalty and allegiance of men and women. It is not always easy to spot them—and many who initially came to faith by way of God's true Word have been led astray by self-styled religious con-artists who concoct a gospel of their own and for their own self-centered purposes. One test that will separate the shepherds from the goatherds, the false prophets form the genuine article, is whether or not they confess and proclaim Jesus Christ as God's Son—God in the flesh, God-incarnate, who has come to redeem us from our sins. If they do not proclaim the Christ in this manner, they, according to John, must be avoided like the plague.

John goes on to say that the proof of our adoption into the family of God is love. That adoption begins with our being drawn into God's gracious love as revealed and granted through God-incarnate, Jesus Christ. We cannot come to God by way of our good works; we come only by way of His grace and by way of Jesus Christ, who communicates that grace to us. It is in response to that grace that we are lovingly compelled to love one another—willingly and joyfully to love our fellow creatures with the love that God's grace sows and brings to fruition in our hearts and lives.

I confess, O Lord, that I am selfish and primarily concerned about my own station and status in life—and that I have been using You to fulfill my aspirations. Forgive me, O God, and teach me anew the meaning of Your eternal love and how to love and accept others as You love and accept me. Amen.

Left Holding the Bag

Repentance and forgiveness of sins should be preached in His name to all nations. v. 47

He lives! He reigns! And He left His disciples "holding the bag." It's a rather colloquial expression. The fact is that what Jesus began the disciples were left behind to continue. Before He departed from His faithful followers, He left with them a commission and a promise: a commission to witness of the things they had seen and experienced, to proclaim the Gospel they had heard, and a promise that they would be fully equipped to do the job they were commanded to do. It was not in God's eternal plan that the visible Christ should try to cover all the bases by Himself. So He "parted from them" only to invisibly, through His Spirit, indwell, empower, and carry out the purposes of His Father through the bodies and brains of men and women who would embrace His salvation and commit themselves to His service.

The disciples of Christ, after receiving the Holy Spirit, proceeded to do this very thing—most of them being martyrized in the process. Thousands followed in their wake. The Gospel of God's saving grace was proclaimed throughout the world, and millions were redeemed and are being redeemed by His forgiving, life-giving love.

Now we are the disciples of Christ, authorized and commissioned to continue the ministry of the suffering, resurrected, and reigning Lord Jesus Christ in our world today. And we are, enabled by His Spirit, equipped to do the job. Our God and Christ, working through our fallible, failure-fraught bodies and spirits, will continue to carry on His purposes in our community and world.

Gracious God, undergirded by Your grace, and filled with Your Spirit, help me to find my place in a revolutionary world, and to put my reputation, job, income, even my life on the line to confront violence with courage and hatred with love, and to be Your faithful child and servant. Amen.

From Dust to Deity

Let not your hearts be troubled, neither let them be afraid. v. 27b

The Genesis story of creation tells how "God formed man of dust from the ground, and breathed into his nostrils the breath of life; and man became a living being." In a strange and wonderful way the living Lord is still involved in creating—taking the dust of this world's darkness and oppression, the wrecks that humans make of their lives, and breathing into them His deity. The very heartaches and agonies, the inscrutable difficulties, the insurmountable problems of peoples' lives are as important in this process of creation and transformation as are the joys, the hours of achievement and accomplishment, that are the portion of God's human creatures.

There is a secure basis for attacking and overcoming, or for learning how to live with, the sufferings and conflicts and dark hours that come our way. For one thing, there is the love of the Father. "If a man loves Me, he will keep My word, and My Father will love him . . ."

There is the indwelling of the Holy Spirit ". . . The Holy Spirit, whom the Father will send in My name, He will teach you all things . . ." The dust of this existence can be inhabited with deity. The Spirit of the living Christ clothes Himself with the very bodies of problematic, sinful fishermen and tax-collectors, men and women of all races, temperaments, and walks of life.

There is the peace of Jesus Christ. "Peace I leave with you; My peace I give to you," said Jesus. "Let not your hearts be troubled, neither let them be afraid." It is not the kind of peace found in some distant world of make-believe, nor is it life separated from the turbulence of this frustrating existence, but the kind of peace that can be ours right here in the very midst of a world of trouble and trial.

Grant to me, O God, this love and power and peace. Amen.

The Big Event

In the Spirit he showed me the holy City Jerusalem coming down out of heaven from God. v. 10

What about that that great Day in which God's kingdom shall be revealed? Is there any way we can picture that glorious event?

Some have had visions; others dream dreams. But it is not possible for our small minds to visualize the glory of God's eternal kingdom. Our images are earthbound. Our words are like the babbling of babies. Our imaginations are utterly incapable of grasping the majesty, beauty, and power of the glory that awaits the children of God on that great Day. We see but minute glimpses of His eternal glory in the elements about us, yet even these are beyond the comprehension of our finite thinking. The pictures we compose are crooked lines or abstract blobs that barely represent ultimate truth.

This, however, we believe: with the dawn of that magnificent Day Christ shall be revealed in all His glory and majesty. All the hosts of heaven will be gathered to sing His praises. And every human creature upon this earth, along with those who have gone before us, will know that this One who walked among us, who revealed God's eternal love and suffered in His own body the consequences of our faithlessness and disobedience, this One, the resurrected Christ, is Lord and King of this earth, the universe, of heaven itself, for all eternity.

It is only those of us who love and serve our God today who can be assured of rejoicing in His manifestation tomorrow. We can regard that great coming event with joyful anticipation.

"Amen! Praise and glory and wisdom and thanks and honor and power and strength be to our God for ever and ever. Amen." (Revelation 7:12)

Jesus' Concern for His Own

Holy Father, keep them in Thy name which Thou has given Me.
v. 11b

This great prayer of our Lord highlights His concern for the disciples He was about to leave behind. His earthly mission was about to be terminated in His betrayal and crucifixion. Whereas His visible ministry was almost completed, the work of God's kingdom as revealed through His Son had barely begun. The expansion of that kingdom, the accomplishment of God's objectives as initiated by Christ, was to be carried out through those Jesus left behind. It was for them, and for us who claim to be the 20th century disciples of Christ, that Jesus expresses His loving concern through His prayer.

We see this concern of our Lord in the fact that Christ prays for us. "I am not praying for the world but for those whom Thou hast given Me," said Jesus. The Good News concerning the past is that Christ has intervened in this realm of suffering and death, struggle and conflict, and made possible our deliverance from the eternal consequences of sin. The most consoling news concerning the present is that Christ intercedes on behalf of His disciples.

We witness Jesus' great concern for us in that He regards us as His possession. "They are Thine; all Mine are Thine, and Thine are Mine," He prays. If we have unwittingly regarded God as some ethereal Being assigned to serve and please us, we have our wires crossed, for Jesus emphatically declares that we belong to God, that we are His possession, that we are expected to enlist our lives in His service. "You did not choose Me," said Jesus to His disciples, "but I chose you and appointed you . . ." (John 15:16). The surest guarantee that we have nothing to fear amid the tempests that batter our world is that we are God's possession, His property, His own forever.

I thank You, my Lord, for this blessed assurance of Your concern and love for me. Amen.

Someone Does Care about Us

Cast all your anxieties on Him, for He cares about you. v. 7

"No one cares for me," agonized the psalmist on one of the "blue Mondays" of his life (Psalm 142:4 TEV). The statement is attributed to David, spoken while he was hiding from King Saul in a dark cave.

There are caves along our sojourn through life, and we duck into them now and then to hide from something that frightens or threatens us, and there we moan out our loneliness and despair—telling ourselves lies about the Divine's indifference and our fellow persons' unconcern about our problems. We may have reason at times for doubting human concern. Our fellow beings are often too preoccupied with their own failures or successes to coddle us in our confoundment. It is true that God's love, usually transmitted by way of men and women who have encountered Him, is often made ambiguous by human insensitivity. Over and above the fallibilities of human beings, however, is the perpetual and eternal truth of God's love and concern for us. "Cast all your anxieties on Him" wrote Peter, "for He cares about you."

It is time for us to emerge from our sorry little caves of morbidity and self-pity to face up to the "King Sauls" that intimidate us. We don't have to be afraid, for God really cares about us.

Pull me out of my cave, O Lord, the self-pity-corner in my life. I don't belong there. Teach me how to accept my status and the validity and power that go with it, and to walk and serve in joy. Amen.

How Much He Loves Us!

[I pray] that they may have My joy fulfilled in themselves. v. 13b

This holy prayer of our Lord was not offered, as was the "Lord's Prayer," in order to teach His disciples how to pray. This prayer is truly the Lord's Prayer, expressing, in view of His coming crucifixion, the deepest feelings of His heart at a very critical hour in His life. The real beauty and the consoling message of these precious words of our Lord are discovered in the rich expressions of love and concern for each of us.

Jesus prays that we have His joy fulfilled in us. He is not referring to the effervescence and ecstasy that accompanies the religious experience of some people, but to true joy, eternal joy, the joy that filled the life of Jesus even while He faced betrayal and execution and that would abide in us even in the midst of this world's catastrophes and calamaties.

Jesus prays that we may be kept. "Holy Father, keep them in Thy name, which Thou hast given Me . . ." In an atrocious world with all of its pitfalls and temptations, we with all our weaknesses and fallibilities are the subject of God's promises and Christ's prayer that we will be kept by Him.

Jesus prays, not that we should be spared the conflicts and struggles of this cruel and contemptuous world, but that in the midst of it all we might walk in the truth. "Sanctify them in Thy truth; Thy Word is truth," prayed our Lord.

How much our great Lord loves us! It is when we really believe in this love, accept and abide in this divine, everlasting love, that we will become lovers and will be enabled to communicate this love to our fellow beings in our world about us.

I stand in awe of the amazing, incredible, incomprehensible love that You have for me, my blessed Lord. May my love for You and all Your human creatures grow daily as I reach out to serve You. Amen.

By This We Know God's Love

God is love, and he who abides in love abides in God, and God abides in him. v. 16b

"So we know and believe the love God has for us." It begins with our acceptance of God's love as it is revealed to us through Jesus Christ. It is further revealed and extended through our love for one another. This is what the God-life is all about. Apart from God there is no real love; apart from love God is not real in us and is not able to work through us. If we assume we can continue to bask in God's love even while we continue to harbor hateful, unloving thoughts about a brother or sister, we are deceiving ourselves.

We live in a fear-ridden world and foolishly allow these fears to permeate our lives and polarize our interpersonal relationships. If God's love truly dominates our lives, this will not happen, because it crowds out all fear and unites us to God and to each other.

God's love is perfect—and He loves us perfectly. Not only should this free us from the fears that plague our world; it should enable us to love our fellow persons without concern for consequences. This is our assignment in our world today: to be, as was Christ in His visible visitation, love-incarnate in our love-starved society.

Let us begin by genuinely loving one another.

Inasmuch as I fail to love, dear Lord, I fail to serve You. Forgive me, O God, and teach me anew the meaning of Your great love for Your children, and grant to me the grace to emulate You in Your love for Your creatures. Amen.

Is Something Wrong with the Church?

The glory which Thou hast given Me I have given to them, that they may be one even as We are one. v. 22

In the great and beautiful "High Priestly Prayer" before His trial and crucifixion, Jesus expressed His foremost concerns about those He was leaving behind to carry on the work He had begun. For one thing, He prayed that there would be unity, "that they may all be one; even as Thou, Father, art in Me, and I in Thee . . . that they may be one even as We are one."

Contrary to Jesus' earnest and devout prayer, unity is not generally known in the church today, and at times has hardly even been sought.

Fortunately, however, there now are many who believe that this unity for which Jesus prayed ought to be more visible to the broken world about them and regard it as their duty to yearn for and struggle toward a more visible and viable unity within God's kingdom.

What is wrong with the church is clearly related to what is wrong in our own lives. Our lack of genuine love for Christ, for our brothers and sisters in Christ, for those for whom Christ died and rose again, even for the institutional church as it exists today, is certainly a part of the root cause for the failure of the church to dramatize and communicate God's saving love to our generation.

Teach us, O God, how to love even as You love us, to love Your children, whatever their race or creed or station in life, to love the church that inclusively, without bias or prejudice, gathers Your children into the sanctuary to proclaim Your love and share that love with one another. Amen.

Hold On—He's Coming Soon

He who testifies to these things says, "Surely I am coming soon."
v. 20

This was the message John was sending to his persecuted, imprisoned, suffering brothers and sisters in the faith: Hold on—Jesus is coming soon! Whatever else his Revelation said to his readers—and there may have been much that they understood but which still remains a mystery to us—it was a message of hope and comfort to Christians trying to hold on to their faith and their lives in that violent world of their time.

Almost every generation, in times when things become unstable and the world appears about to go out of orbit, produces its prophets that herald something of the same message: Hang in there; Jesus is coming soon! The crowds they gather give some indication of how much the message is needed, of the fears and anxieties that harass people even today.

Some prophets, unfortunately, prophesy too much. They twist John's Revelation into saying or meaning something never intended by the writer—thereby confusing rather than clarifying the end-time message. The "Jesus is coming soon" message ought to be proclaimed to every generation, but it needs to be ungarnished, freed up from the tantalizing frills and thrills offered by popularity-seeking prophets and their overworked imaginations. Jesus is coming soon; that is all we know or need to know. There will be an end to violence, to all that is evil and ugly. There will be healing and joy, peace and rest, for those who "hold on" in faith—or allow God to hold on to them—and walk in obedience with the invisible Christ who directs their lives. The day is soon upon us when He will be fully revealed.

"I consider that the sufferings of this present time are not worth comparing with the glory that is to be revealed to us" (Romans 8:18).

I am "holding on" by Your grace, my loving Lord. I want to do more—to celebrate Your coming soon even now—and to march boldly into the future whatever its dangers and its pitfalls. Amen.

You Shall Receive Power

You shall receive power when the Holy Spirit has come upon you.
v. 8a

We are about to leave behind the Easter season even while we continue throughout the year to rejoice in and meditate upon the Easter message. From now on, however, we deal primarily with the consequences of the resurrection of Jesus Christ in our own lives. Like those first disciples, we are thrust out into our world or our specific arenas of life and activity to communicate to the inhabitants of our world the Good News of God-incarnate, Jesus Christ, and His salvation made possible for all through His death and resurrection.

We are not left unarmed or unequipped. Jesus spent forty days following His resurrection talking to His disciples about the kingdom of God and their responsibility in building that kingdom. Just before His ascension He promised that the power they would need for this task would be granted them by the indwelling of His Spirit. Then Jesus disappeared, vanished, ascended into heaven. God in the visible Christ had inaugurated His kingdom upon earth. From now on it was God and Christ working through the mortal, fallible, failure-fraught bodies and spirits of their redeemed children who would carry on His plan to consummation, building the kingdom of God that would ultimately include His created children from all nations of the world.

The disciples did not fully understand Christ's final words, but they held on to His promise. It was a promise or a prophecy that had been proclaimed years before by John the Baptist. It was now about to be fulfilled.

I praise You, my God, for the blessed privilege of Your child and servant in this kind of world. I pray that I might be faithful and obedient in claiming Your grace and power to carry out Your objectives in this world. Amen.

The Birthday of the Church

It is to your advantage that I go away . . . If I go, I will send [the Counselor] to you. v. 7

We are now on the threshold of the longest season of the church year—the Pentecost season. Pentecost proved that God became flesh not only by way of the womb of Mary and in the earthly ministry of Christ but, in a sense, also by infilling, indwelling, and empowering, the flesh of His human creatures. It is Pentecost that inaugurated the perpetual presence of Christ in our world—through you and me and all of our brothers and sisters who follow Christ. Whereas Christmas celebrates the event whereby God became man, Pentecost initiates the event when men and women became the vehicles and channels, the very temples of God Himself. It is Pentecost that makes us Christs-incarnate in the world today.

The fact is, we are the only visible "Christs" that God has to advance His kingdom and carry out His purposes "concerning sin and righteousness and judgment," and concerning His great love for His creatures. We are in the blessed struggle of carrying on the work of God, so that He in His love for us and through our love for others, may communicate divine love and healing to the lonely, unloved, frightened, and fractured people all about us.

And He has already equipped us for this task. Setting us free from sin's guilt and power and eternal consequences and reconciling us to His divine family, He has given us His Spirit. The power that brought the visible Christ into our world through the virgin Mary and raised Him from the dead on the day of Resurrection is the same power, the same divine energy, that abides within us. This is our equipment as the sons and daughters, servants and ministers of the living God, and it is more than adequate for the task our God has set before us.

Thank You, Lord, for the gift of Your Spirit. May He enable me to walk in Your ways and accomplish those things You would have me to do. Amen.

Pentecost—It Has Happened to Us!

And they were all filled with the Holy Spirit. v. 4

Many people who frequent our churches are quite comfortable with the manger scene and Calvary's cross—and especially with Easter and its grand tidings of victory over sin and death—but Pentecost is something totally incomprehensible. There must be the Christmas, Good Friday, and Easter experiences in the life of every Christian, but this is to prepare the way for Pentecost. It is the culmination everything that went before it.

The birth of Christ took place at night in the seclusion of a stable; Pentecost blazed forth in broad daylight with hundreds of people to witness this fantastic event. Unfortunately, the giving of the Holy Spirit is often still associated with particular signs—such as speaking in strange tongues or miracles of healing, and according to some people must be initiated by a second religious experience or second baptism. God may very well be the initiator and perpetrator of certain phenomena. But to insist that these mysterious, ecstatic experiences are necessary or synonymous with the Holy Spirit's infilling and control of Christ's followers is contrary to God's Word as declared through Jesus Christ. Wind, tongues of fire, and foreign tongues did indeed accompany the initial Pentecost event. God may occasionally use such phenomena today. It may take such happenings to move some people off dead-center and get them going for God.

Neither you nor I, however, have to sit around and wait for such strange, supernatural signs. Pentecost has happened to us; the Holy Spirit has been given. He continues to abide within the lives of those who follow Jesus Christ. God is about us and within us this very moment.

Help me, O God, to acknowledge the fact of Your daily presence about and within me and to continue to faithfully carry out Your objectives around me. Amen.

If Anyone Is Thirsty

If anyone thirst, let him come to Me . . . v. 37a

The last day of the feast commemorated the amazing incident that happened during the Israelites' long trek through the wilderness when, while camping at Rephidim, Moses at God's command smote a rock to bring forth water to satiate his thirsty people. In celebration the priests poured out sparkling water with choral song. While they stood with their empty vases, the temple's silence was pierced with a loud voice that proclaimed these words: "If any one thirst, let him come to Me and drink." It was Jesus, the son of a carpenter and, unknown to the temple crowd, the Son of God, who spoke these words.

The scene and the ceremony change. Today there are thousands of rites and ceremonies—all geared toward the same goal, the quenching of thirst, the satisfying of humanity's desires, the fulfillment of the human creature's inner longings, the universal quest for meaning.

"If anyone thirst . . ." The basis of humankind's longing and desire is thirst for God. Jesus presents Himself as the answer and fulfillment of that thirst: "Let him come to Me." His first invitation and directive is to *approach Christ.* Our Lord stands before the human race as that One who knows its deep thirsts, takes account of the impotence of any created thing to satisfy humanity's inner needs, and assumes the divine prerogative by saying: "He who believes in Me shall never thirst" (John 6:34).

Jesus' second injunction is to *appropriate Christ.* "Let him come to Me and drink." It isn't enough to come to the Fountainhead; one must drink—embrace, enter into, commit oneself to, appropriate Christ and the life He offers to all. It is the Holy Spirit working in and through us who makes all this possible in our lives.

O Lord, may I always be thirsty even while satiated by the living water which only You can grant. Amen.

And Now Pentecost

When the Counselor comes . . . the Spirit of truth . . . He will bear witness to Me. v. 26

Pentecost is the culmination of everything that went before it. It is Pentecost that inaugurated the perpetual presence of Christ in our world—through us and our fellow-disciples in the Christian faith. Whereas Christmas celebrates the God-become-man happening, Pentecost initiates the event whereby man and woman become the vehicles and channels, the very temples of God Himself.

It appears that it was the ascension of Christ, His return to His Father, which made Pentecost possible. "It is to your advantage that I go away," said Jesus to His disciples. "If I do not go away, the Counselor [the Holy Spirit] will not come to you . . ." The disciples understood nothing of this at the time. Now they learned through actual experience what Jesus was prophesying. While Jesus was with His disciples, the divine, supernatural power so necessary to the salvation of humankind was confined within the visible Christ. After He performed His mission on this planet and returned to His heavenly Father, the same divine, supernatural power responsible for Christ's resurrection and essential to the building of God's kingdom upon earth was to return to inhabit and empower His disciples.

Pentecost has happened. The same divine Spirit that ministered in the creation of the world, producing cosmos out of chaos, that had ministered through the visible Christ, has now returned to indwell and pour Himself out through the lives of all those who would in faith and obedience lend themselves to His infilling and outflowing.

We are supposed to be the contemporary evidence of the Holy Spirit's presence in our world, O Lord. We pray that You will through Your Spirit work in and through us today. Amen.

It Came to Pass

In those days, I will pour out My Spirit. v. 29b

Much of what the Old Testament prophets had to say to their people appeared to be obscure. Many contemporary prophets and their imaginative interpretations of the ancient prophecies only further obscure the messages of these prophets of the past. Among the blessings and woes which the prophets pronounced upon the Israelites, however, were numerous gems of profound insight from the very heart of God. At least portions of God's plan for the distant future were and are revealed through their prophecies.

It is those prophecies of the Old Testament that are fulfilled in Jesus Christ and the times following His resurrection that are most significant to us. They underline the authority of the Bible, these Scripture lessons we meditate upon each day, and assure us that God indeed speaks to us through the written Word.

What Joel prophesied came to pass. On the day of Pentecost Peter immediately linked what was happening to him and the believers around him to the ancient prophecy of Joel. God's Spirit was being poured out upon human flesh, and accompanying that Spirit were supernatural gifts and powers such as healing and tongues and prophesying, making it obvious to all present that God was acting and His human creatures were being edified and equipped to carry on His purposes in the world about them.

It came to pass—for them and for us. The Spirit who was promised through Joel, and poured out upon the apostles and other believers on the day of Pentecost, is the very same Spirit who abides in each of us. As we truly believe this, it ought to make a real difference in the way we live and walk and act today.

Enable us, our Lord, though we cannot see You, and even when we cannot feel Your presence through some mystical or supernatural experience, to know that You dwell within us and are with us in our fellowship together. Amen.

The Breath of God

I will cause breath to enter you, and you shall live. v. 5

One is tempted to out-prophesy the venerable prophet in his astounding vision, to mark this as God's promise that all of Israel, once cut off from God's grace and apparently without hope, will be raised from the dead to honor and serve the God of their fathers.

Such a temptation put aside, it is possible to find in this vision excitement and hope for the church-at-large, for the "spiritual Israel" which includes true believers out of all nations and tribes throughout the world. Is it possible that scores of people who attend our churches and dutifully confess their faith are still comparable to "dead bones" because they have not allowed God to have His way in their lives?

The excitement and hope transmitted through Ezekiel's vision is that this does not have to be; this can be changed. Church institutions throughout our world are being brought back to life again as their members who once confessed only with their mouths begin confessing with their hearts the forgiving love of God. Many are returning to the covenant made between them and God at their baptism; and God is breathing upon them, restoring them to life and truth and joy and purposefulness by way of His Spirit who is taking control of their whole beings.

This is the incomparable experience: restoration to the love and grace of God. It includes forgiveness, reconciliation, assurance of life eternal, peace and joy, purpose and meaning. It is like a resurrection from the dead, a new birth.

May God continue to breathe upon us.

I have not always been faithful to You, my loving God, but You have never lost faith in me. You continue to accept and forgive and draw me back into a loving relationship with You. I praise You, my God, from whom all blessings flow. Amen.

Response to a Suffering World

Go therefore and make disciples of all nations . . . v. 19a

The world is sounding off. A thousand quivering moans herald each rising of the sun. If one is sensitive, one can almost hear the sighing of the oppressed, the whimpering of the starving, the pleading of the sick. Less evident but very real is the spiritual need in which so many millions find themselves. Idolatry, superstition, unforgiven sin, lack of purpose in life are everywhere.

What is to be our response to these manifold needs? It is not to hide behind the walls of our affluence and prosperity or even within the walls of our hallowed sanctuaries. It is to "Go . . . to all peoples everywhere and make them My disciples" (v. 19 TEV). Our Lord did not enjoin us to reach for the moon; He ordered us out into the world. He did not instruct us to stay close to our manmade sanctuaries and altars; He sent us into the world to relate to the oppressed and the affluent, of every color and race and creed, and to tell them about the salvation planned by the Father, wrought by Jesus Christ, and brought to us by the Holy Spirit. "Go therefore and make disciples of all nations."

O Lord, I have often cheapened Your eternal love and grace by selfishly accepting Your love and claiming Your promises for my benefit alone. Forgive me, O God, and help me to take up my cross and to follow You in service to the despairing and oppressed, the suffering and sorrowing in the world about me. Amen.

Live in Peace

Greet one another with a holy kiss. v. 12

"Live in peace, and the God of love and peace will be with you."

We may not always nor need always to "agree with one another," nor have we yet all embraced Paul's injunction to "greet one another with a holy kiss," but it is possible and important to all of us that we "live in peace."

We are products of Pentecost. We are indwelt with the same Holy Spirit. We are confronted with the same overall command of Jesus to "Go . . . to all peoples everywhere and make them My disciples" (Matthew 28:19 TEV).

With the love of God the Father, the grace of Jesus, and the fellowship of the Holy Spirit empowering us, we can do great things in spreading God's kingdom.

We can be assured that "the God of love and peace will be with [us]," and we can confront each day of our lives with the determination to love one another and allow the Spirit of God to bring His eternal love and grace to those who cross our paths.

Heavenly Father, may Your great, eternal love so flood my life that, not only will my self-serving be forgiven, but that it will be eradicated from my life and I may become an open channel of that love and peace to others about me. Amen.

How to Start Over Again

Unless one is born anew, he cannot see the kingdom of God. v. 3

It is one of life's most precious gifts: the opportunity and the privilege to begin anew, to start over again.

We are born into a discordant, disease-ridden humanity. We inherited a sinful, error-prone nature. Inculcated into our souls, however, was the longing for better things, the grasp for perfection, the urge for something that hovers tantalizingly beyond our reach.

We flail the air with desire but fail to obtain. We run but never arrive. We seek but do not find. We grovel or grapple with the things of this life only to lapse into depression and defeat, our souls empty and unfulfilled.

Our great God has shown us how to start over again. It begins with a new birth, a reentry into this finite dimension with the realization of divine acceptance and grace. It is the gift of the ever-loving Father. It is revealed through our redemption made possible by His Son. It is received and appropriated by faith through the power of the blessed Holy Spirit.

We may still be haunted by failure and plagued with defeat. The new birth does not promise the end to guilt feelings or to the sins and weaknesses that cause them. But even while clothed in the blemishes and flaws of mortal flesh, we are the adopted sons and daughters of God. Our failures do not damn or destroy us. They drive us back to the sufficiency of God. There we find forgiveness and acceptance. There we are granted the opportunity to start over again.

I claim, O God, Your forgiveness for the failings and faults of my earthbound nature. I seek, O Lord, the grace and the courage to begin again. May I remember always Your victory over sin and death. Amen.

His Spirit within Us

You have received the Spirit of sonship. v. 15b

"For the Spirit that God has given you does not make you slaves and cause to be afraid; instead the Spirit makes you God's children . . ." (v. 15 TEV).

Can you imagine people dying of malnutrition with hundred-dollar bills stuffed into their mattresses? And yet it happens from time to time. A similar malady is common among Christians. While God through His indwelling Spirit provides us with all that is needed to live contributive, joy-filled lives, we are often afflicted with spiritual malnutrition.

It is indeed necessary that we are "born again." While this happened to us in the covenant God made with us in our baptism, we need daily to confront our finitude and failures and return to that covenant and embrace God's forgiving love anew. We need, as well, to be continually reminded and assured that Pentecost has happened, that God's Spirit dwells within us. It is this that establishes our credentials as God's children and equips us for the service we are called to render unto Him as His servants.

The faith that justifies us, that by God's grace enables us to tie into and respond to that grace, is the same faith that accepts our inheritance as God's children and the indwelling of His Spirit. "God's divine power has given us everything we need to live a truly religious life . . ." wrote Peter (2 Peter 1:3 TEV).

I thank you, my loving God, that You will not allow my flaws or failures to damn or destroy me. I pray that they may always drive me back to Your love and grace, to remind me of Your forgiveness and acceptance and to enable me to rise and renew my relationship with You. Amen.

Power to the People

When the Spirit of truth comes, He will guide you into all the truth.
v. 13a

We hear a great deal about power today. Our lives are enriched or frustrated, and may even be destroyed, by the various energies and powers that surround us. Whether we wake or sleep. we are sustained or threatened by the powers that press in upon us.

There is, however, another power, a far greater power, available to us: the Spirit-given power to love, to discover truth, to create and to heal, to bring light into darkness, beauty into ugliness, goodness into evil, sweetness into bitterness, joy into grief-stricken situations. Apart from it we could well become monsters that murder: with it we can become men and women who minister, sons and daughters of the living God destined to reflect and channel His love and grace to a broken, distorted world. The power of the Holy Spirit indwells us as God's special and divinely endowed representatives assigned to bring Christ's powerful gift of salvation into the fractured lives of the ailing and lost all about us.

It is time that we cease being clods that clutter up the church of Christ and become what we are destined to be—vibrant, pulsating vehicles of spiritual power. That power is within us. We need only to submit to the Source, the invisible Christ, and yield ourselves totally to His control and use.

O God, You took Your Son from our midst only to return to us by way of Your invisible Spirit. We thank You for the gift of Your Spirit. May we allow Him to make out of us what You intended us to be, and to work through us the accomplishment of Your purposes. Amen.

Accepted by God

Through Him we have obtained access to this grace in which we stand. v. 2

The truth of the matter is—and this in spite of those fine religious people who attempt to placate God by means of laws and rules and traditions and customs—the truth of the matter is that we *have been* accepted by God through Jesus Christ. This is where "we stand." This is what we ought to celebrating.

We can well afford to celebrate this even amid the difficult circumstances that harass us. Whether it be physical pain or mental anguish, material loss or excruciating sorrow, this does not separate us from God or alter our relationship with Him.

When we accept and cling to what God has done for us through Christ, irrespective of our human feelings and frailties, then the very conflicts that beset us and may even threaten to destroy us become God's tools to grind and polish and temper our spirits and prepare us for loving and obedient service.

This is no vain hope; it's the Gospel truth. God's love and Spirit *do* abide within us. Let us move into this day before us under this conviction and by the power of God's Spirit, for we are the very children of God, and no one can take that truth and experience away from us.

O God, now I know who I am. You gave me my identity in the moment of my baptism. You touched me with Your cleansing power and indwelt me with Your Spirit. I thank You, God, for accepting me as I am and for making me valid and significant as Your child and servant forever. Amen.

There Is No Other

Therefore you shall keep His statutes and His commandments.
v. 40

"Know therefore this day . . . that the Lord is God in heaven above and on the earth beneath; there is no other."

This Old Testament text is from one of a series of addresses made by Moses to his people prior to their crossing over the Jordan to occupy the new land to which God was leading them. The book of Deuteronomy is a record of Moses' inspiring pronouncements ranging from commandments and rules his people were to obey to prophecies of what would happen to them on the other side of the Jordan River and promises of God's care and guidance that would accompany them if they put their trust in Him. Throughout these lengthy discourses run Moses' constant reminders that their God is the only true God, a fact often proven throughout their long wilderness journey, and the guarantee of God's judgment upon all who create gods or graven images of their own to worship. "Lay it to your heart," said Moses, "that the Lord is God in heaven above and on the earth beneath; there is no other."

This injunction of Moses is as relevant to us as it was to the children of Israel. We need to be reminded from time to time that God, as revealed through God incarnate, Jesus Christ, is the only true God. "There is no other." False shepherds are persistently hailing and propagating false gods, cults, sects—sometimes well-intentioned groups that use divine names and sacred Scriptures and take on a "form of religion but deny the power of it" (2 Timothy 3:5). There are, as well, the more obvious "graven images" that tempt Christ's followers, such as wealth or position and various philosophies that promise self-fulfillment.

Lest we be seduced by those gods that seek our allegiance only to betray and possibly destroy us, let us begin this day's journey with the reminder "that the Lord is God in heaven above and on the earth beneath; there is no other."

O God, You truly are my God as revealed through Christ. There is no other. Amen.

Salvation—Then What?

Not everyone who says to me, 'Lord, Lord,' shall enter the kingdom of heaven. v. 21a

I have been a Christian all my life, but it wasn't until my late teens or early twenties that the implications of God's free gift of salvation really began to take hold in my life. A transformation began in my thinking and feeling that was as dramatic as is the initial conversion experience to scores of "born again" people in our society. I began to realize that I needed to take seriously some of the hard words of Jesus such as those recorded in our Gospel portion for today. The purpose was not to assure me of my salvation or to pile up credits in some future life, but to respond to God's grace, to accept the implications of my sonship with God. As Jesus bore the cross on my behalf, so I have been chosen to bear a cross on behalf of others in my world.

The words of this Gospel portion are indeed difficult, and sometimes disturbing, for Jesus may be speaking to us. We need to understand that our Lord's words are not suggesting that our salvation is dependent upon our good works. He clearly implies (v. 17) that these do not make us right with God. Our Lord insists, however, that those who abide in God's grace must respond to it in terms of hearing and doing the words and will of God.

"Conversion, in its original meaning," according to Jim Wallis, "meant that those who had been transformed by Jesus Christ, experienced a change in all their relationships to the world, to their possessions, to the poor and dispossessed, to the violence in their society, to the idols of their culture, and to the false worship of the state."

Maybe some of us need a second conversion, one that embraces our Lord's will as well as His life and salvation.

We must learn, our Lord, that our service to You must be rendered to Your human creatures about us. Enable us by Your grace to be Your faithful and effective servants. Amen.

Back to Square One

For we hold that a man is justified by faith apart from works of law.
v. 28

"They are justified by His grace as a gift," said Paul.

"The Gospel of the grace of God awakens an intense longing in human souls and an equally intense resentment . . . ," said Oswald Chambers. "I will give my life to martyrdom, I will give myself to consecration, I will do anything, but do not humiliate me to the level of the most hell-damning sinner and tell me that all I have to do is to accept the gift of salvation through Jesus Christ."

We are reminded again that we cannot earn or win anything from God, that we must either receive it as a gift or do without it. Before we go back to the office, the marketplace, the school room, or the household chores, on the first working day of any week, it is well that we go back to square one, the fundamental of our faith, the grace of God—His unmerited, undeserved love for us, and this irrespective of our frailties and failures. We will deal much with good works, our response to grace, to God's love for us, and our resultant enlistment in His will and purposes for us as His children and servants. But we will be reminded again and again that our salvation, our justification, is "by His grace as a gift."

Let us celebrate that precious truth on this day—and always. If our celebration is genuine, it will result in the dedication of our lives to glorifying God through Jesus Christ and to communicating His love to those around us.

Help me, O God, to understand that faith results, not simply leisurely abiding in what You have done for me, but also in striving to lay hold of the gifts You offer and carry on the commission to utilize those gifts in the extension of Your kingdom. Amen.

Law Without Love

The sabbath was made for man, not man for the sabbath. v. 27

The Pharisees were guided by law, not love. Jesus introduced an entirely new element, one that superseded the laws and rules concocted by the religious leaders of Israel, who proceeded to make them absolutes that dictated the ethics and action of the people. The Law was centered around the Ten Commandments and was intended to clarify and dramatize the ancient and essential commandment to "love the Lord your God with all your heart, and with all your soul, and with all your mind, and with all your strength" and "your neighbor as yourself" (Mark 12:30–31). Though the prophets at times indicated some understanding of what that kind of love was all about, it was Jesus who personified it, proclaimed it, and dramatized it.

The Ten Commandments continue to be essential to our life and growth as Christians, but they are superseded by love—the kind of love taught and exemplified by Jesus and the kind He expects of His disciples. This kind of love becomes an absolute for us. It means that our standards must supercede the Law as stated and interpreted in the Old Testament. It is the kind of love that sets us free from the bondage of the Law in order to love as Jesus loved and thereby communicate God's love to people about us.

This does not come naturally. We will often fail to love one another as Jesus loved us. Having received God's eternal love and grace, and this by way of Christ and the cross, we who are the objects of His never-ceasing love are to dedicate our lives in love to the needs of our fellow beings and discover in God's great love for us the compulsion to love our neighbor.

O Lord, it is my self-centeredness that prevents Your love from flowing through me to the lonely, unloved, deprived people in my path. Forgive me, and teach me how to love. Amen.

Enjoying the Disagreeable

*For while we live we are always being given up to death for Jesus'
sake.* v. 11a

The selling point in much of the hustling that is going on in the
name of Christian ministry today is joy, happiness, the highs and
ecstatic feelings that are suppose to result from such a religious
experience. This is not necessarily wrong. After all, Jesus certainly
underlined joy as one of the prime fruits of "abiding in the Vine"
(John 15:1–11), and John wrote his letter in order that "our joy may
be complete" (1 John 1:4).

This is not the whole picture, however, and Paul tends to wet-
blanket some of the excesses and extremes in this respect by
pointing up a few of the disagreeable things that befell him and his
colleagues as a consequence of their faithful witness: "afflicted in
every way . . . perplexed . . . persecuted . . . struck down . . ." There
doesn't appear to be a great deal of joy in these episodes that
happened so often in their ministry. Yet these painful experiences
did not smother out the joy of their relationship to God and their
ministry for Him: "afflicted . . . but not crushed; perplexed, but not
driven to despair; persecuted, but not forsaken; struck down, but
not destroyed . . ." Even these things inadvertently resulted in joy:
"We are always being given up to death . . . that the life of Jesus
may be manifested in our mortal flesh."

Is it really possible to enjoy the disagreeable? Only if our joy is
divinely inspired and matured in the enthusiasm and delight of
allowing "the life of Jesus" to be "manifested in our mortal flesh."

We are not about to seek out or choose the disagreeable,
hurtful things that will happen to faithful disciples. If, however, they
come as a consequence of obeying God and serving our fellow
creatures, they will enhance and temper our joy as children and
servants.

Teach me, dear Lord, how to accept and cope with struggle
. . . and yet to walk and serve in joy. Amen.

The Gospel for Body and Soul

And when those who had been sent returned to the house, they found the slave well. v. 10

There are many instances when Jesus preached—particularly to His closest followers—so that they might be purged and prepared for future service. For many people who came to Him, however, His ministry took the form of tangible acts of mercy in terms of problem-solving, pain-relieving miracles: turning water into wine, giving sight to the blind, healing the lame and the ill, exorcising demons, and so on.

Some of us were brought up under the illusion that the problems of people and their world would be solved or eliminated by simply preaching the Gospel, that our commission as Christians was only to talk about Jesus, to witness as to our faith in Christ, to get people ready for heaven. Whatever the source of such a misconception, it didn't come from God's Word. The early Hebrews recognized the difference between the sacred and the profane, but they did not divide the social from the spiritual. The social concern of the prophets is well known: "Seek justice, relieve the oppressed, judge the fatherless, plead for the widow," were their stern injunctions. Christ gave priority to the spiritual emphasis—salvation, God's forgiving grace, eternal life—but He did not neglect the social emphasis.

When we are truly committed to Jesus Christ as our Savior and Lord, both the spiritual and the social needs of our fellow beings become our concern. We are genuinely evangelistic only when we begin to demonstrate that kind of concern in our relationships to God and to the human family about us.

Loving Christ, You identified with us in our sins and sicknesses, You embraced us as Your brothers and sisters, You commissioned us to be Your servants, now help us to fulfill our servanthood in identifying with the needs of our brothers and sisters and in communicating Your love and grace to them. Amen.

Subverted Christians

There are some who trouble you and want to pervert the gospel of Christ. v. 7

It is astonishing and disconcerting when people are easily subverted from the Gospel as Jesus proclaimed it to chase after some subjective ecstasy, or go traipsing after a sign or miracle or vision, or fall prey to some half-truth that promises to make their lives more secure and exciting. One doesn't have to look far to discover false prophets twisting the Scriptures to say what they want them to say. They enclose our great God within their own shallow concepts and pass this sometimes poisonous concoction on to their avid followers. Paul had no kind thoughts about such individuals: "Let [them] be accursed," he said.

While we may not be inclined to judge so harshly such promoters of a religion, we need to avoid them like the plague and to make certain that the Gospel we submit to is the Gospel of Jesus Christ and not the pathetic mouthings of foolish and dangerous self-styled prophets.

All Christians are tempted at times to interpret the Gospel in ways that fit their assumed needs or that appear to be most reasonable. Perhaps we need to be shaken up from time to time to make sure that our reach for eternal truth far exceeds the grasp of human understanding and to continue resisting attempts to package or bottle-up God in a closed system of select rules, regulations, or rituals that can be handled without too much discomfort or pain.

God, as revealed through Jesus Christ, is the true God whom we accept and serve; He is the One who loves and accepts and commissions us for service.

There is, O God, no way to be reconciled to You except through Your Son, Jesus Christ, and the cross He bore on our behalf. Forbid, our Lord, that we should ever turn away from that blessed truth. Amen.

Blessing or Curse

Behold, I set before you this day a blessing and a curse. v. 26

Life or death, heaven or hell, good or bad, black or white. Maybe the issues were simpler in Moses' day. Issues and decisions appear to be far more complicated in our time. While our intentions are honorable, things don't seem to turn out quite the way we expect them to.

Apparently, the same was true for the children of Israel. They carelessly or deliberately disobeyed God or attached their lives and fortunes to other gods along the way. The history of Israel is a history of human sinfulness and faithlessness and of God lovingly but sternly attempting to draw them back into a relationship with Himself. God did not have to zap them with frightful disasters; they aptly created their own by their refusal to listen to and obey the commands of their God.

We are the recipients of the Good News that the ultimate curse that is promised God's unbelieving, disobedient, sinful creatures has been borne by God Himself in His Son, Jesus Christ.

So, too, are the sins of our lives, the bad decisions, the failures and flops of yesterday or last week. We may still have to bear some of the consequences in one way or another, but God Himself forgives and forgets, and such unfortunate experiences do not stand between us and our loving God.

Tomorrow—and next week—afford us the opportunity to start over again. And all the while that we struggle to live according to His will and to reflect His attributes in our relationships with His creatures around us, He is with us to comfort, guide, admonish, and enable us to work out His purposes through us, and to forgive us when we fail.

I so often fail, O Lord, despite my firm resolutions and determined efforts. And yet I dare to believe that this does not come between me and You. I praise You for this blessed assurance. Amen.

The Call of Christ

And He said to [Matthew], "Follow Me." And he rose and followed Him. v. 9

The most astounding, incredible fact of all history is the call of Christ to sinful men and women, the invitation to follow Him. It is extended to the meanest, greediest, most unpromising creatures on the face of the earth. No matter how fractured or distorted, failure-fraught or inadequate we may be, we are invited to follow Jesus Christ, to become the sons and daughters of God, servants and disciples of our Lord and Savior. It is, moreover, not an invitation to casual acquaintance or weekly worship. It is not simply an offer of outside help when we are in trouble. It is the call to follow Him, to become exclusively attached to the Person of Christ, to love Him, serve Him, and crown Him Lord of every phase and facet, attitude and aspect of our lives.

Of course, we *accept* Jesus Christ. This ought to flood our lives with the joy of sin forgiven and the assurance of life eternal. But if we are to be effective as Christians and obedient as God's children, we must *follow* Jesus Christ. Our Lord is not only inviting us to respect Him or honor Him or appreciate Him; He is calling us to follow Him, to join with Him, become one with Him, to die with Him and be resurrected with Him, and to reign with Him in that eternal kingdom He has come to establish and build.

It's incredible! It's true! As He called Matthew, that despised tax collector, so He calls us—raising us out of our sin and despair to become, with Him, the very sons and daughters of God. "I came not to call the righteous, but sinners," said Jesus to the Pharisees. We are eligible; let us rise up to follow Him.

I pray, my loving Savior and Lord, that You will never give up on me, that I will continue to hear clearly and respond gratefully to Your call to follow You. Amen.

Hope against Hope

No distrust made him waver concerning the promise of God . . .
v. 20a

"In hope he believed against hope . . ." Abraham portrayed a very stubborn faith in God's promise "that he should become the father of many nations." This is the kind of faith we often need in our kind of world. The Holy Spirit, according to Jesus' promise, will accomplish the purposes of God in and through us. Abraham "did not weaken in faith when he considered his own body," but we often do. It is not particularly our age that concerns us, as it did Abraham, but our inadequacy. We still rely so very much on our human attributes and faculties and, by all appearances, they are incapable of carrying out God's objectives—especially in the role we are called on to play on this stage we call life. It is difficult enough to consistently believe that we are forgiven, accepted, loved by God, that we are through Christ righteous in His eyes. To believe that He is working out His will through us, that the seed we sow will bear fruit to the advancement of His kingdom, is well-nigh impossible.

It is, at times, a matter of "hope . . . against hope," of taking God as His Word and letting the chips fall where they may. Abraham's faith was "reckoned to him as righteousness." We are, through Jesus Christ, accounted as righteous; it is not at all a matter of how strong our faith is. And yet our faith is the means of embracing and believing that through Christ we are forgiven. It is also the means of overcoming our frailties and feelings of inadequacy, and it enables us to rejoice in the blessed truth that God will work out His purposes in and through us today.

My loving God, I need Your grace to keep on believing, to hold firmly to the glorious Gospel of my salvation, and to dedicate daily my life to thanksgivings and praises even as I serve You in the process of serving Your children about me. Amen.

The Family of God

Who are My mother and my brothers? v. 33

"Whosoever does the will of God is My brother, and sister . . ."

We strongly affirm the emphasis on family life in these days when the forces of evil seem so intent upon and successful in their attempts to divide and destroy this all-important unit of society. Our Lord, early in His ministry, also referred to family life. It was, however a far different family that concerned Him. He was speaking about something thus far incomprehensible to His listeners, that was related to another dimension: the family of God. Human relationships were still important to Jesus, and He continued to reveal a human concern for His own family, noted especially in respect to the pain and sorrow His crucifixion was causing His mother (John 19:26–27). But even at that critical hour He was regarding the family relationship on a different level that we generally understand or experience.

We ought to cherish much our families and our relationships therein. We need, as well, to grow into an understanding of Jesus' pronouncements concerning the new family He had come to construct, the family of God. He said, in effect, that those who are related to God as their heavenly Father are brothers and sisters to one another—and are the very brothers and sisters of Jesus, the Son of God.

Whatever our race or heritage, class or status in society, our gifts or abilities, we are all the members of the family of God and are, with Jesus Himself, brothers and sisters in that family. It is an eternal relationship that is far more significant than the human family relationships we cherish here on this planet. The Christians in our church, the members of Christian churches down the street, the hundreds of thousands of Christ's brothers and sisters all over the world—they are our brothers and sisters.

We sing our praises to Your glory, our eternal Father, and as Your children shout our thanksgivings. Amen.

Do Not Lose Heart

So we do not lose heart. Though our outer nature is wasting away . . . v. 16a

We are "earthen vessels," clay pots, in the hands of God, Paul said in the verses preceding this Scripture portion. And while every vessel has its flaws, God has chosen to deliver His eternal gifts to this world through such vessels. He may have to break and remake us from time to time, but use us He will—with our cooperation and obedience. He only requires that we gratefully submit our bodies and beings for His use and consecrate our efforts and energies to His purposes.

Of course we will have problems. There will be times when we are flattened by despair. There will probably be executioners about seeking to nail us to some cross. It is quite possible that we will lose status, popularity, friends, if we dare to let God have His way with us. Whatever we lose, however, we will regain a thousandfold in this life or in the next. This is the promise of our God. And He doesn't shortchange anyone.

The truth is, we don't have to be discouraged. We can be free even from fear of failure. Only then are we free to live—or to die—to joyfully spend and expend our lives for Jesus' sake.

So "do not lose heart." It's a great and wonder-filled life.

My loving God, I am still learning how to walk on this great journey of faith before me. Yet I believe that You walk beside me even in my mundane, ordinary, everyday living. Grant, O God, that I may never lose heart. Amen.

Rise Up and Live!

And He said, "Young man, I say to you, arise." v. 14b

This Gospel portion deals with Christ's confrontation with human grief and the event of death—and with His power to overcome both grief and death. It is designed to assure God's children of such power in respect to their lives and to eradicate once and for always their fear of this ultimate event. Death is a part of life, one single step from the front stoop of this three-dimensional world into the living room of everlasting union with God—one that Christians may well anticipate but certainly need not fear.

The fact is we are not likely to be of much use to God in this world until our eventual exodus from it, though at times fraught with apprehension, holds no real fear for us.

"Do not weep," Jesus compassionately exhorted the mother of the deceased man. "Stop crying," He is saying to doubting, griping, fearful, complaining Christians today. "Arise!" He said to the deceased man and is saying to all who claim His salvation and yet are sick unto death amidst the pains and pressures of our uncertain and insecure world.

Is it possible that some of us still haven't learned how to live, how to lay hold of the love and life made available through Jesus Christ and the death He died on the cross, a life that grants His supernatural peace and joy even in the midst of doubt and pain and insecurity?

It is only when we rise up and live in the joy and power of Christ, the resurrected Christ, that we can lovingly and helpfully respond to the doubts and fears, the burdens and sufferings, of dying people about us. It is when we do this that we are really living.

Grant, O God, that Your eternal Spirit may replenish the dry wells of my life that I may be a spring of living water to others around me. Help me to "rise up and live!" Amen.

The True Gospel

I did not receive [this gospel] from man . . . it came through a revelation of Jesus Christ. v. 12

"For I would have you know . . . that the Gospel which was preached by me is not man's gospel." Nor is the Gospel we listen to in churches we attend on Sunday. There may be some question about some of the popular media religious presentations that fill the airwaves at some time on almost any day, but most of us are secure in the knowledge that our pastor is preaching the Gospel of Jesus Christ.

It is true, nonetheless, that those of us who preach or witness have often been guilty of something less than spiritual motives in our presentations. While we often sense this to be true about some of the popular evangelists who charismatically draw viewers and listeners into their fold, we ought to be aware of the possibility that we may be doing the same thing in our little groups. God uses the message we proclaim because of us or in spite of us. We need to be sure, however, that we are mouthpieces, instruments, in the hands of God, and rid ourselves of any intent to seek our glory or the adoration of our fans or followers.

Responsible preachers of and witnesses to the faith pray sincerely that they may not come between people and God, but that they be channels of God's Word of comfort and challenge to people about them. Only then can they be assured that "the Gospel which was preached by [them] is not man's gospel."

We become God's servants by His grace alone. We preach and witness effectively only by that grace. The Gospel which we preach and to which we witness is the true Gospel.

I pray, my God, for the grace and the compulsion to preach "Christ crucified . . . Christ the power of God and the wisdom of God." Amen.

God Is Faithful

Let us know, let us press on to know the Lord . . . v. 3a

God is faithful even when we are not. Like the foolish, unfaithful wife of Hosea, we turn from our loving God to pursue the foolish pleasures and temporal treasures, the creature comforts, within reach around us. We find ourselves, at times, in mind if not in body, whoring after the ephemeral delights of this world. Even then the love of our eternal God never ceases. He allows us to discover for ourselves, sometimes tragically, the emptiness of our lives and to taste the suffering we bring upon ourselves through our rebellion and unfaithfulness. God knows well that we may not find our way back to Him, so in His loving mercy He pursues us, suffering in Himself the judgment we incurred through our infidelities, seeking to draw us back into His forgiving heart and to restore us to a loving relationship with Himself.

God will not give up on us. Even while we insanely call down judgment upon ourselves, He is ready to forgive us. When we stumble into the pits that await us, He is waiting and ready to draw us back to His loving heart. God stands by to forgive the infidelities and heal the faithlessness of His wandering children. If only we will confront our emptiness and loneliness, our great need for our true and eternal Lover, He will restore us to a loving relationship with Himself and within the family and kingdom of God.

Let us cease playing God with our own lives and return to the true God, our God who created and redeemed us. He will heal the wounds caused by our faithlessness. He will forgive and cast aside our iniquities. He will love and securely hold on to us forever.

"Great is Your faithfulness! Morning by morning new mercies I see. All I have needed Your hand has provided. Great is Your faithfulness, Lord, unto me." Amen.

Christianity: Escapism or Involvement?

Heal the sick, raise the dead, cleanse lepers, cast out demons. v. 8a

This Gospel portion presents a concept of the Christian life that is sometimes lost among the soft, sentimental approaches that are often promulgated.

Jesus tells us that discipleship means involvement. He set the pace, and He expects His disciples to keep it. He identified with the agonies of humankind. He became involved in their crying needs. He even went so far as to bear the consequences of their sins. To be a disciple of Jesus means that we who accept Him as our Savior must also accept Him as our Lord and Master. We are expected not simply to criticize the distortions of humanity from the pews and pulpits of our churches, but to become involved in the blood and tears, the sorrows and sufferings, of God's creatures wherever they may be found.

Because we are involved in the sickness of our world, we must, as the disciples of Christ, become involved in its cure. Discipleship means involvement. As our Lord suffered on our behalf, we are expected to suffer on behalf of others, to lose our lives in service only to truly find life anew in the incomparable joy of being the children and servants of the living, loving, eternal God.

"As the Father has sent Me, even so I send You" (John 20:21).

Forgive me, Jesus, for not always taking You seriously. I have so often taken what You have granted me—forgiveness, eternal security, the comfort of knowing that You are my Shepherd—without really following You as my Lord and Master. May my love for You resolve in the courage to follow You whatever may be the consequences. Amen.

What God Has Done for Us

While we were helpless, at the right time Christ died for the ungodly.
v. 6

The preceding Gospel portion underlines the necessity of involvement in the purposes of God by dedicating our lives to the good works of proclaiming and demonstrating God's love to the inhabitants of our world. This is followed by this Epistle portion that draws us back to the center and core of our religion. Faith does not save us because it is a good work, but because it is the hand that reaches out to take the salvation God has prepared for us. Daily repentance will not make or keep us Christian but is our realization of and response both to our unworthiness and to what God has done for us in Jesus Christ. Nor does our obedience to God make us right with Him, but the suffering, death, and resurrection of Jesus Christ make us right with God. It is by the supernatural miracle of God's grace that we stand justified before Him, not by sorrow over sin or confession of faith or consecration to divine purposes.

This will always be a great mystery, something we can never quite comprehend, but it was Jesus Christ who reconciled us to God. What we cannot comprehend we can still celebrate. Through the sacrifice of our Lord, God's act of grace and gift of love, we have been made the very sons and daughters of God. We were once the enemies of God, totally estranged from Him, sick unto death with the disease that pervaded and permeated the whole human race. God's love for His creatures, however, is far greater than the evil that brings death and destruction. His grace is more powerful than human wickedness. This is the grace that was wrought and revealed by Jesus Christ, and it is this that grants us everlasting life.

Every day should be a day of celebration, my loving God, a day to sing or shout or write or proclaim Your eternal salvation through Jesus Christ, my Savior and Lord. May my church, my home, my life resound with the glad, joyful sounds of celebration. Amen.

God's Patience with Us

But when the grain is ripe, at once he puts in the sickle, because the harvest has come. v. 29

"He spoke the word to them, as they were able to hear it."

According to Mark, Christ's proclamations to the general public were almost always in the form of parables, "but privately to His disciples He explained everything." From the ancient prophets of Old Testament times through the apostles of the first-century church, God patiently unfolded His eternal truth in the measure that they were able to hear it and thereby experience and proclaim it. In this very day, even concerning the truth as revealed through the Scriptures, it becomes our own in knowledge and experience as we increase in spiritual growth and maturity.

God has dedicated time and eternity to the project of making us what He intended us to be. He has redeemed us through Jesus Christ. By way of the Law and the Gospel, we have heard and made our own the truth of His eternal love for us. Yet God is not finished with us. As we are "able to hear it," He continues to let us find deeper insights about ourselves and about Himself and His purposes for us.

Thus we grow and mature as His sons and daughters, assuming that we are ever alert and obedient to His truth as He enables us to recognize and embrace it. Some of our brothers and sisters in the faith appear to grow more rapidly than others, and are enabled to hear and proclaim new dimensions of His eternal truth that may still be unknown or obscure to us. God won't give up on any of us. He loves each one of us and takes His time with each of us in order that all of us may be what He wants us to be. Some of this unfolding He does "privately," in our personal relationships with Him; much of it is done through our relationships with one another in the great family of God.

Almighty, all-wise, and everywhere-present God, may we always keep ourselves open to You and to one another that we may hear, recognize, understand, and respond to the truth as revealed through Jesus Christ. Amen.

The Walk of Faith

So we are always of good courage ... We walk by faith, not by sight. vv. 6, 7

"We walk by faith, not by sight."

The few years we have on earth are precious to us. They are what we can consciously comprehend. But the same God who gave us this three-dimensional experience has promised us eternal dimensions far above and beyond anything we can imagine or comprehend. He asks only that we trust Him and demonstrate that trust in all-out commitments of all we are and have to Him and to our fellow persons for His sake.

This is what faith is all about. As a matter of fact, if we really knew what lay ahead of us in that eternal world that is to come, we would be too anxious to enter its portals and much too impatient about the few years and many tasks and hard problems of this temporal existence.

We can stop being cowards and begin taking risks for God. We are the inheritors of His great kingdom, heirs and joint-heirs with Jesus Christ Himself. Whatever we tenaciously hold on to in this life eventually turns to ashes. Whatever we painfully, responsibly, and lovingly give away really enhances our lives, and in the process of thereby serving others we serve our gracious God.

I know, O Lord, that it is not so all-important that I be successful, but that I be faithful in my daily walk, that I belong to You, represent and glorify You, and allow You to have Your way in and through me. So be it, Lord. Amen.

Some People Can't Love

He who is forgiven little, loves little. v. 47b

I have always assumed that the "unpardonable sin" referred to out-right blasphemy against the Holy Spirit. I now wonder if one's hatred or even disregard or unconcern for a fellow human being approaches this kind of blasphemy. Simon was a man who apparently could not love. Meticulous, well-disciplined, highly respected, extremely scrupulous, yet completely detached and noninvolved, he was like a cold fish. He demonstrated no affection whatsoever toward Jesus. He did not stoop to perform the host's function of providing water and washing a weary traveler's feet. There was no kiss of welcome, no oil for anointing. The only emotion he showed was an exclamation of horror or disgust over the entrance of a sinful woman and the manner in which she was acting toward the Christ.

There was, however, a woman who did love, a street-woman carrying with her a tool of her trade, a flask of ointment. She heard that Jesus was near and sought Him out to express her love for Him. Ignoring the rules of tradition or etiquette, she broke into that small assembly and in passionate devotion poured out her tears upon Jesus' feet and wiped them with her hair. Then, with utter disregard for the economics of the act or the restrictions of propriety or decorum, she poured the expensive contents of her flask of precious ointment upon Him and stooped to kiss His feet.

"Therefore, I tell you, her sins, which are many, are forgiven, for she loved much," said Jesus about this woman, "but he who is forgiven little, loves little." It becomes obvious to me that I need God's forgiveness of my sins and His loving acceptance of me. Then, perhaps, I can learn how to love.

"Most merciful God . . . for the sake of Your Son, Jesus Christ, have mercy on us. Forgive us, renew us, and lead us, so that we may delight in Your will and walk in Your ways . . ." Amen.

Signing Away Our Rights

It is no longer I who live, but Christ who lives in me. v. 20

"I have been crucified with Christ . . ."

We vociferously and sometimes belligerently insist on our personal rights—to property ownership, free speech, the pursuit of happiness, or whatever else promises to please us. Not so, testifies Paul: "I have been crucified with Christ." This means many things, much of which we don't really understand, but it adds up to our signing the death warrant for the disposition of sin and self-rule in our lives, and the yielding over to Jesus Christ of every right that we claim for ourselves. We do not simply determine to imitate Christ or try to follow Him when it suits us; we have been identified with Him in His crucifixion. All that is accomplished for us on Christ's cross is also to be accomplished in us. We "die" to sin and our right to run our own lives and, by the grace of God, become His loyal and faithful disciples forever.

We remain human beings, each one unique and individual, but the mainspring is radically altered. Once estranged from God and His purposes, we are through Christ reunited to Him, made one with Him, restored to His orbit for our lives. We no longer insist on our own rights but carry out the rights and objectives of our Creator and Redeemer and discover that this is what we were meant to do from the very beginning.

"The life I now live in the flesh I live by faith in the Son of God . . . " wrote Paul. This is really living! The limited satisfactions that are occasionally experienced by claiming our rights in this fractured world are small indeed when compared to the incomparable joy of allowing Christ to live out His life in and through us.

"Have Your own way, Lord, have Your own way! You are the Potter; I am the clay. Mold me and make me after Your will, while I am waiting, yielded and still." Amen.

Remember Who You Are

You shall be to Me a kingdom of priests and a holy nation. v. 6a

"You shall be My own possession among all peoples . . ."

Thus God speaks to Christians today as He did to the people of Israel in ancient times. The conditions as spelled out to Moses on the mountain were quite clear: "If you will obey My voice and keep My covenant . . ." The people failed miserably and, except for a remnant, were dispossessed by God. Then through Jesus Christ, God not only spoke but acted to make His creatures His possessions once more. God Himself fulfilled the necessary conditions. Humanity's rebelliousness and disobedience, the sins of every man and woman, were atoned for in the suffering and death of Jesus Christ. It is now possible for all of God's human creatures to be repossessed, to be drawn back into the circle of His love, to belong to Him forever.

It almost takes one's breath away, the fact that God would want to possess us, that He would give Himself over to suffering and death that such a thing might be possible. We just are not that much of a prize that God should go to such lengths to lovingly draw us to and keep us for Himself. His ownership was established at our creation. He permitted us to break out of His circle of loving care and foolishly try to make it on our own. He seeks always to repossess us and make us His own for all eternity.

We who have been repossessed and reconciled to God abide in the sweet comfort that we are His possession, and "no one is able to snatch [us] out of the Father's hand" (John 10:29). Let us remember that, as we face the temptations that seek to trip us up today or the adversities that cause us anxiety and pain.

Gracious Father, help me to be what I am, to accept myself as a part of that vineyard that bears fruit for You and to grow and bloom where I am planted. Amen.

Christians on Trial

Do not fear those who kill the body but cannot kill the soul. v. 28a

Many of us, as Christians, have coasted along with an anemic, bargain-basement kind of faith, worshiping a sort of mother-God who pacifies our hungers and secures our future. It has been respectable to be called Christian. It has been a warm, comforting, consoling, safe kind of faith that demands almost nothing in return. This may be the reason that we have difficulty understanding or identifying with the words and inferences of Jesus in our Gospel portion, or with the words of a 20th-century martyr, Dietrich Bonhoeffer, who wrote: "If we refuse to take up our cross and submit to suffering and rejection at the hands of men, we forfeit our fellowship with Christ and have ceased to follow Him."

For this reason the words of Christ in this lesson may not mean very much to many of us. For those who seriously and sincerely obey Him, however, and who truly become His servants in our chaotic, hate-infested, sin-bound world, our Lord's words are words of encouragement. "It is quite possible that you will lose your lives if you follow Me, but don't be afraid," our Lord is saying, "you are of more value than many sparrows." He speaks words of warning. "There is an enemy that you must contend with," He may be saying to us today, "the apathy and neglect, the selfishness and self-centeredness that can destroy your souls and rob you of eternal life."

We remain the children of God because He is a loving, forgiving God. We pray that He will graciously and patiently lead us into a relationship with Himself that will honor and glorify Him by demonstrating His love and His life to the world about us.

My loving God, grant to me the courage to face up to the demands of discipleship, and the grace to meet and deal with them. May I begin today to relate as Your child and servant to someone whose path I will cross and whose life I may influence. Amen.

Don't Blame Adam

And so death spread to all men because all men sinned. v. 12a

While it is true that "sin came into the world through one man," the old "blame Adam" gimmick some of us have used to explain away some fault or failure in our makeup is sheer nonsense. According to one writer, sin is not explained as an accumulation of immoralities or wrongdoings in our lives, but is in reality our foolish and disastrous claim to our right to ourselves. It is, in essence, casting our God-Creator off the throne of our hearts and enthroning and enshrining self-will as god and master. It is this immoral and rebellious act that estranged us from God. Created to be His sons and daughters, we instead turned into tyrants and traitors, the very enemies of God.

We can't blame Adam. We are sinners with or without the contributions of our ancestors, for "all . . . are under the power of sin . . . All have turned aside, together they have gone wrong . . ." (3:9, 12). We are responsible if we do not embrace the gift of forgiveness, the deliverance from the sin and guilt that holds us fast, the righteousness that Jesus came to grant to us. "And this is the judgment," said Jesus, "that the light has come into the world, and men loved darkness rather than light, because their deeds were evil" (John 3:19).

How great is the grace of God! It is sufficient to cover all the sins of the human race—including yours and mine. The knowledge of this is that light which, through Jesus Christ, has come into our world. May that knowledge become our experience today and every day of our lives.

"Just as I am, You will receive, will welcome, pardon, cleanse, relieve; because Your promise I believe, O Lamb of God, I come, I come." Amen.

God's Grace amid Life's Storms

Do not fear, only believe. v. 36b

World population is exploding. Our economy is on a rampage. Our environment is endangered through carelessness and waste. Our natural resources are being depleted. Our government is often ineffective and sometimes corrupt. Crime is increasing toward frightening proportions. Millions in our country are jobless. Hundreds of millions throughout our world are starving. Drought, earthquake, natural and man-perpetrated calamities are wracking our world. I think we are beginning to feel something of what those disciples felt as the "storm of wind arose and the waves beat into the boat," and they awakened the sleeping Christ crying out, "Teacher, do You not care if we perish?"

Maybe Christ is saying to us what He, in essence, said to those disciples: "Why are you such cowards? How little faith you have! I have created, redeemed, and appointed you for just such times as these. I am always with you, working out My will through you. Trust Me; I won't let you down. There is a quiet harbor somewhere at the end of your journey, but for now you are to abide in Me and work for Me in the midst of storm."

What this Gospel portion is saying is that God truly does care about us and, in the midst of our insufficiency, His grace is sufficient—and it is available. It is not something we have to earn, merit, or work for; it is grace, His great gift of love. While He does not promise to cancel out all the storms of our lives as He did that storm on the Sea of Galilee, He does promise to be with us as we face and endure the storms that whirl about us. We need only, in faith, to recognize and accept His promises and power and to lay claim to His loving, supernatural peace even in the midst of these raging tempests that beset us.

Help me, O God, to lay hold of that grace which is sufficient to keep me steady and faithful whatever the storms that ravage my small craft. Amen.

Abandoned to the Love of God

If any one is in Christ, he is a new creation. v. 17a

"For the love of Christ controls us . . ." A good question to begin any day with: Am I controlled by the love of God as He is revealed through the loving Christ? I ought to be because "He died for all, that those who live might live no longer for themselves but for Him who for their sake died and was raised."

Or one might consider the same question concerning yesterday: Was I controlled by the love of God, or did some other desire, passion, lust, or prejudice control my attitudes or actions?

Some of us fell far short of Paul's experience yesterday. We were tempted or tainted by some idol or graven image, or we were led astray by our focus on lesser values, or propelled by self-interest, or we rebelled in the face of adversity or failed to show love among unlovable people.

"We are ambassadors for Christ, God making His appeal through us." We are a "new creation," God's redeemed creatures, reflecting God's love in whatever circumstances may come our way. Is this transpiring in our lives? Is this what happened yesterday?

Yesterday is past and forgiven. Today is another day—and a new opportunity to be what we are in Christ, what God would have us to be every day of our lives. This will happen only if we are truly abandoned to the love of God and allow that love to purge away all inordinate affections and self-interests, all lesser values and loyalties, and to be clearly portrayed and manifested through us. Our determination alone will not enable us to do this, but the grace of God will draw us closer to this noble goal as we abandon ourselves to His love and determine day by day to make this our foremost objective and allow Him to have His way in and through us.

I love You, my loving God. I pray that such will be reflected in my relationships to my fellow persons along the journey of life. Amen.

From Milk to Meat

If any man would come after Me, let him deny himself and take up his cross daily and follow Me. v. 23

When Jesus invited His disciples to spell out their feelings concerning Himself, the most encouraging statement came from the lips of Peter, who identified and accepted Jesus as "the Christ of God."

Peter's confession was immature at this point, but it was genuine. Jesus accepted it as such, so much so that He dared at this stage in His ministry to predict His coming suffering and death and to reveal to His followers something of the price they would have to pay when continuing the ministry He had begun. They, of course, had no comprehension of what Jesus was talking about. They were still living on milk while Jesus was pointing out to them the real meat of Christian discipleship.

They were destined to mature quickly in the following months, however, and soon understood well the meaning and extent of Christ's predictions and promises. The very men who fearfully denied their friendship with Christ or went into hiding when He was indicted and sentenced to torture and execution were the very same men who gladly and courageously embraced persecution and martyrdom as a consequence of proclaiming the risen Christ as the world's Savior and Lord.

We may have regarded ourselves quite fortunate in being able to rise above the obvious immaturity of Christ's disciples prior to His crucifixion. We now confess that there is still a lot of milk left in our spiritual diet. We, along with Peter, can confidently proclaim Jesus to be "the Christ of God." Contrary to the post-resurrection Peter, we are not so confident or eager about denying self, taking up our cross, and risking all to follow Jesus Christ.

I do confess, O Christ, my immaturity and childishness in respect to my understanding of and commitment to Your will for my life. Forgive me, and continue to draw me into the very center of that will whatever may be the consequences. Amen.

Abraham's Offspring

In Christ Jesus you are all sons of God, through faith. v. 26

"If you are Christ's, then you are Abraham's offspring, heirs according to promise . . . you are all one in Christ Jesus."

Paul's declaration may not have been very popular in his day—perhaps not today either—but ought to be gladly acknowledged and heralded by Christians of every race and color throughout the world. We are one family, one kingdom, whatever our national origin or ancestry, our church or denomination. Our baptism into Christ brings us into the family of God.

Our adherence to the Law does not make us or keep us the children of God. The Law is still of value in revealing our spiritual poverty and our absolute need for God's grace, but it can in no way make us right with God. It continues to be the basis and guide for daily living, but it is never a means of salvation. We are baptized into Christ, who has kept the Law in our stead and freed us from its stringent demands and consequential judgments to freely and joyfully love and serve God as His beloved children and servants.

Our faith in God's acceptance of us, His gift of forgiveness and grace, makes it possible for us to celebrate our eternal union with Him and with all those who belong to Him. As a consequence of that faith and that relationship to God as He is revealed through Christ, we embrace a morality or standard of ethics that is far superior to the Law as interpreted by legalists, ancient or modern. This is the standard or morality of love—God's love for the whole human family—imparted to us and reflected through us to our fellow beings throughout the world in which we live.

My almighty and gracious God, blast out the bias and bigotry which threatens my relationship to my fellow persons and to You. Grant me the grace to demonstrate to my brothers and sisters something of the love You have demonstrated to me. Amen.

When the Nights Are Dark

*The Lord is with me as a dread warrior; therefore my persecutors
. . . will not overcome me.* v. 11

The prophet Jeremiah appears to bounce back and forth
between complaints and praises. He honestly proclaims his gripes as
well as his gratitude. He was often depressed and discouraged. And
so are we. We feel at times that God has given up on us, that while
we are children of His grace, we fail to meet His demands for
servanthood, we fail to effectively carry out His purposes in
stemming the tide of wickedness overwhelming our world, we fail
to proclaim and manifest God's love to people about us.

Yet we know, deep within us, that His love for us never ceases,
that when our faith falters, He is ever faithful, that He cares for us
and will never let us go.

We need to be reassured that the world is in God's hands and,
despite the persistent rebelliousness of its children, He will
accomplish His purposes within it. It is not important that we see
the results of our servanthood; it is important that we trust God and
His Spirit within us—and that we quietly and patiently wait for the
revealing of His kingdom.

Let come what may—adversity or affliction, enmity or
opposition, feelings of defeat, even the ridicule of our peers, we are
the redeemed children and chosen servants of our God, and we are
His forever.

"Sing to the Lord; praise the Lord!"

I pray, O Lord, that my foolish complaints may be transformed
into celebration, my sinning into singing Your praises, my
gripes into gratitude and thanksgiving for all Your love-gifts
to Your child and servant. Amen.

Peace or Violence?

Do not think that I have come to bring peace on earth. v. 34a

"I have not come to bring peace, but a sword." Our first reaction to Jesus' words is bewilderment. We are often tempted to regard this as one of the great paradoxes of the gospels and respectfully pass on to those portions of Christ's teaching that are more agreeable to our frame of mind. "But Jesus elsewhere blesses the peacemakers," we protest.

Jesus did promise peace: "Peace I leave with you; My peace I give to you," He said in John's gospel (14:27). But within the same three years of Christ's ministry He proclaimed: "I have not come to bring peace, but a sword."

We spent most of our Sunday school years picturing our Lord as a gentle, meek peacemaker. This is not the whole picture. When Jesus dealt with the poor, the ill, the simple-minded, the sinners, the publicans, the fishermen, He spoke words of comfort and challenge, peace and promise. But when He addressed the sanctimonious, hypocritical establishment of His day, He spoke like a revolutionary. His words were like a sharp sword, slicing into the hides and hearts of those oppressive and self-centered leaders like a knife into soft butter.

We cannot avoid or ignore the violent events that transpire about us any more than did our Lord and His faithful followers in the face of Israel's legalism or Rome's paganism. Our responsibility is to put our reputations, jobs, incomes, even our lives, on the line to confront violence with courage and hatred with love.

I can never, my God, be perfectly at peace in a world so fraught with pain and suffering. And yet I can claim Your eternal gift of peace even as I seek out and try to heal and comfort the victims of this world's violence. Comfort and strengthen me in this effort, O Lord. Amen.

Dying Daily—Living Forever

We were buried therefore with [Christ] by baptism into death . . .
that we too might walk in newness of life. v. 3

Regardless of our past, no matter how abominable our wrongdoings, whether such sins be unconscious or deliberate, our Lord's sacrifice is sufficient, and God's forgiveness is complete. This does not, however, cancel out our responsibilities in respect to the present and the future. The fact that we are not totally dead to sin, whatever our intention and determination, is indicated by Paul himself when he stated in his first Letter to Timothy: "I am the foremost of sinners" (1:15). This has become obvious in our own lives as we look daily to the cross to realize anew God's gracious forgiveness. We are, nevertheless, in the daily process of dying. That dying will not be completed until we are set free from these mortal coils, but it continues as we cease yielding to self-interests and self-concern, cease seeking our own gratification at the expense of others, as we become increasingly successful at overcoming our lusts, covetousness, bigotry, impatience, apathy, and whatever else clouds our relationship with God and fellow creatures.

We have, in effect, been crucified with Christ and raised with Him from the dead. We are new people, focused upon new goals, compelled by new motives, committed to new objectives. We have been reborn. All things have become new. Having been delivered from sin's destructive bondage and having received God's love and the gift of everlasting life and made available through the resurrected Christ, we are now free to love and accept ourselves and to dedicate our lives to loving our fellow persons as ourselves.

We die daily—to the control of sin and self-righteousness; we live forever in loving service to God and our brothers and sisters in the human family.

Revive my flagging spirit, O God. Restore to me the joy and assurance of a right relationship with You. Reinstate me in Your purposes—all this that I might live forever. Amen.

The Power of Faith

Your faith has made you well; go in peace, and be healed . . .
v. 34

Christianity is a faith religion. No other religion in the world makes so much of faith. "Abraham believed God," we read concerning the father of believers, "and it was reckoned to him as righteousness" (Romans 4:3). "Behold, God is my salvation; I will trust, and will not be afraid," proclaimed Isaiah" (12:2). "Let not your hearts be troubled; believe in God, believe also in Me," stated Jesus (John 14:1). "Daughter, your faith has made you well," He said to the woman of our text, and when hearing about the death of Jairus' daughter, "Do not fear, only believe."

Many of us who profess to follow Christ have never really grasped this, the prime essential of the Gospel. We press upon Jesus Christ as did the crowds who gathered to witness His miracle-working power, but we often fail to embrace Him in a reckless, all-out, totally trusting faith. We believe in God; we pray when we are desperate; we try to follow the example of Christ, yet we hardly know what it means to allow this Christ to be living and active at the very center of our beings. We come to Him; we hear Him speak to us through the Word; we express our needs through the liturgy and the prayers; we proclaim His praises in the hymns we sing; we indeed touch Him in the Service of Holy Communion—and yet we are still assailed by guilt-feelings, plagued with weaknesses, defeated and overcome with failures, incapacitated by tragedies, and very much in doubt about the outcome of it all. The reason? Perhaps our touch has not really been the touch of faith. We may be jostling Christ rather than embracing Him.

We believe, O Lord; help us with our unbelief!

May my faith, O God, be not just "belief in spite of evidences, but life in scorn of consequences." Amen.

From Rags to Riches

As it is written, "He who gathered much had nothing over, and he who gathered little had no lack." v. 15

"For your sake He became poor, so that by His poverty you might become rich."

When we think about the amazing grace of God as demonstrated by His Son, Jesus Christ, who enriched our lives through His willingness to embrace poverty, we then see something of the course He has laid out for us. In the measure that God pours out His riches upon us, we ought to channel them into areas of need about us. We are not created to be reservoirs that accumulate, but pipelines that direct and conduct the flow into poverty-stricken lives about us. As we are the recipients of divine gifts through our Spirit-filled parents and peers, so we are the transmitters of such gifts to the human family with whom we have contact. This is the way of God in our world today, and it is thus that He advances His kingdom through His children. He intervenes in the lives of the poor and oppressed through His interveners. We are such interveners; we can limit God's flow of power and wealth into other lives by our selfishness or bless that flow by our sacrificial acts of love.

How privileged we are to be His stewards and trustees in the great task of making His love known and experienced on this planet! The one who gives much receives much, and the one who holds fast to what he or she possesses has very little to give to others. It is the latter person who is truly poverty-stricken.

Let us love generously; we have nothing to lose but our self-centered notions of what is of true value and worth. We have everything to gain and the guarantee that we will be rich indeed in terms of those things that really count in this life and the next.

Keep me, O Lord, from being a sponge that sops up, and make me into a vessel that pours out Your blessings to Your human creatures about me. Amen.

Followers or Fellow-Travelers

I will follow You wherever You go. v. 57

There was no lack of fellow-travelers dogging Jesus' footsteps, but He was not pleased with this kind of popularity. It therefore became necessary for our Lord to call forth out of this group a band of "inner circle" disciples, men and women who would follow Him out of love and loyalty, selflessly and sacrificially.

There were several "takers," those who responded enthusiastically to Jesus' invitation, but few who could pass the test and measure up to His prerequisites. "I will follow You wherever You go," exuberantly exclaimed one young man. Instead of opening His arms in glad welcome, Jesus deliberately discouraged this fine young fellow. He recognized the enthusiast's words as the words of one who had not counted the cost, and Jesus wanted it clearly understood that there is a battle to fight, a price to pay, a cross to carry, a life to lose, in the business of following Him.

Our Lord's message to us is disturbing as well as challenging. It indicates that we who call ourselves by His name must throw out our adulterated concepts of discipleship and become authentic in our Christian lives. There is nothing easygoing about Christianity— the kind of Christianity that Jesus lived and proclaimed. It is costly and demanding. It promises not softness but suffering, not comfort but challenge, not safety but sacrifice. There is peace; there is also persecution. There is security, joy, and abundance; there is also blood, sweat, and tears.

May God grant us the grace to live valid Christian lives.

I understand, O God, that my response to Your great love must be commitment. I understand, as well, that the grace that embraced me in salvation must also be present to enable me to truly and committedly follow You. Grant to me, O Lord, that grace. Amen.

Free to Love

For freedom Christ has set us free . . . love your neighbor as yourself.
vv. 1, 14

While we live under law, our relationship to God is not dependent upon the Law or upon the rules and regulations inaugurated by men. Having submitted to the redeeming love of God, we have been set free from the Law's demands as a means of salvation to embrace a higher law, a higher morality, the morality of love, which ought to guide our lives and issue forth from them as a consequence of God's love and indwelling. Whereas we are responsible for keeping man's laws that do not come between us and God's higher Law and purposes, our eternal salvation does not come through such obedience.

Christ has set us free—to love. It is in this freedom that we are enjoined to lovingly relate to one another, to share with, to serve, to support one another. Thus freed from the need to gratify our fleshly concerns, we can invest in the physical and spiritual needs of others. In this freedom we can shed our anxieties, our guilt feelings, even our concern about our identities, and freely, haphazardly give of ourselves in loving service to the human family.

Let us always be aware of subtle temptations to regress into periods of self-concern and self-service. They are always with us, these tendencies and temptations, and we know what happens when we court them and ultimately yield to them. We have been set free from these shackles that bind us, for a deeper investment of our lives in the service of others, a determination, by God's grace, to put the needs of our fellow persons even before our own.

Christ has set us free to love. It's a freedom we need to exercise daily at home, school, at work, and elsewhere—if we are to grow in our Christian lives.

You have seen and have forgiven my sin, O God. Now enable me to demonstrate my gratitude in loving acceptance of my fellow beings irrespective of their failures and faults. Amen.

Run for Your Life

I, even I only, am left; and they seek my life, to take it away. v. 14b

Elijah was on the run. He had stood up against the ungodly forces of Ahab and Jezebel and had revealed the far greater forces of his God over the followers of Baal. The victory was bitter-sweet; it did not accomplish what he expected; the ruling powers did not turn to the Lord, and now Jezebel was out to get Elijah. He was frightened, and he took refuge in a cave. But not for long. He met God there. "What are you doing here, Elijah?" (v. 13). Elijah poured out his complaints: the whole world, or so it seemed, was against him; he alone remained faithful to the true God; he was afraid that he might even die at the hands of the enemy.

Something of this sort happens to all of us at times, and we, too, crawl into a cave or a corner to moan out our complaints. We sincerely try our best to do what God would have us do; but nothing of consequence happens, and we are defeated and despondent.

We discover, sometimes to our amazement, that God meets us there. It may not necessarily be a consoling meeting. He may tell us, in His "still, small voice" (v. 12), that the consequences of our ministry during the past week are not to be our primary concern; He will take care of them. And then He may well order us out of our cave to get on with the job of advancing His kingdom. There is another day, another week, ahead of us. We are not promised great victories, but are commanded to sow small seeds. All He requires is that we be faithful to Him; He will be responsible for the results.

Forbid, O God, that I should ever be so broken, so beaten down, that I fail to come limping back to You. Raise me to my feet again, O Lord, with the assurance of ultimate and eternal victory at the end of my earthly journey. Amen.

Invitation to Fulfillment

Come to Me, all who labor and are heavy laden, and I will give you rest. v. 28

We read in the first book of the Bible that God "breathed into his nostrils the breath of life; and man became a living being" (2:7). Man and woman were created in God's image, spiritually, but lost that image and became disjointed, distorted invalids. Thus the breath of creation was followed in the New Testament by the breath of redemption, and then of sanctification: ". . . and they were filled with the Holy Spirit." This means that a human being plus the Spirit of God equals a total, complete, fulfilled person, and it is this that gives identity and meaning, purpose and fulfillment to the individual lives of men and women.

This is the kind of life and experience that our Lord calls us to. He extends the invitation to this fulfillment. "Come to Me, all who labor and are heavy laden, for I will give you rest," said Jesus. We must recognize that we are sick before we will accept the prescription of the Great Physician; we must realize that the heavy burdens we carry and the labors we struggle through are too much for us, before we lay them upon that One who will carry them in our stead.

Then Jesus follows His invitation with a command: "Take My yoke upon you . . ." What is the "yoke" of our Lord? It is the world, the sin-sick, disease-ridden, catastrophic world about us. It includes its starving, deprived, oppressed, its addicted and enslaved, men and women in need, whatever their color, race, or religion, and wherever they may be found. This is the yoke of our Lord, the yoke He commands us to take upon ourselves. Until we do, we have little or no claim to His promises and may never "find rest for [our] souls."

I thank you, my Lord, for Your incredible invitation, and for the "rest" that is granted when I assume the "yoke" You have placed before me. I pray for the grace to shoulder that yoke and carry on Your purposes. Amen.

A Message for Wretched People

Wretched man that I am! Who will deliver me from this body of death? v. 24

Our allegiance is to God through Jesus Christ. Our relationship to Him is based not on what we have done for God, but on what He has done on our behalf. Christ has measured up to God's standards and has taken upon Himself the penalty for our imperfections. We have been declared righteous, perfect in Christ, apart from the Law. We still need laws to direct and protect the lives and destinies of people, but they are incapable of turning sinners into saints.

The ancient, yet always relevant, Law does portray goodness and justice. It portrays, as well, my utter inability to be truly good and just. I simply do not have within my nature the capability of reaching those high standards. God knows I have tried. He knows how I again fail. I have the desire, even the will, to do what is right. I do not, in myself, have the power. Thus there is conflict, agonizing conflict, and I am driven to the wall in despair. It is a conflict which in one measure or another will persist as long as I live upon this planet.

The answer is in Jesus Christ. God through this Christ adopted me as His son apart from the Law. I am set free from the Law's demands, and free from its judgment, free to immerse myself in God's great love, and free to serve Him forever.

This is Paul's testimony. It is mine. It continues to be the testimony of every man and woman who follows Jesus Christ.

I praise You, my gracious Father, that while I am fallible and imperfect, I am still an object of Your love and concern, and because of Jesus Christ, there is no question as to my eligibility for Your grace and forgiveness. Amen.

Some People One Cannot Reach

He marveled because of their unbelief. v. 6

There were some people Jesus could not reach. This Gospel portion deals with what was possibly the second time our Lord preached in His hometown synagogue. And for the second time, His message and ministry there were heckled and rejected. His first visit resulted in a riot that drove Him out of the city and might have taken His life save for God's intervention. The second visit continued to rile the synagogue crowd; they simply could not understand how this man Jesus could speak with such authority and wisdom. After all, was He not just a carpenter, the son of Mary, and a brother to her children, some of whom were still living there? Thereafter Jesus issued the well-known statement often used to this very day: "A prophet is not without honor, except in his own country, and among his own kin, and in his own house."

"They took offense at Him . . . And He could do no mighty work there . . . And He marveled because of their unbelief." He left His mark, nonetheless, for He laid hands on and healed a few sick people. Whether it is in our hometown or at some other point along our sojourn, in home or office, Main Street or market place, we will come across people whom we apparently cannot reach, who turn deaf ears to our verbal witness and unresponsive hearts to our God-inspired intentions.

So be it. We can, nevertheless, leave our mark with them, a witness of love and concern that may eventually find its way into their hearts. They can put down but cannot entirely obliterate the truly good deeds we leave behind, and there are times when our deeds of love proclaim more loudly and effectively the Gospel of God's love than do our words.

I need, O Lord, Your grace to proclaim effectively Your Word of salvation. I need even more that grace to witness in my attitudes and activities Your saving love for my brothers and sisters about me. Amen.

The Paradox of Paradoxes

My grace is sufficient for you, for My power is made perfect in weakness. v. 9a

"When I am weak, then I am strong."

Over against the ecstatic high points of irrepressible joy—and we cherish them for ourselves as well as for others—are those balloon-puncturing experiences that flatten us in despair. It may well be that we need both in our lives to keep us close to our Creator and Redeemer. The remarkable thing is that the Spirit of God is often more obvious and more capable of using us during those low, thorn-in-the-flesh points in our lives.

The thing that most often drives us into depression is some pernicious, unconquered fault or weakness in our makeup. We are certainly not expected to revel in our weaknesses; we need to overcome or control these inbred distortions that afflict us and may even harm others around us; but we need not crumble in defeat or falter in despair.

They may actually, though indirectly, be the means by which we can recognize and learn to rely on God's promised, all-sufficient grace. God is great. He accepts us as we are. He can work out His purposes through us—even in spite of us. We need only to continually submit to Him our whole beings—strengths, weaknesses, and all—and let Him have His way with us.

May God speak to you as He did to Paul: "My grace is sufficient for you, for My power is made perfect in weakness."

O Lord, I am often belabored and weighed down by my weaknesses and imperfections. I thank You that despite these things in my life, You continue to grant me value and significance as Your beloved child and servant. Amen.

Authentic Evangelism

Go your way . . . I send you out as lambs in the midst of wolves.
v. 3

Like the seventy disciples of our Lord's day, we, too, are meant to be thrust out, like "lambs in the midst of wolves," into our secular and revolutionary world. Our immediate assignment may not be to preach God's Word of judgment or grace to those we meet. Nor are we assigned or equipped to convert people. We are to seek out those people to whom we can relate, who will respond to our friendship. We are to share with them, listen to them. When we have gained their confidence and they begin to share their pains as well as their joys with us, we are to "heal the sick" or to use every means within our power, and the power that God provides, to meet those people and minister to them at the point of their immediate and recognized need. Perhaps we can help to heal their loneliness, to raise them out of despair, to restore their dignity, or to provide for some of their material needs in order to alleviate their suffering. And then we are always to seek to relate them to that One who is the answer to their deepest needs, to proclaim the Good News that "the kingdom of God has come near" to them—that God is here, that Jesus went to the cross on their behalf, and they can be set free from their sins and hang-ups and be guaranteed eternal life.

Daniel Niles defined evangelism as "one beggar telling another beggar where to find bread." It is most certainly introducing people to and communicating to them the concern of a loving God—and the power He offers to bring healing and enrichment, meaning and purpose into their lives. Evangelism is our task. Jesus outlines an effective method. There are risks involved, and we may seldom see the results of our witness. May God find us faithful and obedient to our calling as His ministers and servants.

Help me, O Lord, to overcome my self-centeredness and dedicate my life to revealing to others Your eternal love and saving grace. Amen.

Front and Center

Bear one another's burdens, and so fulfill the law of Christ. v. 2

"Far be it from me to glory except in the cross of our Lord Jesus Christ."

Paul certainly rejoiced in the resurrection of Jesus Christ, but he "gloried" in the cross of Christ. The cross is not something we experience once and for all and then leave behind to concentrate totally upon the resurrection. Without the resurrection the cross would be of little significance. Likewise, without the cross of Christ there would be no resurrection. Both are essential to genuine Christianity and effective Christian living. An overemphasis on the cross apart from the resurrection might promote a negative, joyless, powerless experience and witness. An overemphasis on the resurrection apart from the cross might result in unrealistic, ecstatic, humanless, heaven-bound antics that would offer a very inadequate witness to the world about us.

We need to pass by the cross on Calvary's hill before we proceed to the empty tomb, and this is a daily experience for God's redeemed children and chosen servants. Pentecost is the consequence of both the cross and the resurrection of Jesus Christ. Apart from either one of these significant events the pentecostal experience is not possible.

We daily leave our sins at the foot of the cross; it is there that we die to self-interests and claim anew divine forgiveness. We commit ourselves to the power of the resurrection; there we are made new creatures and are guaranteed our ultimate resurrection as the eternal sons and daughters of God. It adds up to Pentecost, the indwelling of the crucified and resurrected Lord Jesus Christ and the power of His Spirit to enable us to be Christs-incarnate in our broken world.

I proceed, O Christ, from the cross to the resurrection and pray that Your indwelling Spirit will daily empower me to walk my journey in joy and loving service. Amen.

The Prophets among Us

Whether they hear or refuse to hear they will know that there has been a prophet among them. v. 5

If Ezekiel should materialize and show up in the pulpit of your church next Sunday morning, what might he say? It would go something like this:

"God will soon gather together His kingdom throughout our world. There are some of you here who are not yet a part of His kingdom. You are deluding yourselves into believing that you are God's children. You make your confessions and professions and assume that your religious exercises are acceptable to God; you have not, however, put aside your materialistic idols and committed yourselves to His purposes. You seek to use Him for comfort and good fortune and some guarantee of immortality, but you have not allowed Him to use you by revealing and demonstrating His redeeming love among the peoples of your world. You continue to live to and for yourselves. While God has through Christ borne the cross for you and through His suffering has set you free from sin's bondage, your response to His grace has not resulted in your taking up your cross on behalf of others. Your religion is an intensely self-gratifying activity, and regardless of the slogans you adopt and the convictions you subscribe to, you are in dire danger of being excluded from the kingdom of God."

Does your pastor ever preach like this? Is it possible that he is inspired by the same God that spoke through Ezekiel of old? There are prophets among us today—and he may be one of them.

Speak to our needs, O God, in respect to our relationship to You. Tear away the facades that camouflage our self-centered concerns and enable us to come clean in our relationship to You and our embrace of Your life and purposes. Amen.

The Search for Disciples

He who has ears, let him hear. v. 9

Jesus began His ministry following His baptism by attracting men to Himself and challenging them to loving service. Now was the time for our Lord to separate the men from the boys, the followers from the fellow-travelers, and to concentrate on equipping His devoted disciples for the great work that lay before them. The great majority of the huge crowds that emptied the villages to see and hear this One called Jesus were curious sign-seekers, looking for spectacular feats. Many brought their sick to be healed; others wanted Jesus to become their king who would make Israel a free, abundant, and powerful nation. There was a small group of loosely attached disciples who followed Jesus from time to time but were in question as to their future loyalty toward Him. Then, of course, there was the nucleus, the twelve, who were the closest to Christ in love and loyalty.

Jesus was not yet to abandon the multitudes, but He was beginning to concentrate upon the few. His teaching in parables was a device for the achievement of this purpose, selecting and stabilizing the loyalty and love of these men who would be so important to the church and the advancement of the kingdom in the near future. To the curious, the sign-seekers, the shallow and superficial, His teachings would be obscure or hidden. To those, however, who hungered and thirsted after righteousness, who persistently sought for truth, His teachings would gradually be revealed and eventually understood.

Jesus was, and is to this day, searching for disciples. The primary goal of the church today is to search for, call, and equip disciples. May our response be the response of Isaiah to God's call to him: "Here am I! Send me" (6:8).

There will always be much in Your Word and will, O Lord, that I will not comprehend. Help me to be open to and act upon that which You will reveal. Amen.

Sufferings versus Glory

The sufferings of this present time are not worth comparing with the glory that is to be revealed to us. v. 18

Paul had no illusions about the Christian faith being a primrose path or a perpetually ecstatic experience. Lest we be phony or foolish in our representations of the Christian life, we need also to be disillusioned about what it means to follow Jesus Christ. It is not a continual mountaintop experience; we have to slog through deep, muddy ravines and around dangerous precipices. Most of us are aware of this by the time we reach some maturity in our growth as Christians. Our testimony becomes that of the psalmist: "Though I walk in the midst of trouble, Thou dost preserve my life and Thy right hand delivers me"(Psalm 138:7). "In the world you have tribulation," said Jesus, "but be of good cheer, I have overcome the world" (John 16:33). We are to "suffer with [Christ] in order that we may also be glorified with Him" wrote Paul in the verse preceding this Epistle lesson.

Paul reminds us that "these sufferings are not worth comparing with the glory that is to be revealed to us." But some immature Christians want the "glory" now. The insistence of those who say they have it, that they are presently living within it, contradicts the witness of Paul and the lifelong experiences of unnumbered saints before us. There is some danger that what they have is self-concocted or self-induced, or is promoted by some foreign spirit that seeks to lead them astray.

God does not intend our sufferings; He involves Himself in them. It is His presence in our trials and tribulations that gives them meaning and purpose. Paul enjoins us to wait with patience for God's total deliverance from all that causes us to suffer. It is soon to take place, and we will then be encompassed "with the glory that is to be revealed to us."

I thank You, my Lord, for the many who through their suffering have brought hope and strength to my life. Amen.

Discipleship Means Involvement

He called to Him the twelve, and began to send them out two by two. v. 7a

Some people cozy up to the kind of Christianity that is equated with plush pews and pious prayers—even if it does involve an offering plate or a weekly pledge. The kind demonstrated by Christ and reflected in His first followers is therefore something difficult to comprehend.

Discipleship means involvement. Our Lord set the pace, and He expects His disciples to keep it. "As the Father has sent Me, even so I send you," Jesus enjoined His disciples following His resurrection. Jesus identified Himself with the agonies of humankind. He became involved in their crying needs. To be a disciple of Christ means that we who accept Him as our Savior must also accept Him as our Lord and Master. To follow Him means that we continue in His course for our lives. We are expected not simply to point up and criticize the distortions of humanity from the pews and pulpits of our churches, but to become involved in the blood and tears, sorrows and sufferings, of God's creatures in suburb and ghetto, town and country, wherever they may be found.

The task we are called upon and sent into our world to carry out includes proclaiming the forgiveness of sins through faith in Christ. It means, as well, that we stand up with the oppressed against their oppressors, that we try to exorcise the "demons" of life and culture that rob people of their self-respect and dignity, their rights and opportunities, even the demons of pride and prejudice and ignorance and apathy within us that serve to inhibit the claim of disadvantaged people to the same rights and opportunities available to us.

Discipleship means involvement. As our Lord suffered on our behalf, so we are expected to suffer on behalf of others.

You have chosen me to be Your servant, Lord. Grant to me the grace to fulfill my servanthood. Amen.

Something to Celebrate

He destined us in love to be His sons [and daughters] through Jesus Christ. v. 5a

Truly, we have much to celebrate as the sons and daughters of God. We have, through Christ, become the recipients of God's whole treasure-house of spiritual gifts. Even before we were born—before the world itself was made—we were destined to be His children. Christ's death on the cross set us free from the Law's demands. Reconciled to the divine family, we are now an integral part of God's plan to reconcile the whole world to Himself.

It is indeed something we cannot comprehend, but God created us and chose us to be His people, and this was God's purpose and plan from the very beginning. It was made known to us and made possible for us through Jesus Christ. Through Christ and His indwelling Spirit, the brand of God's ownership was burned indelibly into our hearts. With the gracious gift of His Spirit comes the guarantee that all of God's gifts, though at present unseen and little understood, are already ours and will be revealed to us in God's own time.

There is much to celebrate, but let us not forget that it could never have been possible except for the tragedy of the cross. Our redemption, our restoration to God, was "through His blood," the blood of Jesus Christ. Forgiveness, which is relatively easy for us to accept, must never be taken lightly. It cost the agony of Calvary. All the riches that we inherit as God's children are ours only because we are forgiven, and for that God paid a price—a price that we will never fully comprehend.

My God, I do embrace Your forgiveness offered through Jesus Christ and the cross which He embraced on my behalf, and I celebrate this glorious gift and all the gifts which You have lavished upon me. Amen.

And Who Is My Neighbor?

And who is my neighbor? v. 29

The lawyer was not about to challenge the revered "love God, love your neighbor" commandment. He also knew that his colleagues could not challenge his love for God. After all, he said the right words. He went through the required motions. He carried on a very respectable kind of life. But the "love your neighbor" part of the commandment stopped him cold. This was where the authenticity of his faith could be challenged. He had only one recourse: "Who is my neighbor?"

I don't know if Jesus' answer was a surprise to the lawyer, but His parable of the Good Samaritan is a revealing and judgmental condemnation upon much that goes under the name of Christianity today. It also tends to make so much of my professed or assumed piety appear to be something less than authentic. As long as I say the right words and belong to the right church, my faith cannot be proved or disproved by mortal man. But the parable of the Good Samaritan pins me to the wall and demands that I "put up or shut up." There is no question as to the why and what for of my salvation. It comes from God; it comes as a gift of His love. It is not enough, however, to say the right words like "I love You, Jesus," or "I accept You, Christ." There must be total committal, a placing of myself at God's disposal, the presentation of my body as a living sacrifice. These are not mere words; it is an act of the will. And the only way I can act in this manner towards the invisible God is to commit myself to the needs of my visible neighbor.

"Who is my neighbor?" Jesus gave the answer—loudly and clearly. Every human being is my neighbor—and that without regard to color, background, or social status.

Deliver me, O God, from bigotry and prejudice that taints my soul and teach me how to love my fellow beings as You have loved me. Amen.

A Time for Gratitude

We always thank God, the Father of our Lord Jesus Christ . . . because of the hope laid up for you in heaven. vv. 3, 5a

"He has delivered us from the dominion of darkness and transferred us to the kingdom of His beloved Son."

How grateful we are to God for what He has done for us, for the clear revelation of His love through His Son, our Savior and Lord, Jesus Christ! Through this Christ we have experienced forgiveness and redemption. By way of this Christ we have been set free from the bondage of darkness and despair. In this Christ we become the very heirs of God and share in the inheritance promised to all His sons and daughters from the beginning of time.

He is full of God, this Jesus, God-incarnate. The Word became flesh, and manifests all the glory and beauty, the splendor and majesty, the love and grace of the Godhead, as St. Paul emphasizes in the verses following our reading. We can know God only as He is revealed through this Christ, and so Christ then becomes for us that One who puts it all together, the Head of the body and of the church, our Lord and Leader, our Shepherd and King.

This is the Christ to whom we have committed our lives. This is the One we will worship and follow today. Let us begin this day with gratitude.

Help me, O God, to put aside all my grumbling and to begin and to conclude this day with gratitude. Turn my groans of despair into proclamations of joy. I am Yours, O God, Yours forever. Make my life a perpetual offering of praise. Amen.

Be a Prophet

Go, prophesy to My people . . . v. 15b

"I am no prophet," said Amos, and yet he most certainly was. "Speaking up for Christ is not only the history, but the whole future of the Church," said Dr. Oswald Hoffmann. "Paul listed a first gift of the Spirit as prophecy, which is proclamation. This means witnessing to the good name and good news of Jesus Christ." In a very real sense, we are all prophets or proclaimers. "But I am a herdsman, and a dresser of sycamore trees . . ." "But I am just a housewife, or farmer, or nurse, or businessman . . . I am no prophet."

Prophesying refers to proclaiming. This has often included revelations concerning some future judgment or event, but is not limited to that. The Word of God is to be proclaimed. In the Old Testament this was usually expressed in terms of proclaiming the Law of God. Jesus measured up to the Law on our behalf, and He proclaimed and commanded us to proclaim the glorious Word of God in respect to His redeeming love, His bounteous grace toward His human creatures. Nor is prophesying only a matter of preaching. It is primarily bearing witness to something great and wonderful that has happened in our lives—to what God through Christ has done for us.

There are people in your daily course through life to whom you cannot preach. Yet you can leave with them a prophetic witness— or prepare them for it in your acts of love and concern toward them. As important as your vocation may be, and they all may be sanctified by God's presence, even more important is your call to be a prophet, a witnesser, a proclaimer, a demonstrator, a vehicle and channel of the blessed Word of God. You are not "just a housewife, or farmer, or businessman . . .," you are a prophet!

Grant to me, O Lord, the courage to witness in word and in deed as to Your love and salvation for humankind. May my response to Your love and grace be servanthood and ministry among those with whom I work and play. Amen.

The Christian in Our World Today

The righteous will shine like the sun in the kingdom of their Father.
v. 43

The parable which makes up this Gospel portion paints a picture of perpetual conflict. The world is a battleground where the forces of good and evil are in constant warfare. There are moments when evil appears to have the upper hand. The atrocities that take place about us cause fright and insecurity. The agony of our own inner beings as we do battle with the rebellious, selfish taints and tendencies of our humanity, leaves us confused and frustrated. We are involved in struggle—fierce, vicious, unabated. The outcome, according to our Lord's analogy, is not in question. When the day of harvest arrives, God will supernaturally intervene and the forces of evil will be eternally defeated.

We long desperately for the day of harvest when evil shall be no more, and we shall know and experience the meaning of ultimate and eternal victory. Jesus does not tell us the "why" of struggle. It may be a necessary part of our redemption. Perhaps this crucible experience, with all of its anguish and agony, is essential to our Christian maturity and development, and there is no other way of learning total surrender to and dependence upon God.

The law of all nature, that life is given and enriched through struggle and travail, is no less true in our spiritual lives. It is our task to learn how to exist within this struggle, how to turn failures into successes, how to develop and mature within the throes of conflict and find therein a measure of joy and effectiveness. And it is here, in the midst of daily conflict and struggle, that we are called and equipped to advance the kingdom of God and to contribute to the great harvest God has promised.

Our great God, teach us as You taught Paul how to "rejoice in our sufferings, knowing that suffering produces endurance . . . character . . . hope. . . ." Amen. (Romans 5:3–4)

Praying in the Spirit

The Spirit intercedes for the saints according to the will of God.
                                                    v. 27b

Prayer is really a spiritual act; it is no wonder that "we do not know how to pray as we ought." It is only when the Spirit of God within our human frames communicates with God, who is spirit, that there can be effective communication between our dimension and that of our invisible God. Human semantics is a very inadequate and imperfect instrument or vehicle of communication between the human and the divine. Therefore, in the act of prayer, sometimes with words, most often through prayers we cannot even utter, the Spirit expresses for us that which is unutterable.

"Do you not know that your body is a temple of the Holy Spirit within you, which you have from God?" queried Paul (1 Corinthians 6:19). There are both conscious and unconscious aspects to our personalities. We are responsible for the conscious aspect, and that means a continual subjection of our bodies and minds to the power of God's Spirit. If that is under His control, we can be assured that those matters of which we are not conscious are in the hands of God. It is then that God listens not only to our fumbling words, but hears the prayers of His Spirit within the temple of our bodies. Our words are fallible and error-prone; not so the unutterable groanings of the Holy Spirit.

Our primary concern must be to keep our "temples" clear and clean of anything that may defile them so that the Spirit may help us in our weakness; then there will arise from our innermost being those intercessions of the Spirit that God does hear and respond to positively because they are "according to the will of God."

"Spirit of the living God, fall afresh on me. Melt me. Mold me. Fill me. Use me. Spirit of the living God, fall afresh on me." Amen.

The Lord Will Provide

He had compassion on them, because they were like sheep without a shepherd. v. 34a

One of Jesus' most striking miracles, particularly in view of the large numbers of individuals affected, is the feeding-of-the-five-thousand, related in the verses immediately following this Scripture reading. In some ways the miracle is a very strange one. The religious leaders of Christ's day were planning a way to get rid of Him. On the other hand, there was a movement afoot, probably known and encouraged by the disciples, to compel Jesus to come forth and declare Himself as king of Israel. Now, as if to accentuate His popularity and standing with the people, He performs this amazing miracle which could only serve to fire up their enthusiasm and intensify their desire to crown Him as their king.

This was not, of course, our Lord's purpose in this miracle. If we were to ascertain just what His purpose might be, we would have to begin with Mark's assertion that Jesus "saw a great throng, and He had compassion on them." His concern for them led to His efforts to teach them, to draw them to Himself and the life He had come to impart to God's human creatures. That, in turn, led Him to reveal His power to meet people's needs in the feeding-of-the-five-thousand.

It is a beautiful expression and example of God's concern for His creatures. The Lord will provide. This is not a trite phrase; it is eternal truth which we have experienced over and over again. It is God's desire that we continue to rely on His promises, to demonstrate the audacity of faith that expects great things though there be nothing visible upon which to build. This is far more reliable than creeping common sense that adheres to facts which are mere shadows and forgets the chief fact, that we have an almighty God and Father, Helper and Friend, at our side who is at all times concerned about our material needs.

O Lord, I pray that my faith will embrace and trust You for my material and spiritual needs whatever the future may hold for me. Amen.

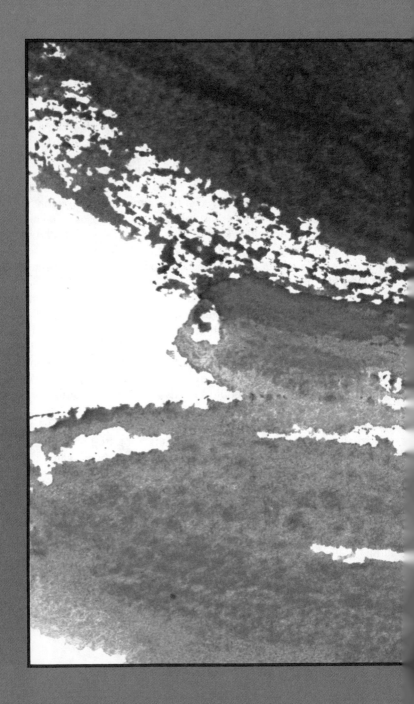

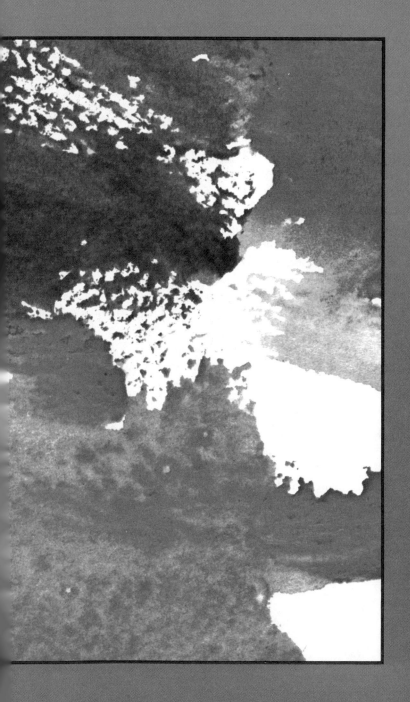

We Belong to One Another

For He is our peace, who has made us both one. v. 14a

Every human being is the object and beneficiary of God's gift of eternal love. Only those who by faith lay hold of this divine offering, however, who accept and live by this saving grace, can discover and experience the salvation that God has prepared for His creatures. Whereas God's love is a gift which cannot be merited by human efforts to aspire to divine standards, God's deliverance from sin and self-service sets us free to give our lives to good works by way of loving God and communicating His love to humanity about us. This is one of the very important purposes of our salvation, that we might serve God and people and thus fulfill the destiny for which we were created.

It is God's love as manifested in Christ that makes us equal, in God's eyes, with all persons and makes all persons equal with us. We differ in many ways: intelligence and talents, training and temperament, background and opportunity. Under God, however, there is no distinction. His all-encompassing love levels all barriers and accounts every human creature of equal value and worth.

There are no "foreigners or strangers" (TEV) in God's family, only brothers and sisters. And all of us are the members of one body, the body of Christ, and are commissioned to work together in carrying out His purposes.

Our loving God, You have accepted us as beggars and turned us into Your sons and daughters. As we love and glorify You together, may we love and serve one another and together dedicate our lives to carrying out Your purposes on this planet. Amen.

The Perils of Distraction

One thing is needful. v. 41a

Two statements are recorded concerning the attitudes and character of two friends of Jesus, Martha and Mary. The first is a *comment from Luke,* the author of this Gospel. "But Martha was distracted with much serving," he wrote. He was suggesting, perhaps, that Martha was so taken up with the bustle and hustle of service that she neglected the quietness of worship. She was so busy giving that she was not open to receiving. She may have been unaware that there cannot be effective outflow unless there is daily intake.

The second statement is a *commendation from Christ.* "Mary has chosen the good portion," said Jesus, "which shall not be taken away from her." "One thing is needful," Jesus said to Martha. This is what He would say to us today. Probably the most difficult task of the church is to convince men and women in this age of distraction that "one thing is needful." Rather than proclaiming "I believe in God Almighty," people today are indicating that they believe in the almighty dollar, the necessity of financial security, the lust of the flesh, the importance of comfort, and in getting for themselves all they can get out of this life.

We are to be servants in our world. We are such by Christ's call and assignment. This assignment begins at the feet of Jesus, and it returns us periodically to that place of quietness and strength. It is here that we get in touch and keep in tune with God and His purposes. It is in the fellowship of saints around the Word and the Sacrament that we are perpetually renewed and revitalized. It is from there that we are launched out into our Monday-through-Saturday journeys into our discordant world to serve humankind through our earthly calling and to transmit some small touch of divine love and power to despairing, suffering, lonely people who cross our paths.

I pray, O Lord, that my day may begin with meditation and proceed always to serving You by serving others around me. Amen.

Suffering for the Sake of Others

In my flesh I complete what is lacking in Christ's afflictions for the sake of His body . . . the church. v. 24b

It appears to be very important for many Christians today to have leaders with striking personalities. They must possess many gifts or some kind of charisma that attracts and holds their fans. These especially endowed leaders must, in turn, draw their strength and encouragement from the adulation of their followers.

Whereas Paul was certainly a gifted and learned man, he was not known for his charm or followed because of his exciting personality. He "rejoiced in [his] sufferings for [our] sake." It was certainly not his personality that gathered members for the church, but the real presence of Christ coming through him.

In our immaturity we may be tempted to indulge in a sort of personality cult and latch on to leaders who entertain and stimulate and appear to have immediate answers to our every question or problem. When we grow up a little, and this often in spite of such leaders, we begin to recognize what real leadership is all about. The kind of leaders that truly communicate the Gospel may not be carbon copies of Paul, but they will demonstrate a willingness to suffer for the sake of the Gospel—to "complete what is lacking in Christ's afflictions for the sake of His body, that is, the church."

If we are followers, let us be aware of whom we follow. If we are leaders, and most of us are at some point in our lives, let us forsake self-aggrandizement and emulate Jesus Christ. We are to be the servants of those we lead, and share gladly in their sufferings in order that the grace of God may be channeled to their lives through us.

Gracious Father, it has been the sufferings of Christ, and many of Your children before me, that have contributed to my welfare. Enable me through Your love to lovingly share the sufferings of others about me. Amen.

Responsible Leadership

I will set shepherds over them who will care for them. v. 4a

"Woe to the shepherds who destroy and scatter the sheep of my pasture!" says the Lord.

It is often difficult to discern the false shepherds who presume to speak for the Lord throughout our world today. Those who preach a gospel other than that which reveals Christ and His cross as the cornerstone of true faith are certainly to be shunned. There are, however, those who do preach in His name and yet are unwittingly drawing people out of the institutional church. Some of them, by means of the electronic media, are creating invisible congregations that turn away from local Christian groups, wherein they might be able to mature into responsible Christians, and tie on to media personalities that promote a polished, popular, and exciting kind of religious presentation. While we can't fault all of the teachings these electronic shepherds expound, we question the final results and wonder if they are dividing and scattering the Christian flock rather than building up the kingdom of God.

"The Lord is our righteousness." This is truly the Gospel, the Good News, proclaimed as far back as Jeremiah. It is this that was revealed through Jesus Christ, who became the righteousness of God for us, and by way of the cross and His resurrection made possible the gift of God's righteousness to us. Any shepherd who promotes any other righteousness or any other way to get right with God is a false shepherd. This may also be true of any shepherd who knowingly or unknowingly promotes his or her own image and abilities rather than the righteousness, grace, and purposes of God.

We thank You, O God, for those prophets and pastors who have patiently and faithfully proclaimed and promoted the Gospel of Jesus Christ who truly is our Shepherd. Amen.

233

Thy Kingdom Come

Have you understood all this? v. 51a

Jesus had come to reveal to this world what the true kingdom, God's kingdom, was all about. It was a new kind of kingdom, a spiritual kingdom, one not of this world, one that would include people of all nations and races, one that would be fulfilled or fully revealed in a time and dimension beyond this three-dimensional world.

The kingdom parables are the way our Lord portrayed such a kingdom. The three parables of this Gospel portion point up two things about this kingdom of God.

First, *the kingdom of God is expensive.* ". . . like treasure hidden in a field, which a man found . . . he goes and sells all that he has and buys that field," or "like a merchant . . . who, on finding one pearl of great value, went and sold all that he had and bought it." It cost God the tragedy of the cross; it costs us our very lives. We are to deny ourselves and take up crosses and follow Christ.

Second, *the kingdom of God is exclusive.* ". . . the angels will . . . separate the evil from the righteous . . ." Not all religious people are in the fold of God. Only those who in faith follow Jesus Christ and confess their faith in Him are included in the kingdom of God. All others are excluded.

The kingdom of God is here. It abides among us. We enter it through Christ—at our baptism. If any have strayed from that kingdom, God grant that in faith they may reenter its portals even today.

I continue, O God, to praise and adore You because You have, through Jesus Christ, made me a part of Your eternal kingdom. Forgive me, O Lord, and draw me back into Your kingdom if I should ever stray. Amen.

God and Our Difficult Circumstances

Those whom He justified He also glorified. v. 30b

"We know that in everything God works for good with those who love Him, who are called according to His purposes."

The miracle-working power of God becomes obvious, not in His intervention between us and our sufferings, though some of us can bear witness to such apparent divine interventions in our lives, but in the amazing way in which "God works for good with those who love Him . . ." We can all testify how some of the terrible things that have befallen us became events or instruments which truly did work for good—drawing us closer to God or serving to accomplish His purposes in and through us. Paul believed that God was with him and would work through him whatever the circumstances that pressed in upon him, and he therefore exhorted us to "give thanks in all circumstances" (1 Thessalonians 5:18).

Of this we can be sure: God is with us whatever happens on our journey through this life. Not only that, but He is able and ready to work out His purposes in and through even the tragic episodes of our lives. When we hurt, God hurts; such is His love for us—even if He does not intervene to shield us from such tragedies. He promises to stay close to us, to help us to cope, and to use our sufferings as well as our joys to accomplish His purposes in and through our lives.

Almighty God, may Your Word speak to me, and Your promises reassure me, Your Spirit work some miracle within me, that I may remain faithful to You and the accomplishment of Your objectives even within the distressing circumstances that befall me. And may You somehow use even those hours and days of sorrow or pain to carry out Your purposes in and through me. Amen.

A Remarkable Love-Offering

How are we to buy bread, so that these people may eat? v. 5b

There is a beautiful incident within the feeding-of-the-five-thousand episode that was remembered and recorded by John alone. Between the famished five-thousand and heaven's supernatural provision was a little boy with five barley loaves and two fish. He had brought a lunch with him on this exciting day. He did a selfless, generous thing. He offered his lunch to Jesus to do with as He pleased. It was a profoundly significant act, for it is here, in this simple little incident, that we come across something of the meaning of the cross and of our commission as followers of Jesus Christ. The bridge between God's abundant provision and the world's desperate needs is the sacrificial love-offering. It was made by God Himself, who through Christ descended from His throne of glory, stooped to the humiliating level of our sin, took upon Himself our guilt, and suffered the wages of sin on our behalf. The lad gave all he had; Jesus accepted and blessed this tiny gift, and fed five thousand hungry bodies.

Today you and I, as individuals and members of Christ's body, stand as God's representatives and agents between this world's poverty and heaven's abundant provision. This is our commission, and God holds us, along with the church-at-large, responsible for channeling His eternal grace to those who are in need. We may appear to be, and feel ourselves to be, as insigificant as the little boy with his fish and loaves, but we are not insignificant to God, and by His grace we will become channels and communicators of His life and love to our fellow persons about us.

I am thankful, my Lord, for the many along faith's journey who have communicated Your love and grace and Your spiritual and material blessings to me. Grant, O Lord, that I may be such a communicator to my brothers and sisters along the journey of faith. Amen.

Help Us to Grow Up

*Until we attain . . . to mature manhood, to the measure of the stature
of the fullness of Christ.* v. 13

If Christ is our Lord and Leader, we had better set our sights on
His prerequisites and standards for our lives and strive to measure
up. "Our life in this world is [to be] the same as Christ's," writes
John (1 John 4:17b TEV). For one thing, it means that we be kind,
gentle, and loving to one another. Why is there so much bickering
among the children of God? We are all members of the same body
and are motivated and guided by the same Spirit. Yet, like jealous,
covetous siblings, we fight among ourselves, jostling, crowding each
other, seeking position or honor above the other.

Our gifts, whatever they be, come from the hand of God. They
are not designed to give honor to one over another but, together
with all who make up Christ's body, to carry out His objectives and
advance His kingdom throughout the world. They are granted to us,
not to make us more important—we already know our identity in
Christ—but for the purpose of serving the human family about us.

It is time we stop acting like spoiled children, pouting, griping,
criticizing, stepping on one another, insisting on our way, or
scrambling for some power or position that will boost our ego. We
ought to grow up, being grateful for our status as God's ministers,
whatever our parish or arena of service, and relate to one another in
truth and love. Only then, as the body of Christ, will we be truly
effective in our community and world.

God help us to grow up!

I thank You for Your gifts to me, O Lord. Forgive me for
jealously coveting those gifts You have granted to others. I
pray for the wisdom to use what You have given to me in
ways that will best serve Your objectives and carry out Your
purposes. Amen.

Recipe for Joy

How much more will the heavenly Father give the Holy Spirit to those who ask Him? v. 13b

Most of us are learning that we will never discover true happiness if such by itself becomes the primary intent and purpose of our lives, that gleaming gems crumble into worthless dust if we center our ambitions and aspirations on them alone. It is only when we focus our lives upon goals and objectives that are far more important than personal happiness that we are surprised by joy. This is the kind of joy that Jesus offers—the kind that is often "sorrow unmasked" and that fills up those agonizing cavities served up by long hours of suffering.

Jesus revealed His recipe for joy in His exhortation to "ask . . . seek . . . knock. . . ." It is really the process of finding God—or being found by God—of discovering and being restored to His orbit for our lives by submitting to His saving grace as revealed through the Christ. It is a reliable recipe backed by an infallible guarantee. "For every one who asks receives, and he who seeks finds, and to him who knocks it will be opened," said Jesus. This is the guarantee that is offered by that One who hung the planets on nothing, who created the waters, the land, and the air, who calmed the tempest, who healed the sick and made the blind to see, who raised Christ from the dead, who sent His Spirit to indwell the hearts and lives of His children. And there is no force in all the universe that can prevent the fulfillment of this, God's promise through Christ, save the force of our own wills and our rank indifference or stubborn resistance to His divine gifts of mercy and love which He presses upon us.

"Ask . . . seek . . . knock . . ." not for the things of this life, but for that which God wants to give us. This is, truly, our Lord's recipe for joy.

I thank You, Jesus, for the "joy, joy, joy, joy, down in my heart." It surpasses anything that this world can offer. Amen.

A Time to Grow

*As therefore you received Christ Jesus the Lord, so live in Him, rooted
. . . built up . . . established in the faith.* vv. 6–7

To be mature as Christians means that we continually grow in
the faith into which we have been baptized. It is not sufficient to
verbally and emotionally receive Christ. We are to be perpetually
open to God as He is fully revealed in Christ and as He continues
to instruct and establish us through His Spirit. As we cannot know
God save through Christ, so we cannot hear God speak or carry out
our allegiance to God unless we listen to Christ's words and follow
His leading in our daily lives and activities. If there is anyone who
claims to have found God apart from Christ or who insists that he
can determine and follow God's will apart from our Lord's
revelations and proclamations, he is a usurper, a false prophet, and
ought to be resisted and avoided.

We must be aware of those legalists about us who attempt to
cramp God into some ethical formula that they pass out as a
requisite for God's acceptance and salvation. Their manmade
religions are popular with multitudes of people because they assume
to provide handles or rungs on a ladder by which human beings
can ultimately approach and please the Deity. They are preaching
Law, not grace, or mostly Law with a smattering of grace.

"And you, who were dead in trespasses . . . God made alive
together with [Christ], having forgiven us all our trespasses, having
canceled the bond which stood against us with its legal demands;
this He set aside, nailing it to the cross."

Meditate on this—and take time to grow.

You have accepted me as I am, heavenly Father, and through
Christ I shall be Yours forever. Now, O Vine, I pray, "keep
me what I was meant to be: Your branch, with Your rich life
in me." Amen.

The Acceptable Prayer

Because you have asked this . . . I now do according to your word.
vv. 11, 12a

"Ask what I shall give you," the Lord said to Solomon when he was about to begin his duties as king of Israel. It may well be that this is the key to an effective, God-pleasing prayer life. We are indeed to "ask . . . seek . . . knock . . .," but the prayer that God grants is the prayer for those things that He *wills* to grant us. As little children our requests, or prayers, to our parents dealt primarily with the things we wanted—food, drink, sweets, something exciting to do, help in doing the things we wanted to do. Many of our prayers to God are basically still on that childish level. Mature prayers by mature Christians are sincere requests for a continual openness to God to receive what He desires us to have.

Solomon's prayer was a mature prayer. More important to him than riches or long life or victory over his enemies was the wisdom he needed to guide and rule over his people. His prayer for this was pleasing to God, and Solomon was granted what he humbly requested. He also received many things that he did not request in his prayer.

God will hear our prayers, no matter how childish they may be; yet He ever seeks to bring us to the place where we, in turn, seek the things He wants to grant us. While we accept the fact that "prayer changes things," closer to the truth is the fact that prayer changes us and then we begin to change things.

No matter what our age may be, physically or spiritually, we still need to repeat the request made by the disciples: "Lord, teach us to pray."

I pray, O Lord, for those things You want me to have; I pray that You will make me what You want me to be. Lord, teach me to pray. Amen.

Now You Do It!

As He went ashore He saw a great throng; and He had compassion on them. v. 14

The feeding-of-the-five-thousand revealed our Lord's compassion and concern for the great throngs that followed Him. It also presents to us a tremendous commission. It portrays, on the one hand, the desperate *needs of the world.* The hungry multitude about Christ represented need, and one does not have to look very far beyond one's own nose to see that the thing most common to all people is need—of one kind or another. There are hundreds of millions throughout our world today who are in need of the most fundamental elements of physical existence—food, clothing, medicine, shelter, security, freedom. There is within all humanity the need for inner assurance and serenity, for meaning and purpose in life.

On the other hand, the miracle in question portrays the mighty, eternally sufficient *provision of God.* Our Lord's first action, in the face of the oncoming crowd, was to turn to His disciples as if to lay the responsibility of feeding the crowd on them. "We have only five loaves here and two fish," they said to Him. "Bring them here to Me," said Jesus, and taking the loaves and the fish, "He looked up to heaven, and blessed, and broke and gave the loaves to the disciples, and the disciples gave them to the crowds.

Jesus gave these people what they wanted: a miracle to thrill them and bread to fill them. But He who sustained physical life with mere bread was here for the real purpose of giving people eternal life with that Bread which came from heaven, the Son of God Himself. He would have these people and us understand that the provision of God is more than enough to fulfill every need of every man, woman, and child, and that He is God Himself come to earth to bring that ample, divine provision to needy hearts and lives.

You have made me, O Lord, a channel of Your provision to the needs of people in this world. Now grant to me the willingness and compassion to meet those needs. Amen.

Eternal Security

Who shall separate us from the love of Christ? v. 35a

Nothing, nothing at all, can come between us and our loving God. Our feelings of guilt and depression may rise up to haunt us, but they in no way alter God's redeeming and accepting love. Not, that is, unless we acquiesce to such feelings and neglect to hear and abide by God's Word. The tragedies and conflicts of this life will discourage us, but they can in no way change God's attitude or stifle His love for us. Failures and defeats may trip us up, but they do not affect our relationship to God.

Our boat will rock; the earth will tremble. Revolutions will shake up governments and institutions. Our traditions may be nullified, our convictions threatened. Every temporal security may crumble. But God's love and reconciling grace are forever, and He will never let us go. If our allegiance is to God and our faith is fixed on Him, the very atrocities that seek to destroy us become the means by which He carries out His will in and through us.

Nothing, absolutely nothing can separate us from the love of God as revealed and proclaimed and demonstrated through Jesus Christ. We are the sons and daughters of God, His servants and disciples forever.

"Now to Him who by the power at work within [me] is able to do far more abundantly than all that [I] ask or think, to him be glory in the church and in Christ Jesus, to all generations, forever and ever. Amen." (Ephesians 1:20)

When Life Has Meaning

This is the work of God, that you believe in Him whom He has sent.
v. 29

"What is life for?" questioned Leo Tolstoy, that famous Russian writer of the last century, "To die? To kill myself at once? No, I am afraid. To wait for death till it comes? I fear that even more. Then I must live. But what for? In order to die? And I could not escape from that circle." "Why was I ever born?" Job asked in the midst of his excruciating sufferings. Job was discovering, as many of us do in this vale of tears, that the most atrocious and destructive type of suffering is that in which the victim realizes no meaning or purpose to his or her suffering.

The primary purpose of our Lord's sojourn on this planet was to point out life's meaning, to reveal order and purpose in life's activity, and to direct men and women inextricably entangled in nets of their making back to the orbit and destiny for which they were created—the eternal purposes of God. He first had to break through the thick crust of materialism that numbs most of God's creatures to eternal and infinite values. "Do not labor for the food which perishes," He exhorts. He is not condoning lethargy and indolence, but is rebuking the excessive attention we place on labor designed to fill one's belly and increase one's wealth of possessions at the sacrifice of spiritual and eternal values. "Do not place the focus of your life or set your ultimate goals upon bread or material worth or anything which may perish within the moment or the hour." Reach out, instead, "for the food which endures to eternal life, which the Son of man will give to you." And then Jesus points this up by saying: "This is the work of God, that you believe in Him whom He has sent."

When Jesus becomes the Bread of Life for us, we become bread to others about us. This, then, becomes our purpose in life and gives present, perpetual, eternal meaning to life.

Thank You, Jesus, for granting life to me, and for teaching me how to live. Amen.

Exercise in Holiness

*Put on the new nature, created after the likeness of God in true
righteousness and holiness. v. 24*

Having become God's children, we are enjoined to live as
God's children. As in a human family, this involves a certain
amount of discipline. Growing up as a preacher's son, I was
supposed to disassociate myself from the world in respect to those
things considered at the time to be unchristian—movies, card-
playing, smoking, dancing, etc. There are many who still feel that
external discipline in matters such as these is necessary to their
Christian growth and witness. We have no argument with them—
until they attempt to measure all Christians in accordance with their
particular convictions concerning Christian ethics.

Nor do we have an argument with Paul's "put off . . . put on"
injunctions in respect to the necessary internal discipline required of
all of us, if we are to grow and mature in the Christian faith. It is a
daily discipline, and such discipline involves an incessant struggle—
in some cases a very painful one. To replace griping with gratitude,
lust with love, anger with kindness, selfishness with selflessness,
pride with humility, insensitivity with compassion, all this, and the
gradual acquisition of those qualities and attributes exemplified by
Jesus Christ, demands a lifelong determination and discipline. Any
real victories come by the grace of God, and total victory in all
these matters will be realized only after we leave the body to be
with God Himself.

Paul encourages us to enter into this daily discipline and
exercise in holiness. Failures must not deter us, only challenge us to
keep going, to keep the faith, to "be renewed in the spirit of [our]
minds." We will lose some of the battles along the way, but we will
ultimately win the war. This is the promise of Jesus Christ, who
already won that war on our behalf.

My gracious heavenly Father, I thank You for Your patience
and persistence in keeping me as Your child and making me
into Your servant. Amen.

Security Can Be Dangerous

So is he who lays up treasure for himself, and is not rich toward God. v. 21

"Take heed . . . beware . . . for a man's life does not consist in the abundance of his possessions."

We are not about to put down security. Some of it is good; a certain amount of it is necessary to human happiness. We need to be reminded, however, that security can be dangerous—even damning—if our sense of security is pinned, like a donkey's tail, on the backside of ephemeral and tangible objects, or upon those material blessings inherited through the toil of others who have gone before us.

While many people still identify sin with the glaring headlines of scandal sheets, we discover it to be anything and everything—materialistic, sensate, or mystical—that causes us to draw our life's energies from anything else than God, that the sin that damns involves the person "who lays up treasure for himself, and is not rich toward God."

It becomes needful for us to take the danger and destructiveness out of our worldly security by seeking that which is truly meaningful for our lives. It must begin with reappraisal or reassessment of our lives' goals; "for where your treasure is, there will your heart be also," said Jesus in the Sermon on the Mount. This is followed by repentance, a recognition of our folly, its renunciation, and a return to the love and grace of God. Repentance must be combined with refocus, a determination to "seek first [God's] kingdom and His righteousness" (Matthew 6:33). There is nothing inherently sinful in the things of this life. The tragedy evolves when the acquisition of such things takes precedence over God and spiritual values. So we must refocus, put things in their proper perspective, lest we lose out altogether on divine meaning and purpose and its resultant order and joy for our lives.

Forgive me, O Lord, for allowing the things of this world to obscure and threaten my relationship with You. Amen.

We Are Really Alive

If then you have been raised with Christ, seek the things that are above. v. 1

I wonder if we understand it, that we truly are the people of God, that He loves us and chooses that we be His people. Now we are really alive. As Christ was raised from the dead, so we have been brought from death to life and shall live forever. We ought daily to set our hearts and fix our minds on this fantastic truth. Faith means that we begin to live and act on this truth, that this really happened, whether we feel it or not.

There are, however, still some things within us that must not be permitted to control our thinking or activities. They are those things that come between us and God and are capable of causing harm to our fellow persons. Still rising out of the darkness to haunt and tempt us are the shadows of lust and greed and covetousness and hostility and deceit. They are like booby traps; they can destroy us and anyone close to us. We must, by God's grace and His power at work within us, blast these insidious demons out of our lives; and we must do it again and again, for they die hard, these agents of death.

It is thus that we grow in faith, allowing the Spirit of God to captivate and subordinate every aspect of our lives under His purging love. We learn how to plug up the loopholes in our lives by allowing God to flood our hearts with His love. We commit ourselves to exercising that inflowing and outgoing love by reaching out to others in concern and compassion.

It's a great life; let's get on with it!

Help me, O Lord, to really act on that which I believe, Your resurrection power in my life and living. Only then will I really be alive. Amen.

"You Gotta Believe"

O man of little faith, why did you doubt? v. 31b

The crowd-gathering religions today, as well as in Christ's day, are for the most part satisfied with the spectacular and the fantastic, the walking-on-water, feeding-the-five-thousand, healing-the-sick, turning-water-into-wine aspects of religion, and there appears to be little relationship between that and the "faith of our fathers, living still, in spite of dungeon, fire, and sword."

Jesus was in the process of creating and nourishing faith in His disciples, the kind of faith that stirs up the daring within the soul, that goes beyond the limits of what is reasonable and rational, and flirts with the risk and gamble of new ventures, that turns its back upon one's well-laid plans for future security and well-being and dares to tread the fringe of danger for the benefit of others. It is a vibrant, living, daring, sacrificial faith, a faith that does not burn out, that does not falter when one begins to sink beneath the waters, but lays hold afresh on the proclaimed and dramatized saving love and grace of God and rises again to joy and service.

"We gotta believe"—not in some vague, positive-thinking type of religion, or in a god who titillates us on demand, but in the God of our fathers, our Lord and Christ, who created and redeemed us and made us His own, who provides us with all we need to be what He would have us to be and do what He would have us to do. We must believe and act like it—not only in spite of evidences, but in scorn of consequences.

Grant us, O God, this kind of faith.

Grant to me, my Lord, the "faith of our fathers," that I, also, "will be true to Thee till death." Amen.

How Much Should One Love?

I have great sorrow and unceasing anguish in my heart. v. 2

It is probable that few of us can love as much as Paul loved his people. How many of us "would wish that [we ourselves] were accursed and cut off from Christ for the sake of [our] . . . kinsmen?" Not only did Paul offer up his life for the sake of Jew and Gentile alike, but he was willing to be cut off from God's saving love—to submit to eternal damnation—if that would result in the salvation of the Jews. We are able to love those who love us, and are learning something about loving those of other races—even our enemies— but we dare not claim the love that Paul had for his brothers and sisters.

Yet Paul reveals in some measure the content and quality of Christ's love for us. Jesus submitted to death on the cross in His love for us. He enjoined us to love others even as He loved us. It is obvious that we have a long way to go. While we may never reach the quality and intensity of love Paul declared for his people, and certainly won't attain the heights and depths of Christ's love for us, this is the goal we ought to be reaching for.

Recognizing, as did Paul, that salvation comes only through Christ and that we can in no way save others by being damned in their stead, we should be compelled by God's eternal love for us and all His creatures to spend and expend all we are and have in order that others about us may hear about and desire to receive God's saving grace. God grant that we may experience "unceasing anguish" for those who have thus far rejected or ignored Jesus Christ. Let us be aware that it can in no way match the anguish in the heart of God Himself over those who turn away from Him as He is revealed in Jesus Christ.

"My Jesus, I love Thee, I know Thou art mine, for Thee all the follies of sin I resign . . ." Help me, O Lord, to demonstrate that love in my concern and compassion for Your children around me. Amen.

The Meaning of Believing

I am the living bread which came down from heaven; if any one eats of this bread, he will live. v. 51

We would hope that the average church member today is not as shallow in his or her concept of the Christ as were those who gathered about Him on this occasion. Is it possible to be united with Christ in baptism, to make weekly confessions and go through the motions of worship, and yet fail to comprehend what it really means to believe in Jesus Christ? Don't we all attempt to take the all-wise, everywhere-present God of the Bible and press Him into the confinements of our small thinking? Like a pilot grabbing for his parachute when the motor of his small plane conks out, don't we grab for some comfortable concept of God, for a piece of the Divine, and state emphatically that we believe in God?

A right relationship to God, an authentic faith in Jesus Christ, is really a two-way street. He gives us His all—even though we have nothing to give but our depraved, sin-ridden hearts. This takes place at our baptism. When we become aware of God's covenant made with us through Jesus Christ and appropriated to us at our baptism, we are consciously to embrace His forgiving love and recognize our adoption as His sons and daughters and our appointment as His servants and disciples. We "eat" and "drink" Him; we identify with Him; we take Him into the center of our very beings. We become one with Him through Christ. His life becomes our life; His love becomes our love; His purposes become our purposes, His goal our goal. Redeemed by His forgiving and sanctifying grace, we become energized and empowered by His indwelling Spirit to be His vessels through which to communicate His love to a fractured world, and we who "eat" of that Bread which was broken for us become broken bread to the hungry lives of men and women about us.

This is what it means to believe in Jesus.

"I believe, O Lord; help me with my unbelief." Amen.

Participators and Imitators

Walk in love, as Christ loved us and gave Himself up for us . . .
vv. 2

We know that we are the children of God. It follows, then, that we are responsible to Him—to emulate Him, follow Him—to soar within His orbit for our lives. It is only as we participate in what God has done for us through Jesus Christ that we are enabled and expected to imitate Him as well. As God, through Christ, demonstrated His love for us, so our lives, controlled by His love, are to demonstrate such love toward people about us. It is this that ought to determine our daily conduct. The way we speak or act, the company we keep, whatever we do—whether working or playing, resting or recreating, eating or sleeping—needs to be measured, not by what most pleases us, but in terms of what is pleasing to God and what is most beneficial to our fellow persons.

The fact is, we are under new management, new orders. Our primary task is now to reflect, administer, communicate God's infinite love to a distorted and disjointed world. While self-surrender underlines our relationship to God, self-disclosure should characterize our relationship toward our fellow persons. We are to "be kind to one another, tenderhearted, forgiving one another, as God in Christ forgave [us] . . . and walk in love . . ." It is this that constitutes the ethics of a Christian. With God's help, and because of His great love for us, let us learn how to invest in one another. This is the key to genuine and everlasting joy whatever the circumstances that crowd in upon us.

O Lord, I cannot imitate or emulate You unless, by Your grace, I by faith embrace Your saving love and participate in Your gifts and commit my life and all that You have given me to the accomplishment of Your purposes. So be it, Lord, for now and forever. Amen.

Divine Words in a Dark World

Do not be anxious about your life, what you shall eat, nor about your body, what you shall put on. v. 22

"Fear not, little flock, for it is your Father's good pleasure to give you the kingdom," said Jesus. These are words of consolation—words that offer an exceedingly reliable prescription for joyful and secure living in a very dark and uncertain world. Jesus did not guarantee earthly security or freedom from all things that might cause pain or sorrow; yet He said, in effect, that we have nothing to be afraid of. As God's children and servants we are blessed with God's divine words and promises in a dark world. We shall not be afraid.

Jesus also speaks words of exhortation. We are enjoined to *sell,* to take our clutching fingers off that which we classify as ours—our possessions, our talents, our very lives. In order to inherit the riches of eternity, we must willingly and gladly disinherit earth and its lesser values. Christ must come first in our lives—or He doesn't come at all. We are enjoined to *give.* What good we have received is from God. This does not make it our sole possession. It is ours to enjoy; it is also ours to give away. It is meant to meet some of the needs of people about us. When we neglect to give, we become dead-end streets, stagnant pools. Where there is no outlet, there ceases to be inflow. He enjoins us to *invest wisely*—in the "treasure in the heavens that does not fail." This investment of lives and possessions must be in the hungry that need feeding, the naked that need clothing, the sick that need healing and comforting, the souls that need saving. It is the kind of investment that will pay off in this life and in the life to come.

"Take my life, and let it be consecrated, Lord to Thee." And I want that to include all that I am and have: body, mind, possessions, will and love. Amen.

The Day before Us

Faith is the assurance of things hoped for, the conviction of things not seen. v. 1

"And he went out, not knowing where he was to go." It is difficult for some of us to face a new day without preconceived plans as to what our errands and actions are to be. It appears that a well-ordered life is a distinct virtue in our times and should not be ignored. Maybe we should experiment with the kind of faith Abraham demonstrated when he "went out, not knowing where he was to go." Abraham obviously scored high with God in obeying His command to "go" without insisting on some revelation as to where he was to go or what God would have him do. Nor should we insist on such a revelation. God reveals Himself to us; He seldom reveals much more. The God-given ability to believe in Him for our salvation includes the ability to trust Him to lead us and accomplish His purposes through us on any day of any week.

Whereas our great God grants to us the ability to have faith, it is necessary for us to utilize and exercise this ability. It means that we focus upon the infinite grace of God, accept His forgiving love won for us by Christ and proclaimed through His Word, and in scorn of consequences place our lives and fortunes in His hands. Without faith there is no way of relating to God. With faith, and its resultant commitment to Christian discipleship, there is joy and meaning, risk and excitement, love and freedom, purpose and objective for every son and daughter of God.

Have a good day!

"This is the day which the Lord has made; let us rejoice and be glad in it" (Ps. 118:24). And as I rejoice, my Lord, I will trust Your guidance and the strength you grant to live this day according to Your will and purposes. Amen.

Strength for the Journey

Arise and eat, else the journey will be too great for you. v. 7b

There are times when even stout hearts will faint and strong men and women will falter. As with Elijah, this could even be a sort of post-victory depression or a letdown after an active and reasonably successful day or week out there in the Sunday-through-Saturday arena of one's life. All too often it is a desperate feeling of discouragement and failure. Elijah wanted to die; he was so frightened and despondent. We have had days like that in our lives. We consider Elijah rather fortunate in that he had a visit from an angel who baked him a cake and provided him with drink. In our pain and misery, we wonder if there might be an angel or two about to aid us in our distress.

Probably not, but we have something far better, for God Himself is with us, whatever the difficulties that befall us. He has filled us with His Spirit and, even when our bodies are wracked with pain and our minds clouded by despair, He is with us always and will take the journey with us, no matter how difficult the course we travel. "Arise and eat, else the journey will be too great for you," the angel said to Elijah. "And he arose, and ate and drank, and went on in the strength of that food."

"The cup of blessing which we bless, is it not a participation in the blood of Christ? The bread which we break, is it not a participation in the body of Christ?" wrote Paul (1 Corinthians 10:16). "Drink of it, all of you," said Jesus, "for this is My blood of the covenant, which is poured out for many . . ." (Matthew 26:27–28). There is indeed refreshment for God's children as they slog their way through the wilderness of this life. It is offered in the Word and granted in a very special way through the Lord's Supper. God may not send us angels; He Himself comes to us through Jesus Christ by way of the Word and Sacrament.

So rise up and move on; God is with you!

I thank You, my Lord, for there is daily sustenance and strength, no matter how long and difficult the journey before me. Amen.

Why Is God So Stubborn?

O woman, great is your faith. v. 28

Why is God so stubborn? It is a question many of us have entertained at one time or another. There are those times when we have felt that God is downright obstinate and seems to be cold, indifferent, insulated, or unrelated to our aches and agonies. He not only allows us to get into complexities and entanglements we have no intention or desire to get into, but He appears at times to be totally oblivious to our struggles and conflicts. We agree that God is in His heaven—lest one be accused of blasphemy or heresy—but there are occasions when He seems to have abdicated our chaotic world.

Why is God so stubborn? Perhaps it is because He loves us too much that He insists on giving us the very best in life. There are times when the only way God has of introducing us to the best is to allow us to prick ourselves on the thorny bushes of this existence, or run amok in its blind allies and dead-end streets, or flail helplessly on its quicksands of ultimate disillusionment and disaster. When we desperately long for deliverance, as did the Canaanite woman, we have taken the initial step in preparing the way for God to grant the miracle of sufficient grace to bear our afflictions or to live fruitfully and effectively with our problems.

It is not enough that we bring our problems to God. We must bring ourselves to Him—yield to Him the reins of our lives, place before Him all that we have. Then miracles will begin to happen in our lives.

I pray, O loving God, that You will pull me out of this swamp of self-pity and depression and teach me how to cope with the struggles and conflicts that I must encounter and deal with today. Amen.

The Gracious Mercy of God

*For God has consigned all men to disobedience, that He may have
mercy upon all.* v. 32

Paul suffered much anguish over the unwillingness of his fellow
countrymen to receive God's mercy as revealed through the Christ.
He points out that it was their rejection of Jesus Christ as Redeemer
and Savior that compelled him to focus the primary emphasis of his
ministry upon the Gentile world. He was living in the hope that the
Gentile acceptance of God's mercy as portrayed and proclaimed
through Christ and His disciples would, in turn, be a blessing to the
Jews and encourage them to receive God's loving mercy and
everlasting salvation.

Of this we can be sure: even if His beloved creatures turn away
from Him, God does not reject them. Whereas divine love can be
resisted, as it cannot be forced upon the objects of such love, yet
those objects continue to be loved. Even while we may eventually
give up on those who shun our attempts to introduce them to Christ,
God never gives them up—at least in this life.

We are obviously not able to comprehend the vast depths of
the kind of love that continues to pursue these runaway children
until they are found and returned to the fold. How grateful we ought
to be that God persisted in His search for our souls! How eagerly
and diligently ought we to unite with Him in His persistent search
for the lost and wandering, the willful and rebellious souls of men
and women, Jews and Gentiles, about us! It was, in part, because of
the rebelliousness of God's originally chosen people that the Gospel
came to us and enabled us to be numbered among the "chosen."
While we celebrate God's amazing and never-ending love for His
human creatures, let us live and act in such a way that we may
communicate that divine love to all people and draw them into the
kingdom of God.

Merciful God, I am Yours because of Your persistent, never-
ending love. May I be as persistent in revealing and conveying
that love to others around me. Amen.

Maybe Our God Is Too Small

He who eats My flesh and drinks My blood abides in Me, and I in him. v. 56

Jesus' contemporaries, flabbergasted by what they had just witnessed in the feeding-of-the-five-thousand miracle, were about to believe that this Jesus really was the promised Messiah and to start a Christ-for-king movement that would put Him on the throne and establish Israel as a great and powerful nation once more. Jesus then set about to disabuse their foolish, fanciful notions of His Messianic ministry and attempted to tell them something of what it really meant to believe in Him, to embrace Him as their Messiah, and follow Him as their King.

As with the people of Jesus' day, so our concept of what it means to believe in, worship, and follow Jesus Christ is often too small, too immature. What our Lord is saying, in today's terms, is that the key to authentic Christianity is faith and commitment. The disciples never really understood this until after Christ's resurrection; some of us still have to discover it. The faith and fervor of those first followers of Christ, the devotion and drive manifested in the waking hours of the church, are hard to come by in our generation. The Christianity that some of us have been a part of is a kind of streamlined, plush-lined facsimile of the real thing, a kind of defensive, crawling-into-our-holes-to-lick-our-wounds Christianity, an escapism, a running away from reality, a place of refuge and hiding. The soft faith that characterizes the religion of our day is obviously not sponsored by Christ but is the invention of the minds of men and women who want the pearl without paying the price; who don't really understand that there is a price to pay, a battle to fight, a life to lose, in the great business of following Jesus Christ.

Maybe our God is too small.

Forgive me, gracious Father, for unwittingly attempting to make you a small god, a sort of spiritual concoction that offers no threat to my self-centeredness. Amen.

Carefully and Gratefully

Therefore do not be foolish, but understand what the will of the Lord is. v. 17

"Look carefully then how you walk . . ." When we are blessed with a new friend or obtain a new job or a new car or a new home, we are generally very careful about how we treat this individual or those things. We "walk" carefully, for they are of great value to us. It may be that we are not nearly so concerned about that "pearl of great price," that divine gift and eternal relationship which is of infinitely greater value than anything of which we can conceive. We tend to take God for granted and therefore become careless and irresponsible in respect to our relationship with Him. This has to do, as well, with our responsibility in respect to our relationships with our fellow beings, the servants and ministers of God. We are careful about the things we love the most; it follows, then, that if we truly love our Lord, and our brothers and sisters in the family of God, we will "look carefully . . . how [we] walk."

While we walk carefully, we are enjoined to live gratefully. It is difficult to understand how even Christians can "always and for everything [give] thanks." But we can learn how to be grateful to God, to live thankful lives, irrespective of dire happenings, realizing that even the painful, tragic things that come our way, can be used to carry out God's purposes in and through us.

We have something of infinite, incalculable value in our relationship to God and His children; let us be careful and grateful.

I am grateful to You, my Lord, for making me a part of Your green vineyard, for mercifully and miraculously using me to communicate Your love and peace to anxious, fearful, despairing, and hate-filled persons along my journey. Amen.

The Radical Christ

I came to cast fire upon the earth; and would that it were already kindled! v. 49

We spent many of our youthful years regarding Jesus as a gentle, meek peacemaker. We subsequently came across portions of Scripture that picture Him quite differently. "Do you think I have come to give peace on earth? No . . . I came to cast fire upon the earth . . ."

Jesus did promise us His peace (John 14:27). He promised, as well, that those who labored for His kingdom would face division, conflict, and persecution. He led the way to the scaffold; most of His disciples followed closely behind. And He has left us with the assuring word that we need not be afraid when we face the courts that seek to snuff us out. He has gone before us—but only to return in order to embrace us and love us in the midst of earthshaking events, staying close beside us all the way.

The point is, the Christian life itself is a revolutionary life, a life fraught with conflicts. It has been such from the beginning; it shall be as long as life on this earth continues. Those people who float peacefully by totally content with their religious experience, oblivious or impervious to the conflict-ridden world about them, desperately holding on to their precious ecstasies or God-in-a-box concepts until Jesus comes to take them to heaven, those people may be on the wrong ship—or are dry-docked in some harbor when they should be sailing the storm-tossed seas of reality where God's servants and fishers-of-men-and-women-and-children are supposed to be.

When we reach out to embrace the peace of a right relationship with God, we must also reckon with the conflicts that come as a consequence of that redeeming, healing, joy-giving relationship; for we are the followers of the radical Christ in a revolutionary world.

Enable me, Jesus, to break through any superficial under-standing of You and Your purposes, and to accept and follow You as You really are and by Your grace to become what You want me to be. Amen.

The Faith that Keeps Us Going

Let us run with patience the race that is set before us. v. 1a

Faith is in itself a gift of God. It is not something we can manufacture. And yet, one of the most powerful incentives to have faith, to trust God, to believe in His gracious promises, is the faith of those who have gone before us.

It ought to be enough to enable us to cut loose from our inordinate attachment to earthbound securities, to cast off our foolish doubts, and to let go, let God do what He wills, and let the chips fall where they may. While our Lord is no longer visibly present, we have His Word and His example and the example and experience of countless saints to nourish and mature our faith.

If we expect only sweetness and light, thrills and ecstasies, as the consequences of our involvement with God and His purposes, we have a wrong conception of what faith is all about. There is an element of risk, a measure of pain, involved in our walk of faith. Faith, no matter how intense, does not shield us from the episodes that wound us or the failures that flatten us in despair. But faith is capable of embracing suffering and despair and molding and maneuvering these into instruments that mature us and make us more sensitive to the hurts of others, even while we learn how more graciously to accept the hardships and difficulties of this life.

Rather than floundering and folding in the midst of every turbulence that engulfs us, we can, by the grace of God, learn how to stand firm against the storm and walk steadily among the vicissitudes of daily living.

Our loving God, You who are always with us and within us and seeking to work out Your purposes through us, grant to us this measure of faith as we face the day before us. Amen.

Beware of Dreamers

How long shall there be lies in the heart of the prophets who proph-esy lies . . . the deceit of their own heart? v. 26

"Let the prophet who has a dream tell the dream, but let him who has My Word speak My Word faithfully."

Our Lord's indictments against the many false prophets of Jeremiah's day are applicable to our generation as well. Scores of cults are led by false prophets who base their credentials on some dream. While they may use our Bible to pad their presentations, it is most often some out-of-context portions that are utilized to support their allegations and promote their purposes.

Dreams and visions are not all bad; some may even be useful; and there are indications that dreams have been effectual in relaying divine messages to a dark world. When, however, they are placed above or on par with God's Word as revealed through Christ and related through the Scriptures, they cannot be trusted and may lead one down the road to disaster.

The dreamers about us are not confined to cults or sects. As the people of Christ's day looked for supernatural signs, even Christians in long-established churches are sometimes tempted to reach for magical dreams or visions to spice up their faith or to satisfy their sensual and emotional hungers or their need for temporal security and serenity.

Whether we be preachers or God's servants in the marketplace or on Main Street, we who have heard God's Word are to "speak [His] Word faithfully." That Word is not always a comforting Word; it sometimes jars and provokes, even as it did the Israelites in Jeremiah's time. Nevertheless, it eventually and resolutely leads us to eternal truth and joy. God forbid that we replace it or confuse it with the silly dreams and proclamations of self-styled prophets!

I thank You, my loving God, for revealing Your eternal love through the Word who is Christ and through His words that reveal to us the way and the truth. Amen.

Genuine Confession

Who do men say that the Son of man is? v. 13b

It is probable that Jesus was discouraged over the responses of the many who had heard Him preach and who witnessed His miracles such as the feeding-of-the-five-thousand. Like people who flock to certain churches today that offer healing or mesmerize their audiences with mind-blowing antics that are geared to crowd-gathering, there were crowds who pressed in upon Christ because He could perform the kind of magic that pleased them or fed them or healed them. They were quite willing to vote Him into office as king if that could be arranged.

Jesus took His most loyal followers aside to question them concerning their attitudes in this matter. He invited them to articulate their feelings toward Him. The larger group of followers that showed some interest in Christ compared Him to Elijah or John the Baptist or some prophet come back to life. From the inner circle of followers, through the lips of Peter, came a more encouraging confession: "You are the Christ, the Son of the living God." It was a true confession, probably immature at this point; nevertheless it was genuine, and Jesus accepted it as such.

"You are the Christ, the Son of the living God." No other confession will do. May it be a genuine confession even if it is, as in the case of Peter, still immature. As Peter developed in his comprehension of Christ's person and purposes and his own committal to Him, so we will grow and mature as sons and daughters of God and disciples of Jesus Christ.

You, my Lord, truly are the Christ—the Son of the living God. I stake my life on that blessed truth that has become so obvious to me by way of the cross and Your glorious resurrection from the dead. And because of this blessed truth, I am Yours forever. Amen.

When There Are No Answers

O the depth of the riches and wisdom and knowledge of God!
v. 33a

"How unsearchable are His judgments and how inscrutable His ways."

This is Paul's response to our unsolvable problems. In his case it was the problem of his rebellious and apparently rejected countrymen who refused to believe in Jesus Christ as their Savior and Lord. The lack of an answer to the problem, his inability to fully discern God's mind or future action toward the Jews who rejected God's Son, threw him back on the wisdom and judgments of God. He was able to rejoice in knowing that God's ways are right and His judgments are perfect.

If we are worshiping a God who reveals all the answers to the problems and conflicts of our lives, we are worshiping something less than the true God. Beware of those religious leaders or religions that have the answers to everything that confounds us; they indicate that they tend to confine the wisdom and judgments of God to their own small minds. Our God is far greater than that—and so are His thoughts than our thoughts and His ways than our ways. Some of God's mysteries may gradually unfold when we become more mature in knowledge and insight. But most of His mysteries will remain such to us as long as we abide on this planet.

We can, however, rejoice as did Paul, "For from Him and through Him and to Him are all things." We will never fully know our God, nor the answers to all our problems, but He knows us. We can well afford to trust Him—and to praise Him.

I am grateful, O Lord, that "[Your] thoughts are not [my] thoughts, nor are [Your] ways [my] ways," according to the prophet (Isaiah 55:8), but I pray that Your thoughts and ways may increasingly become mine as I mature in my love and service to You. Amen.

The Gospel that Offends

This is a hard saying; who can listen to it? v. 60

"After this many of His disciples drew back and no longer went about with Him."

The Gospel of Jesus Christ does indeed offer comfort. Something we may hesitate to accept and may find difficult to proclaim is the fact that the Gospel also offends. Many are ill at ease with its paradoxes and demands and make foolish attempts to reduce the Christian faith to simple and often maudlin categories that they can handle without too much pain or discomfort. Others find it downright offensive; it demands too much, and they seek elsewhere for spiritual solace. Christ's preaching resulted in sifting out the fellow-travelers who followed Him for material or political benefits. Jesus ignored their earthbound concepts and invited them to "eat" and "drink," to identify and become one with Him, to commit themselves totally to Him and His purposes. The crowd melted away, and Jesus was left with His original following of twelve men.

Anything that strikes at the very core of our self-centered lives is bound to cause offense. We recognize our sin and are driven to the offense of the cross. We yield, sometimes very painfully, to God's forgiving love. Then we meet up with the offense of yielding control of our lives to Jesus and His purposes, dying daily to sin and self-centeredness to live for the sake of others. Offense will dog our footsteps until there is a genuine surrender to the blessed will of God and to servanthood as His ministers in our world. Thus we discover God's orbit for our lives, and offense is transformed into abundant joy—even in the midst of suffering and persecution.

"Lord, to whom shall we go?" said the disciples. "You have the words of eternal life."

I pray, O Lord, that my self-centeredness and greed might be offended to death in order that Your love and power will have free course through my life. Amen.

Our Interpersonal Relationships

Love [one another] as Christ loved the church and gave Himself up for her. v. 24

"Be subject to one another out of reverence for Christ."

Some of us may have a problem with Paul's injunction to wives and their relationship to their husbands. It is my opinion that Paul, who was certainly upgrading wife-husband relationships in his day, would say some things a bit differently if he were writing letters to our churches today. He would, nevertheless, still underline his initial statement: "Be subject to one another out of reverence for Christ."

Whether we think of marital or family relationships, or our relationships to one another as the sons and daughters of God, Paul most certainly points up Christ's injunction to love one another. A by-product of that kind of love has to do with our concern for and consideration of the needs of the other even above our own needs. This is the responsibility of husbands and wives, sisters and brothers, parents and children, and is to be the dominant note in our relationships with all of God's children.

Subjection or submission of one to another is a two-way street. I often subject myself to my wife, sometimes reluctantly, in those matters where she is gifted and qualified to make decisions. She, by the same token, subjects herself to me and to what I feel is important in our relationships to one another and to God's purposes for our lives. This is the fruit, and a necessary aspect, of our love. Both of us are slowly learning how to subject ourselves to the needs of others about us. This is in response to and is the consequence of God's great love for us. And this is what belonging to the family of Christ is all about.

We know, O Lord, that our relationships to each other within our personal families must be primary. But we pray, O Lord, that our love for each other may stretch our souls and give us a greater capacity to love others. Amen.

When Label Becomes Libel

Many . . . will seek to enter and will not be able. v. 24b

Most of our daily activities are guided by labels of some sort, whether we be eating, driving, working, or learning. When something is purchased under a particular label, but turns out to be far different than the label led one to expect, then the label projected a lie.

Jesus says, in effect, that it is quite possible to wear the label of Christianity without living its life, to don its uniform without fighting in its battles, to claim its benefits without carrying its cross.

We stand convicted—many of us at many times. We may have worn the label; it may have come out as libelous. There has been considerable foliage, but too little fruit. We may have faithfully and piously carried out our religious exercises in the sanctuary only to demonstrate our selfishness and self-centeredness in the home, the office, the marketplace. "Not everyone who says to me, 'Lord, Lord,' shall enter the kingdom of heaven," Jesus said on another occasion, "but he who does the will of My Father" (Matthew 7:21). Profession apart from genuine expression is just so much moist air. It may dazzle and awe a few people; it doesn't get through to God.

In order to take the libel out of our label we need constantly to recognize our call to servanthood, the necessity of divine grace in the carrying out of that servanthood, the importance of a perpetual and total commitment to the living Christ as Savior and Lord, and the courage to live and act as He would live and act in our circumstances.

My Lord and Savior, I really want to be open, aboveboard, honest and genuine in my interpersonal relationships, but my ego and self-concern so often get in the way. Blast these things out of my life, dear Lord, that I may be Your child and servant forever. Amen.

Grace Rather Than Fear

You have come . . . to Jesus the mediator of a new covenant. v. 24

We have, at times, tended to become rather chummy with God, to regard Him as "the man upstairs" or a kindly grandfather in the sky, a big brother of sorts, and to ascribe to Him a familiarity, an indulgent nature that tolerates our idiosyncrasies even while He tries to keep us in line. This is far removed from the God of the Old Testament whom people regarded with great fear and trembling. There are times when we ought to put a little of that ancient fear of God back into our worship services and daily activities and demonstrate some holy respect for our Creator and Judge.

While we are enjoined to fear or to be aware of the consequences of acting contrary to the will of God, we need never fear approaching God, no more than a child would fear coming to the arms of a loving mother or father. God is ever approachable, and His everlasting grace has forever opened the door of the inner sanctuary where we can confess, confide, and reconsecrate our lives to Him and His purposes. This has been made possible in Jesus Christ, through whom God came to us and is ever available to us.

We who have come to God through Christ have indeed drawn near "to Mount Zion and to the city of the living God, the heavenly Jerusalem, and to innumerable angels in festal gathering, . . . and to a judge who is God of all, and to the spirits of just men made perfect . . ." and all this through "Jesus, the mediator of a new covenant . . ."

Grace has taken over where trembling, terrifying fear once occupied the hearts of men and women in their relationship to God.

I thank You, my gracious God, that whereas I have come to You in shame, I never need to come to You in fear. And so I come, my Father and my King, through Jesus Christ, for forgiveness and reconciliation and renewal in my relationship to You. Amen.

A Matter of Response

As for me and my house, we will serve the Lord. v. 15b

The Israelites were challenged to make a clear-cut choice. They were to submit to God's will or to go traipsing after the gods of some other nation or tribe. They had nothing to do with God's choice of them to be His people, but they, in turn were able to reject Him.

We have some difficulty with the semantics of the large number of churches or denominations who beseech their constituents to "choose" Jesus, to make a "decision" for Christ. We sometimes wonder if they are aware that we did not choose Christ, but He chose us that we should be the children and servants of God forever. Those who are baptized into Christ as infants have no awareness of choosing to receive God's infinite and eternal love. God chose us and gathered us into His graciousness.

Yet, decision of one kind or another eventually becomes paramount for most of us. We inevitably encounter crossroads or rivers to cross in our sojourn through this life. Whether conscious of it or not, we do make decisions. Some of them are in tune with God's Spirit within us; others appear to cloud up or obscure His will and purposes for us. The point is, we are capable of resisting God's will or ignoring the direction of His Spirit. True faith, that faith which justifies, is receptivity—the acknowledgment, reception, and appropriation of God's grace bestowed upon us through Jesus Christ. God grants us His love and forgiveness; we are privileged and enabled to respond to it—or to make the dreadful decision not to respond to it.

You have chosen me, O Lord. Grant to me the grace and wisdom to respond today and every day in ways that are pleasing to You and enriching for me and for others about me. Amen.

The Centrality of the Cross

Whoever loses his life for My sake will find it. v. 25b

Our lives as Christians begin with the cross. It is central; it is essential; it is the center and core, pivot and apex of Christianity. It is because of the cross that Jesus accepts us as we are—with all of our sins, failures, and hang-ups. In this Gospel portion, however, our Lord talks not only of its centrality and essentiality, but of its perpetuity. "If any man would come after Me, let him deny himself and take up his cross and follow Me."

What does this mean to you and me in this day and hour? It means accepting our fellow beings where they are in order that we may patiently and lovingly lead them to where God wants them to be. It means to stoop to the feet-washing level of our neighbor's need in order that we may lift him or her to the glorious heights of God's loving acceptance. It means to identify with humanity about us, irrespective of race, color, or creed—to be truly human in the presence of our human brothers and sisters. It means involvement with the sufferings and sorrows, conflicts and consternations, failures and defeats, of our fellow persons. It means that we bear one another's burdens and share in their despair. It means that we listen—and then put our lives on the line in loving and sacrificial action to bring justice and dignity and opportunity and validity to every human being within our reach or circle of influence. It means that, whenever and wherever possible, we proclaim the blessed Gospel of God's love and grace through Jesus Christ.

It will mean other things as well, but these will certainly demand self-denial and cross-bearing for the disciples of Jesus Christ.

You went to the cross on my behalf, dear Jesus. Enable me, my Savior and Master to take up my cross and follow You. Amen.

God Gives—We Respond

Present your bodies as a living sacrifice, holy and acceptable to God. v. 1

Our great God gives; we are expected to respond to His gracious gifts. This response, according to Paul, is to be the offer of our lives, the placing of ourselves at God's disposal, for the accomplishment of His purposes in our world about us. It means that we turn our hearts, minds, and bodies over to God's ownership and dedicate our abilities to His service.

We have all received gifts from our God. They are not given to us to enhance our beauty or assure our worldly security, or even to make us more desirable or respected among the people with whom we love and labor. They are committed to us in order to be committed back to God in and through and by way of service to our fellow beings for God's sake. This is precisely the way in which our God meets the needs of our neighbor—through us and through the gifts entrusted to us.

Not all of us have the gifts that would enable us to administer or preach or finance important projects. But we all have specific gifts and abilities—love, energy, persistence, patience, sincerity, concern, creativity. We are to exercise these things upon one another and on behalf of one another. We are to care for each other even as much or more than we care for ourselves. We are to allow our God to reach and touch others, even our very enemies, with His care and concern for them through us.

"We are His workmanship, created in Christ Jesus for good works," wrote Paul (Ephesians 2:10). The sacrifice we are to make to God as our response to His saving grace is our very selves. The altar upon which our sacrifice is to be made is the altar of our neighbor's need. Let us celebrate and serve!

"Take my life, and let it be consecrated, Lord, to Thee." And teach me how to spend and expend myself for the sake of others. Amen.

Worship That Is Acceptable

In vain do they worship Me, teaching as doctrines the precepts of men. v. 7

One day, thousands of years ago, two men brought their sacrifices to their crudely made altars to offer them to God. The first man was Abel; he was a keeper of sheep. His sacrifice was the best of the flock. The second man was Cain; he was a tiller of the soil. His sacrifice was the fruit of the ground. Both men brought sacrifices; both brought of what they had; both offered them to God. Yet there was a significant distinction, one made by God Himself: "And the Lord had regard for Abel and his offering, but for Cain and his offering He had no regard" (Genesis 4:4–5).

While some have attempted to explain the dilemma by referring to the necessity of a blood-offering, which Cain's was not, I suggest that it goes deeper than this. The difference in God's attitude toward the sacrifices of the two worshipers lay in the heart attitudes of these two before God. Cain was going through a religious exercise. Abel's offering was sprinkled with the incense of lowly trust and came from a heart which desired to love God and obey His commandments. It was therefore a joy to God.

Customs and traditions change, but not the attitudes of men and women before God. There are, on the one hand, the lip-worshipers: "This people honors Me with their lips, but their hearts are far from Me," said Jesus; "in vain do they worship Me . . ." There are, on the other hand, those who demonstrate heart-trust. They bring the acceptable offering, the offering of Abraham, who portrayed his heart-trust by his obedience to God; or of David, who prayed: "Create in me a clean heart, O God"; or of Isaiah, who responded to God's call with the answer and committal: "Here am I, send me"; or of Paul, who "counted everything as loss because of the surpassing worth of knowing Christ Jesus."

Is my worship this day acceptable to You, dear Lord? It is so only if I come to You as Your child and go out into this world as Your servant. Amen.

Off to the Wars

Put on the whole armor of God, that you may be able to stand against the wiles of the devil. v. 11

The Christian walk is never easy. There are enemies to contend with, obstacles to confront, and these are to be opposed or overcome in the power and Spirit of God. Whether these enemies, these spiritual forces of darkness, work through the power structures over us or the numerous loopholes that plague our individual lives, we must learn how to recognize who and what they are and resist them whenever they appear.

If we are to be strong and courageous in the face of enemy forces far stronger than we are, it will necessitate our leaning on or drawing from the power made available to us through Jesus Christ. For one thing, we will have to be intense in our search for truth. Christ has revealed to us all we need to know in order to experience daily God's saving love. Yet we should be open always to ever deeper insights and experiences of His divine love. We are clothed in God's righteousness, gifted with His salvation. Nothing can change that—save our neglect to act upon it. We are to walk in God's path for our lives, the path of loving service to our fellow persons for His sake. We are to fill our minds and commit our lives to His Word and His will for us, and our bodies will act accordingly. We must continually shun the ever-grasping tentacles of the Law that seek to draw us back into its stifling embrace, and walk and run, work and serve, with our faith centered upon that One who made us His own through Jesus Christ.

We are off to the wars. Let us keep awake and be aware—and joyously and freely abandon ourselves to loving God and communicating His love through our love for those we meet along the way.

My great God, I am still learning how to walk on this journey of faith. Help me to fix my eyes and my heart upon You and Your objectives and faint not nor fear the forces of evil that seek to lead me astray. Amen.

The Main Course: Humble Pie

For every one who exalts himself will be humbled. v. 11a

The way to God is the way of humility. "He who humbles himself will be exalted," said Jesus. And the way to humility is the way of a broken heart. "The sacrifice acceptable to God is a broken spirit," said the psalmist; "a broken and contrite heart, O God, Thou wilt not despise" (Psalm 51:17). This has been true throughout the history of Israel. From Abraham, the father of the Jews, to the insignificant tax collector beating his breast in the temple, the sign and seal of God's presence has always been brokenness.

It is the same with us. When God comes near, we find nothing in ourselves to cling to. Our aims and ambitions are transformed into gaping idols. Our merits and manners become like dead leaves before the wind. Our sins and shortcomings blot out the very sun. Before we can be of use to God, we must be broken, crushed, sometimes even to the point of despair. Some people enter into this experience in almost imperceptible ways, under the preaching of the Word or the prick of the conscience. Others need to be frightened by an earthquake or drained dry by some physical disease or emotional trauma. Only then will they recognize their fallibilities and insufficiencies and humble themselves before the almighty, all-loving God.

It is then that the divine Potter reaches out to gather the broken pieces and mold them into a vessel beautiful and precious in His sight. The way of humility is the way of a broken heart. It is also the way to true significance and worth.

O God, I am often belabored and weighed down by my weaknesses and imperfections. I thank You that despite my fallibilities and failures You have granted me value and significance as Your beloved child and servant. Amen.

Advice for God's Children

Do not neglect to show hospitality to strangers, for thereby some have entertained angels unawares. v. 1

We are to guard carefully our relationships with one another and regard even those who are unknown to us as possible emissaries of God. Every interpersonal relationship is a sacred trust—especially those within the family of faith. We need to remember our comrades who are facing problems and conflicts that are even more severe than our own. Our leaders, as human and frail and error-prone as we are, need our respect and our prayers. When they are compelled to make unpopular decisions that are necessary to God's purposes, let us contribute to their courage and respect by giving them our support. We are to do this joyfully, not fearfully, for we are all God's ministers and must learn how to suffer and rejoice together.

We are all God's emissaries to one another—and through us He shares His grace with the members of Christ's body. We march together through a hostile world as the children of God—reaching out to the wanderers and stragglers by the way to draw them into God's family. There will be a price to pay and pains to bear, but we will be able to cope with these because we have a great God whose love for us never changes and who promises that eternal joy which we even now have found in some measure and which we shall experience fully and eternally when our march has been completed.

"Let brotherly love continue."

My almighty and gracious God, there are many of Your children and servants throughout this world who are suffering loneliness and rejection and depression that is far greater than my small problems and conflicts. Reveal to them Your love and concern and perpetual presence with them in their difficult times. Amen.

We Are His Forever

For I am with you to save you and deliver you. v. 20b

"If you return, I will restore you, and you shall stand before Me."

We feel at times that God has given up on us, that while we are the children of His grace, we as His servants have failed to measure up to our responsibilities to effectively carry out His purposes in stemming the tide of wickedness overwhelming our world and in proclaiming and demonstrating His redeeming love to the people about us. Yet we know, deep within us, that His love for us never ceases, that when our faith falters He is ever faithful.

We must daily remember that He cares about us, that He is with us, that He will never withdraw His grace from us. The world is in His hands, and despite the persistent rebelliousness of its inhabitants, He will accomplish His purposes within it. It is not important that we see the results of our servanthood; it is important that we trust God and His Spirit—that we wait quietly and patiently for the revealing of His kingdom. Let come what may, adversity or affliction, enmity or opposition, feelings of defeat or the ridicule of our peers, we are the redeemed children and the chosen servants of our God.

We will fail; we will flounder and fall—but only to arise again and stand before God as His forgiven and restored children and servants, for we are His forever.

Forgive me, O God, when I fail, and raise me up again when I fall on my face. And help me to remember that You accept me fully through Your Son, Jesus Christ. Guide and empower me and work through me in order to reach others with Your promise of love and forgiveness. Amen.

God and Government

Love does no wrong to a neighbor; therefore love is the fulfilling of the law. v. 10

We are God's children now. We have been set free from the stern requirements of the Law, even the screaming demands of our self-centered natures, in order to live and celebrate and serve as the sons and daughters of God. We are, however, to live our lives responsibly. Even the secular authorities over us are to be God's instruments through which He governs and directs our lives. When we disobey these, or fail in our obligations to them, we must expect to suffer the penalty for our disobedience.

Nevertheless, our responsibility is first and foremost to God. The authorities we choose to govern us are expected to govern in accordance with His goals and objectives. If their rule is unjust, we must seek to bring justice to all men and women. If they seek to usurp God's will for our lives, we must obey God's will in scorn of consequences. They may be God's instruments, but they can by no means take God's place in our lives and force us to carry out their wishes and objectives if these run contrary to God's will and Word for us. While we must surely honor our governing authorities, God forbid that we deify them in respect to our lives or the welfare of humanity about us.

We have been set free from the demands of the Law in order to relate to and be governed by a higher, more perfect law. It is the law or the requirement of love. We are to love God, and we are to love our fellow persons even as we love ourselves. It is that law which enjoins us to demonstrate true love in our fractured world.

O Lord, if it ever becomes necessary for me to disobey the laws of my country in order to serve You and my fellow persons, may Your will for me be clear and Your grace abundant that I may have the courage and the strength to act wisely irrespective of the consequences of my actions and activities. Amen.

The Touch That Transforms

And his ears were opened, his tongue was released, and he spoke plainly. v. 35

This gospel portion affords us a glimpse of the miracle-working touch of Jesus, our Lord and Savior. By His touch eyes were made to see, ears to hear, tongues to speak, feet to walk, hands to serve again. It means more than that. He came to disentangle the broken strands of life, the discordant harmonies of fear and despair and hopelessness. He came, that by His miraculous touch, men and women might again be brought into pitch with God and walk once more within divine order and orbit for their lives.

A woman was taken in the act of adultery and dragged before Jesus to be judged. By His touch she became a loving and loyal disciple. A tax collector turned from his cheating and robbing to feel His touch and became a warrior for Christ. A hater of Christians who sought them out for imprisonment or execution felt the touch of Christ and was transformed from the cruelest persecutor into the greatest propagator of Christianity this world has ever known.

And things like this are happening every day throughout the world. Alcoholics, drug addicts, criminals, sick, lonely empty, suicidal people are being touched by the Spirit of God and transformed into His loving and serving sons and daughters.

The touch of the Master has come upon each of us. It first came through His Spirit in our baptism. It became real to us when we decisively and willfully committed ourselves to the Christ of the baptismal covenant. This did not bring with it the dissolving of all our problems or the eradication of all our conflicts, but with Christ's touch came new order and harmony and joy and power and meaning and purpose into our lives. Truly, His was the touch that transforms.

Grant, O Lord, that touch that will result in the extension of our lives into the unbearable, unendurable conflicts of others about us where we may become the loving and healing touch of God upon their lives. Amen.

Growing in Faith

Be doers of the word, and not hearers only, deceiving yourselves.
v. 22

We have much to learn as the children of God. The most difficult, perhaps is to learn how to regard our trials and tribulations, even the tragedies that beset us, as capable of enhancing and enriching our lives. Whereas God does not send them, He does permit them—or chooses not to intervene between us and the sufferings that afflict us. Yet He can use them to draw us closer to Him and thereby accomplish His purposes in and through us. We need the wisdom to accept these painful happenings with graciousness, even with joy, knowing that whatever they may be, God can transform them from ugliness into beauty, from the plots of Satan designed to destroy into the purposes of God destined to fulfill. The key is a genuine faith in a loving God, a faith that frees us and strenthens us to endure whatever may come our way. We won't win every battle in this incessant war against the powers of the night, but the ultimate victory is, in Jesus Christ, already ours.

There is something else we must learn as God's children. It is not enough to be listeners and proclaimers of the Gospel; we are commissioned to be doers. Christian faith that falls short of loving performance in respect to the needs of suffering people about us falls far short of what it should be.

Turn up the flame within me, dear Lord, that my life may glow again—that my faith be rekindled and burn bright with joy and obedience. And may the lives of others be warmed through me. Amen.

Call for Commitment

*Whoever does not bear his own cross and come after Me, cannot
be My disciple.* v. 27

Jesus constantly called for commitment. He never allowed or
expected that His followers would get by with anything less. And it
was this kind of preaching that limited His following to a mere
handful of publicans and fishermen. "You had better count the cost
if you are going to be My disciple," He said. "My purpose for your
life must take precedence over your country, parents, mates,
children—even your own life. Indeed, if you are not willing to
renounce everything you have, you simply cannot be My disciple."

Abraham was called to leave his country and his father's house,
that he might be of use to God. Moses was called to turn his back
on those who brought him up, that he might be free to serve God.
Jeremiah was asked to deny himself many of the greatest joys of life,
such as wife and children, in order to follow God's plan for his life.
God may never call on us to do what He expected of Abraham or
Moses or Jeremiah—or of Christ's disciples, most of whom were
martyred for His sake—but whatever His word to us and and His
will for us, it may be better to make no decision at all to follow
Jesus if that decision is to be a halfhearted one.

Our response to God's great gift of love and to Christ's call to
servanthood must be commitment. There are risks involved as to our
lives and possessions. And there will be failures in our
determination to live committed lives; but there is always
forgiveness and renewal when we fall, and the grace to get up and
try again.

O Lord, in obedience to Your Father's will and in love for
each of us as God's creatures, You entered our wilderness
and submitted to the agony and misery of this earthly domain.
Such is the measure of Your love for us. Grant to us, O God,
the grace to live valid Christian lives. Amen.

Our Equality Before God

*No longer as a slave but more than a slave, as a beloved brother
. . . both in the flesh and in the Lord.* v. 16

Our relationship to our fellow beings within the body of Christ
is of paramount importance. Our roles as the ministers of Christ, our
assignments as His beloved servants, may vary. Some of us are
leaders who have been granted positions of authority over others.
We ought to be aware that our social or educational status,
regardless of what it means to our peers, does not impress our Lord;
every one of His children is equally important to Him. And we need
to be reminded from time to time, that with leadership comes
responsibility, the responsibility to treat those who work under us as
our equals before God, and to love them as such, our brothers and
sisters in Christ.

We are, every one of us, the ministers of God. God works
through us. We need each other, parent and child, employer and
employee, master and servant. We must together submit to the
Master of masters, the Lord of lords, our Redeemer and King, our
Father and our God. Together we seek to fulfill His objectives and
advance His kingdom. We do so as members of the same family,
the family of God and Christ.

If, O Lord, I am ever called upon to lead others, I pray for
the grace that will bring me to the feet-washing level of servanthood to them. For we are all, as Your children, servants
one to another. Amen.

God Forgives—Can We Forgive?

*So also My heavenly Father will do to every one of you, if you do
not forgive your brother from your heart.* v. 35

The servant within our Gospel portion was graciously released
from his impossible-to-pay debt to sally forth and harass a fellow
servant who owed him a small sum. The king had pronounced him
forgiven, but that had not altered the resentment and hostility in his
heart, and he turned right around to take it out of the hide of his
fellowman.

Something of this sort often happens in the Christian frame of
reference. Maybe such an attitude is apparent in our prejudices
toward other races or social classes, our snobbishness, our looking-
down-our-noses at the weaknesses and failures of others. If this is
true, it may well proclaim to the world that something is out of
kilter in our relationship to God. God has done His part; He has
bestowed His love and forgiveness on every one of us. If we, in turn
cannot genuinely portray a like spirit of love and forgiveness toward
our fellow persons, it indicates some basic insincerity or lack of
receptivity in respect to the forgiveness of our sin. The forgiving and
accepting love of God is the basis for our forgiving and accepting
and loving our fellow beings. If the first does not result in the latter,
that, according to Jesus, puts us at odds with God. "To be
reconciled with God," writes Stewart James, "is to see all mankind
with new eyes." It is to have the living Christ within, which means
to feel towards others as Christ would feel and act toward them.

Our recognition and declaration of our own bankruptcy, and of
God's acceptance of us as we are, certainly ought to result in
making us tender, acceptive, understanding, and forgiving toward
our fellow persons.

"Have mercy on me, O God . . . Wash me thoroughly from
my iniquity, and cleanse me from my sin! Restore to me the
joy of Thy salvation . . . Then I will teach transgressors Thy
ways, and sinners will return to Thee." Amen. (Psalm 51)

We Are the Lord's

Whether we live or whether we die, we are the Lord's. v. 8b

No matter how strong our convictions, or how ecstatic our feelings in respect to our faith, God forbid that we attempt to compress Him into set forms or shapes that we expect others to swallow and digest. God is too big for our little boxes or our personal convictions. Whereas He is most certainly revealed through the Christ, He is not confined to the regulations and revelations that we wrap around Him. What may be good for us in respect to the means and methods of sustaining and demonstrating our faith is not necessarily appropriate for others.

We have no right or obligation to deny or demean another person's experience. Others cannot dictate what we can or cannot do as Christians. At the same time, Christian love will not permit us to unnecessarily hurt or offend them. Our freedom in Christ enables us to respect another person's convictions even if they don't make much sense to us. Few of us will agree on all interpretations of God and His will for our lives. We can and ought to agree on the prime requirements of every Christian—that we learn how to love and care for one another.

"We are the Lord's." Whatever we do, live or die, eat or drink, indulge or abstain, we do as children of God. May our love be large enough and generous enough to embrace one another regardless of the manner in which we assume to understand or endeavor to worship and serve our God.

Eternal God, I thank You because there is no question as to my eligibility for Your grace and forgiveness. I know that I am Yours, that I belong to You. Grant me the grace to accept and love others even as You love and accept me. Amen.

Have We Been Identified?

Who do you say that I am? v. 29a

Peter identified Jesus as the Christ, the Messiah, the One who was promised. We have, as Peter ultimately did, identified Jesus Christ as God-come-to-earth and as our Lord and Savior by way of His cross where He died for our sins and the empty tomb from which He was raised as victor over sin and death. We declare with conviction that He is the Way, the Life, and the Truth, and we claim our redemption and salvation through Him.

Now the question is, have *we* been identified? Jesus said it plainly: there must also be a cross in our lives. Does our faith in what God has done for us through Christ and His cross result in our taking up our cross to follow Christ—in giving and losing our lives for His sake and the Gospel's? If it does not, are we truly, can we truly be, identified as Christians?

We are, of course, identified as God's sons and daughters at our baptism, but does that identification hold true today? While God never reneges on that covenant He made with us in our childhood, we can, and often do, as we mature into adulthood. We may continue to make our confessions of sin and faith, but these do not necessarily identify us as the followers of Christ. To be properly identified as such, we must proceed from confession to cross-bearing. It happened in the life of Peter; it is supposed to happen in our lives. We must begin with the cross—the cross of Jesus Christ. It is because of that cross that we are accepted just as we are. It is on the basis of what Christ did for us that we are to deny ourselves and take up our cross on behalf of others and to commit our forgiven and cleansed lives to servanthood.

It is as we do this that we are truly identified as the disciples of Jesus Christ.

I thank You, O God, for adopting me as Your child and for empowering me to be Your servant. Grant to me the grace to be faithful to my new name and commission. Amen.

When Our Faith Is Genuine

Faith by itself, if it has no works, is dead. v. 17

It may appear to be a small matter, but it translates into a gigantic flaw in the lives of scores of Christians. They dare to call themselves believers in and followers of Jesus Christ, and yet they act like outright bigots in their relationships with people who cross their path. If we look carefully—and honestly—we may recognize this to be one of our problems, that we are at times among those who talk limitlessly about loving humanity but are really very selective about whom we accept as the objects of our love and concern.

We are enjoined to love our neighbor as ourselves. When our judgment of people and our actions toward them are determined by the color of their skin, the cut of their clothes, or the size of their bank accounts, we are not acting like the children and servants of God. Indeed, we are sinning against God and endangering our relationship to Him when we neglect to give equal respect and value to all of His children around us. We need to reexamine our concepts of morality, to blast out some of the silly notions that apparently influence our responses to life and people, and learn how to be loving and compassionate.

Some of us may still be hooked on the ridiculous notion that religious faith is something to be exercised primarily through the rituals of a worship service. We can be all mouth in terms of confessions and testimonials while the rest of our bodies may be paralyzed by unbelief or disobedience. We need to tear away the fictitious labels and have the courage to confront the painful truth that we can't talk faith unless we have faith; and when we have the faith that Jesus proclaimed and demonstrated, we in turn will live it and demonstrate it in sacrifical love for the human family about us.

It is not so important that I be successful today, my Lord, but that I be faithful to You and Your purposes for my life. Restore and strengthen my faith. Amen.

The One Who Was Lost

There is joy before the angels of God over one sinner who repents.
v. 10

I am the one who was lost. There is only one antidote for the poison that taints my soul and binds me to the insufficiencies and inadequacies of this existence. It is revealed in Jesus Christ and the Gospel He proclaims, the Gospel that Christ is seeking the one who is lost. Until I realized that I could not escape, that I was lost, it wasn't likely that I would ever be found. The very purpose of Christ's coming, of His cross and the empty tomb, is to find and redeem the lost, to receive sinners, to draw me and others like me back into His orbit for our lives.

It is when I am up against something that is too much for me— when there are problems, weaknesses, sins, distortions in my life that I cannot solve or overcome, when I am truly lost in the wilderness of my failures and insufficiencies—that I become the object of God's search and may hear the divine call of the Good Shepherd and be restored once more to His loving care. It is then that He delivers and heals, forgives and empowers, and draws me into the experience of joy and health and strength and courage that puts point and purpose back into my life and living.

I have been found. I have been drawn back into God's will and purpose for my life. It is a place of refuge in a tempestuous world. But my Lord is still out in that world, seeking those who are lost, the creatures for whom He died and rose again, reaching out, touching, embracing, healing, loving, guiding men and women and children back into His loving will for their lives. And there is where I must be—alongside my brothers and sisters—as the vehicle and instrument through which Christ's Spirit may find others who are lost, in order to touch them with His love and grace and restore them to His order and purposes.

I thank You for finding me, my great Shepherd. And thank You for making me Your servant in seeking out others who are still lost to You and Your purposes for their lives. Amen.

The Law versus the Gospel

Christ Jesus came into the world to save sinners. v. 15b

Though it may never have been intended as such, this lesson is a remarkable sequel to yesterday's Gospel portion. Paul certainly considered himself as one of those who was lost, and this even though he faithfully lived by the Law he once subscribed to, and vigorously attempted to stamp out the followers of the Christ who proclaimed Him as the way of salvation. Paul's amazing conversion experience qualified him to say "that Christ Jesus came into the world to save sinners," and he was quite sure that he was the "foremost of sinners."

Our salvation does not come, nor is our relationship to God assured, by our subscription to particular rules and orders, be they traditional or contemporary, that are being peddled as Gospel today. We are saved by faith—by our total acceptance of what Christ has done on our behalf, with a resulting commitment to God and His will for our lives. In a society where crime and corruption, family breakdowns, sexual promiscuity, and disregard for human life are on the rise, in a nation where much-relied-on structures are crumbling, it is indeed tempting to correlate laws and rules and orders with the Gospel of love and freedom that was proclaimed and demonstrated by Jesus Christ. We need to be guided, and sometimes inhibited, by laws and rules. It is when we make them a part of the Gospel we proclaim and live by that we endanger our faith and promote a system of beliefs that may corrupt the faith of others.

We thank You, our Lord, as did Your servant Paul, that we, whatever our past sins and errors, have been restored to Your mercy and are counted worthy in and through Christ to be Your children and servants. Amen.

The Greatest Miracle of All

Fear not . . . God meant it for good. v. 20

"You meant evil against me; but God meant it for good." I wonder if Paul had Joseph's experience in mind when he wrote, "We know that in everything God works for good with those who love Him, who are called according to His purpose" (Romans 8:28). The greatest miracle of all, in my estimation, is not that God somehow engineers or manipulates our circumstances, but that He is with us through them and in them and can miraculously bring them about or turn and use them to accomplish His purposes in and through us.

To believe that God programs us like some kind of computer, that the tragic happenings in our lives are instigated by Him in order to keep us in line or to mature and equip us for His service, is to reduce the miracle-working power of God and regard Him as a puppeteer of sorts. He thrust us into our chaotic, sin-ridden world and, allowing for some remarkable exceptions, permits us to deal with its gifts of joy, but also its hours of horror and pain without some supernatural intervention to shield us from its potential ugliness and misery. The miracle is that His children are never without His loving presence or His gifts of strength and courage, which enable them to face whatever befalls them. If we cling to Him, He will bring beauty out of ashes and springs of water out of parched sands—in His own good time and in response to our faith in Him and His promises.

This is what He did in the life of Joseph, miraculously using him as a vehicle of blessing to the people of Israel. It is this sort of thing that He has done and will do in our lives.

"Jesus, Savior, pilot me over life's tempestuous sea; unknown waves before me roll, hiding rock and treacherous shoal; chart and compass come from Thee, Jesus, Savior, pilot me." Amen.

Idle Hands

You go into the vineyard too. v. 7b

"Why do you stand here idle all day?" Why is it that so many who claim the experience and title of Christian are not carrying out their ministry as the servants and priests of God? They have the calling and the assignment. They are the recipients of God's grace and power through His Spirit. They have a field of service, a parish or arena in which to proclaim Christ through word and to demonstrate and transmit His love through word and deed. "Why do you stand here idle . . .?"

Maybe we need to understand again just what Christianity is. It is not a mere philosophy, a conglomeration of virtues, a system of ethics, but a radical, revolutionary experience. It is not confined to having our sins forgiven, or a guarantee of heaven and eternal life, as basic and necessary and glorious as all this is. It is a losing of our lives that we may find them, a denying of self and taking up the cross and following Christ, a pledging of loyalty and unhesitating obedience to Christ as King and Lord and Commander-in-Chief, a following of that One who commands us to "go into all the world . . . preach . . . bear fruit . . . love . . ." It means that, by virtue of our redemption, we become debtors to every human being on the face of the earth until they, too, are brought into the redemption of Christ.

Martin Buber once said: "He who ceases to make a response ceases to hear the Word." Is Jesus real to us, or is He just a fad, a crying-post, a pious notion? If He is real to us, we will head for the vineyard to work for Him.

I am grateful, my loving God, for my arena of service, for a place to put my feet, for burdens to carry and lives to touch, for a vineyard in which to serve. Amen.

Alive and Serving

Let your manner of life be worthy of the gospel of Christ. v. 27

It is truly amazing, and it should be encouraging to all of us, the way God is able to turn the unhappy things that befall us, even our foolish errors and failures, into stepping-stones toward the accomplishment of His purposes in our world. We have much to celebrate. God has not given up on our world. He is here—and sometimes because of us, sometimes in spite of us, He is working out His purposes in our world.

Our greatest concern should be that we may fail to give God our all, and to risk our all, so that His purposes may be accomplished through us. This means that we should be willing to put our lives on the line, to live and, if need be, to die in order to fulfill our commission as God's children and servants. We have nothing to lose and nothing to be afraid of. It is not surprising that we cling so tenaciously to this life. It is all that our natural senses can comprehend. Nevertheless, if we knew what God has in store for us, we would have no fear whatsoever of death and whatever may follow death. We would probably be most eager to leave this vale of tears for the indescribable glories of life eternal.

We are, however, here in the valley and under divine orders. Let us be alive and courageous and joyful and obedient as we faithfully carry out God's commission to us.

Grant me, O Lord, the will and the courage, not only to listen to Your Word as revealed through Christ, but to risk all in the blessed endeavor to put it to work in my arena of service and responsibility. Amen.

The Secret of Greatness

If any one would be first, he must be last of all and servant of all.
v. 35

Still thinking of the new kingdom that they visualized, and still assuming that their Master was about to launch a new and all-powerful kingdom with the people of Israel, the disciples conjectured among themselves about who might be the greatest and the most honored among them in the new kingdom Jesus was about to establish. We are perfectly capable of understanding and identifying with the disciples in this instance because we are very much like them. The difference between our world-order and God's order is that our ambitions in terms of this world are usually for being number one or being superior to others in some aspect of life. This concept is as American as motherhood or apple pie. It is encouraged in our educational programs, our sports and athletic extravaganzas, in politics, the business world, the entertainment world, the arts. Competition and winning are the name of the game. It has almost become the primary religion of our lives.

Jesus knew what the disciples were thinking—and what we are inclined to feel. He took His disciples aside and said to them and to us, "If any one would be first, he must be last of all and servant of all." This is the secret of greatness in the new order that Jesus came to establish. It happens when we learn how to be servants. We are not here to lead or dominate or simply serve our private interests, but to serve—in our community, in our world—by taking sides with the poor and oppressed against this world's forces that ignore them or seek to manipulate them, by responding to their desperate needs. Those needs are primarily spiritual in terms of hearing and responding to God's Word. They are also physical and temporal—their needs for freedom and justice and daily sustenance.

As with Jesus, so with us, this kind of servanthood involves a cross. And this is the secret of greatness.

I come to You, my Lord, by way of Your cross. Now grant to me the grace to take up the cross on behalf of others on our journey amid this bleak wilderness. Amen.

The War within Us

Is it not your passions that are at war in your members? v. 1

There is a war of sorts being waged within us which, if not adequately handled, is capable of creating a war around us. It is initiated by the ever-present inner urge for self-gratification and glorification. There seems always to be something on the inside that rebels against and even attempts to dethrone the God who created us and claims us for Himself. It began with Adam; it continues within each of us.

More often than not, we yield to those self-serving instincts and desires and thereby crowd the Spirit of God into some small corner of our lives wherein His influence and control upon us and through us is severely limited. The evil force within us, when unleashed, is capable of turning us into the very enemies of God—of rupturing our faith and drawing us back into darkness again.

We cannot totally escape the siren calls of the natural man and woman, and we shall fall prey to those destructive powers if we do battle on their own ground. We can, however, resist these urges and instincts, and resist them successfully, if we do so with the grace that God grants His children. He grants this grace to those of us who submit to His loving intervention in our lives and who give Him permission to conquer, control, and remold our passions into vessels for His daily use.

It is a day-by-day, week-by-week battle, but it is one that Christ has won—and will win for us if we remain faithful to Him.

You know my conflicts, O God, and how fierce, vicious, unabated they sometimes are. You know how incapable I am of fighting my battles alone. Grant me the grace to endure, to mature, and to manifest loving concern for my brothers and sisters along our journey of faith. Amen.

Accumulators or Stewards?

No servant can serve two masters . . . you cannot serve God and mammon. v. 13

Christ in this parable relates how some people who are not of His kingdom make use of wealth in ways that secure their existence upon this world. They see to it that some of their material riches are used for the welfare of others. They are wiser, in their own way, than many of those who claim to follow Jesus.

One does not enter God's kingdom by generously sharing gifts with others—though a person may thereby benefit by the love and devotion of those whom he or she serves. No one can come to the Father except through Christ. However, all who come unto Him and become a part of His kingdom will accept their calling as stewards of God's great gifts and utilize them to bring light and joy into the lives of God's creatures about them. They will find their greatest joy in serving others, because in serving them they are truly serving God.

What we have acquired and accumulated is not ours; all the good things that have come our way have come from the hand of the Father. While we readily assume they are given to enrich our lives here upon earth, they are also granted for the purpose of enriching and blessing the lives of others. When, however, we make God's gifts the object of our loyalty and devotion, they take His place in our lives and become a curse rather than a blessing and may render us ineligible for that life and kingdom which He has prepared for us. In that event, we are, in the midst of our grand accumulations, truly and eternally poverty-stricken.

All that I am and have is Yours, my Lord. I pray that, by the daily gift of Your grace, I may overcome my self-centeredness and give of myself and my possessions to the needs of my brothers and sisters about me. Amen.

Let Us Pray

I desire that in every place [we] should pray . . . v. 8

Salvation does not come to us by way of the Law or by our participation in religious exercises, but our acceptance of God's forgiving and redeeming love does place upon us certain responsibilities. We are to live through loving, and that requires that we be nonviolent, peaceful, kind, humble, nonjudgmental, caring, fair-minded, self-giving, and persistent seekers for equality and dignity, freedom and opportunity, for everyone. This may well begin with prayers to God on behalf of every human being—from leaders and executives in high places to the laborer, the poor, the uneducated, the oppressed.

We are most certainly enjoined to pray for these people. Then we must get off our knees and do whatever we possibly can, by the grace that God grants, to become His means of answering our own prayers on behalf of these people. We need to select leaders who will fulfill the requirements of just leadership. We are to support them in these endeavors, and to do everything possible to feed the hungry and house the homeless and assure equality and dignity, freedom and opportunity, for all.

God knows far better than we the needs of every human being. While our prayers for others offer no new information to Him, they may prepare us to be the vehicles through which He can meet people's needs with His loving grace.

My Lord and God, may my responsibilities to You and Your human creatures be manifest and carried out, not only in many prayers, but in genuine acts of concern and compassion for those I meet along my journey of faith. Amen.

Time to Think

Hear this, you who trample upon the needy. v. 4a

The prophet Amos compared the Lord's speaking to the roar of a lion (1:2, 3:8). Is it possible that this lion has been domesticated for most of us—even those of us who are in the church? In this Old Testament lesson Amos rails against his people "who trample upon the needy and bring the poor of the land to an end" in their efforts to make the best deals they can in buying and selling and the securing of their own futures. Is it possible that the Lord through Amos may be roaring against us?

Most of us are comparatively rich in view of this world's masses that struggle so desperately for survival. So often we refuse to accept responsibility for helping them in their plight. We assume that we deserve our good fortune, and we overindulge in food and drink and luxurious living as if we were the favored children of God. Apart from occasional "hunger offerings," we busy ourselves with our small problems and all but ignore the multitudes who are starving to death.

While we have no immediate answers to the problem of the poor and oppressed, we are responsible for doing our best to relieve the conditions that make and keep people poor. Amos said what he certainly had a right to say, and his words may upset our day, but it is time that we and our churches take note of his political analysis and contemplate what we can do about world poverty. How can we remain Christians without relating to the prophet's and our Lord's concern for the oppressed people of our world?

It is something to think about. It may result in our seeking for ways to do something about it.

Help us, our Lord, to sense something of Your agonizing concern for Your suffering children, and grant to us the compassion and the wisdom to reach out to those whom we can help. Amen.

From Prattle to Practice

He answered, "I will not"; but afterward he repented and went.
v. 29

As we worship in our churches today, we utter very precious words. Through our singing and praying, confessions and creeds, we proclaim penitence and belief and pledge love and loyalty to our eternal God. Some of the most precious and significant words of the Bible are words of pledge and promise from the lips of those who committed their lives to God and Christ. "As for me and my house, we will serve the Lord," promised Joshua (24:15). "Deliver me from blood-guiltiness, O God . . . and my tongue will sing aloud of Thy deliverance," wrote the psalmist (51:14). "Here am I! Send me," exclaimed Isaiah (6:8). "I will follow You wherever You go," said an enthusiastic young man to Jesus (Luke 9:57). "I will lay down my life for You," proclaimed Peter (John 13:37).

The fact of the matter is, however, that words alone do not constitute a commitment, and there is a distinct precariousness in making such verbal commitments. We know this well by our innumerable failures to follow through on our commitments— failures to translate them into obedient activity in our everyday living.

Nor did Peter follow through on his heroic commitment, but after Christ's resurrection He was restored to a loving and obedient relationship to Jesus Christ. Perhaps this is the lesson of this Gospel portion today. Not only is it precarious to make verbal commitments, and they should not be made unless we are truly sincere, but there is the privilege of repentance and restoration when we fail to follow through. Even when we renege on our promises to follow Christ, He never ceases to reach out to us, seeking ever to restore us to a loving and obedient relationship with Himself.

O Lord, may our worship today and every day, include the restoration and recommittal of our lives to You and Your purposes. Amen.

Living for Others

Though He was in the form of God . . . [He] emptied Himself, taking the form of a servant, being born in the likeness of men. v. 6

There is a way to test the authenticity of our relationship with God. It is by examining our relationships to our fellow beings. When we are short on compassion and concern for our brothers and sisters, it is probably because we haven't fully grasped or experienced God's infinite love for us. God is not holding back; His love is available. And so is His great wealth and power and all the other gifts needed to enrich our lives. They are, however, gifts that must be shared with others lest they turn to ashes in our hands.

There are, unfortunately, ambitious Christians who are more concerned about their own image than the needs of their fellow persons. They attempt to corral their God-given gifts for their own egocentric purposes. This was not true about Jesus Christ. Even though He was filled with the power of God, He never used it for His own glory or gratification. He became the servant of the very beings whom He and His Father created, using His divine power only to heal their hurts and free their spirits and reveal to them their rich inheritance as the children of God. As God-incarnate, Christ walked as man upon this earth—even through the experiences of torture and death—that He might touch human creatures with the love of their Father in heaven.

Now we are assigned to be Christs-incarnate—proclaiming, demonstrating, and communicating God's healing, reconciling love to one another and to His wandering, lonely, lost children around us. As Jesus "[took] the form of a servant," so we are to become the servants of God to people about us in order that "every tongue confess that Jesus Christ is Lord, to the glory of God the Father."

Loving Christ, You identified with me in my sins and sicknesses and commissioned me to share Your servanthood with my brothers and sisters on this planet. Help me to fulfill my servanthood in communicating Your love and grace to them. Amen.

Confession or Camouflage?

Have salt in yourselves, and be at peace with one another. v. 50

Our Lord's words are radical. He invites us to take a radical stance, to make a radical decision, the grand event of becoming His disciples. What He may be saying is that the business of following Him involves some pain. He first talks about the pain of amputation, the removal of hand or foot or eye, and is suggesting that life itself is more important than the individual members of the body. He is talking about the power of sin and death through invisible and spiritual appendages at work within us, and the necessity of removing these appendages, of suffering the pain of being separated from them and all that stands between us and God's will for our lives. Confession is very painful for a proud person, for this means the stripping away of the camouflage, the hypocrisy, the self-will that blocks God out of a person's life. It is spiritual surgery; it is radical surgery.

While our Lord's first illustration has to do with radical surgery, His second is medicinal and has to do with salt. The first has to do with the radical and sometimes painful separation of ourselves from those things that stand between us and God and are capable of destroying our relationship with Him. The "salt" illustration (salt=the Word) refers to the perpetual pain or discomfort of growing and maturing as God's children. However much it hurts when it is rubbed into fresh wounds, it is good, said Jesus. It helps to subdue and control the fire that rages within us. It sometimes burns like hell, but the burning is not forever, and it will help to keep us from going to hell, where the "worm does not die, and the fire is not quenched."

Suffer the amputations that are necessary! Let the salt do its work! It will render us wholesome and happy as the sons and daughters, servants and ministers of God.

Let it happen to me, my Lord. I truly desire to be what You want me to be. Amen.

Lest We Throw Stones at Others

Do not speak evil against one another. v. 11a

Sometimes we feel like nagging. Most often it takes the form of slicing, deprecating jibes, belittling, unappreciative attitudes toward other people's characters and contributions. What is so disconcerting is that it is usually not the incompetence of our victims that makes us critical toward them. It is often some disturbance or distortion within ourselves. It is a kind of projected form of self-deprecation. Because we feel small, inferior, invalid, inadequate, we find ourselves hacking away at somebody else until he or she is demoted to our assumed dimensions.

"Let him who is without sin among you be the first to throw a stone at her," said Jesus concerning a woman who was caught in a sinful act (John 8:7). When we recognize our own inner weaknesses, we are less likely to judge one another or to say things that may harm another person. Acknowledging our own humanity, we will not be so apt to play God with our own lives or toy with the emotions and affections of another.

God grant that we be truly human, acknowledging our frailties and failures, and yet authentic in our persistent search for and acceptance of God's control of our lives and destinies. May God's love and mercy for us cause us to drop our stones and be loving and merciful and tolerant in our attitudes toward others.

O Lord, whereas I need to be critical in respect to my attitudes and actions, enable me to be generous and kind in my consideration of and response to my fellow persons. Amen.

Get the Hell Out

If they do not hear Moses and the prophets, neither will they be convinced if some one should rise from the dead. v. 31

When the American Version of the Bible appeared over a century ago, a man came into an English book shop and asked for a copy of the "new Bible without any hell in it." The attitude expressed thereby has been characteristic of many people throughout the history of Christianity who are trying "to get the hell out" of theology and Christian teachings. Hell is indeed a repugnant doctrine—if one dare call it a doctrine. The fact that it does exist, however, is obvious all about us. Those who would like to "get the hell out" of the teachings of Christianity probably have little idea of the enormous price God has already paid to remove the fact of hell when He through Jesus Christ became man and died by torture in order to break the hold of sin and its consequences upon His creatures. Herein is the problem—and the tragedy: there is so much mercy, and still there is hell.

The good news of the Gospel is that there is deliverance from the hell that afflicts people today. It begins with the acknowledgment of sin, failures, mistakes in our lives. Having recognized with sorrow and confession our personal involvement in the hellish conditions that exist within and about us, we need no longer to brood over past errors but rather to accept God's acceptance of us as we are and to commit ourselves to His reign and control of our lives. This means that we must dedicate ourselves to God's purposes as well, to be Christs-incarnate, channels and communicators of God's love and power into the hell that exists around us.

All who trust in Christ as their Savior can eliminate forever any fear of hell in that glorious life eternal that Jesus guarantees through His death and resurrection on behalf of all God's creatures.

Grant to me, my God, the wisdom and the courage to confront the hellish conditions that exist about me with the good news of eternal life and joy that comes through Jesus Christ. Amen.

The Abrasive Truth

They shall now be the first of those to go into exile . . . v. 7a

"Woe to those who are at ease . . . who feel secure . . ." Our day begins (or ends) on a woe-filled note. There is much in Scripture that is not comfortable or comfort-giving. We would like to relegate the "woes" of Amos to the Old Testament, where we think they should stay. After all, the life of a Christian ought to be a life of peace and joy, and one needs a little of both after a day on the front lines of life's daily battle.

But do we dare, as concerned and conscientious Christians, to "rest easily," to be smugly secure in our kind of world? Unless we shut our eyes and clap our hands to our ears, or crawl into some dark cave to shut out the ugly sights and abrasive sounds of this world's suffering people, it is just about impossible to be at ease or to feel secure.

If we are to be healthy, maturing Christians, we will have to learn how to live in tension. It is an ongoing, never-ending tension between the peace and joy and comfort of a sin-forgiven, life-giving relationship with God through Christ and our tremendous, often frightening responsibility as His children and servants in our kind of world. For some Christians this has meant imprisonment; others have faced torture and death. We are all being challenged to change our affluent life-style in order to feed and house the millions who are hungry and unsheltered. How can any of us really be "at ease" or "feel secure" if we are awake and loving enough to be humane and Christian in this global village we call our world?

Maybe tomorrow's meditation will be more comfort-giving. For today, however, let us painfully consider the "woes" of Amos and muse on what they ought to mean to us.

Open our eyes and ears, O Lord, to the horrendous suffering that exists all about us, and open our hearts to those who cry out for help. Amen.

We Are Involved

He lent out the vineyard to other tenants who will give him the fruits in their season. v. 41b

Jesus had various reasons for doing so much of His teaching by way of parables. In some instances it was to hide the true meaning from those who were immature and undiscerning. He must have had the latter in mind when He told this parable. It was during His last week upon this earth. The ever-increasing hostility of the religious authorities was about to culminate in His execution. Our Lord, in very picturesque language, levels with His disciples, and there is little doubt that some of them understood full well His meaning.

The parable points up the responsibility of our nation and our church before our Creator and God. Our greatest concern, however, is what He may be saying about us as individuals about our responsibility as His avowed followers. As the householder of the parable sent his son into the vineyard, so Christ is in our midst. And His presence demands a response. We are not as neglectful as were the tenants of this parable; we sing hymns, spell out our creeds, make the the elaborate motions of worship, and are respectfully aware of altar and cross. But what does Jesus find in our hearts? He does not find the hatred of the parable-tenants, but He might find something just as insidious—preoccupation, procrastination, neglect to fully embrace Christ and His life-style, unwillingness to give Him prior devotion or to dedicate our lives to working within His vineyard and living out His purposes in our day-by-day activities because of the discomfort or inconvenience or personal sacrifice this may entail.

I pray, O Lord, that You will break through the dominion of sin and self-centeredness in my life and make me a vineyard that will yield fruit to Your glory and toward the salvation of others. Amen.

Let Us Press On

I press on toward the goal for the prize of the upward call of God in Christ Jesus. v. 12b

Jesus Christ is sufficient—and so is the righteousness He imparts to us. We don't earn or merit or gain it by following certain rules or rituals; we receive it as the gift of God's love. We possess this righteousness even now by faith in Christ Jesus. We have no need for any other.

This by no means indicates that we have arrived—that we have already reached a state of perfection. We do indeed belong to God; we are His possession. And yet we struggle constantly to surrender our beings to Him and let Him have His way with us. This does not come easily. It involves the crucible of conflict—even failure and defeat. But even when we fall, we fall only to rise again. Acknowledging but never nursing our failures, we claim God's gracious forgiveness and press on, knowing that our loving God understands and perpetually reaches out to draw us to Himself.

Even while we are God's sons and daughters, we are in the process of becoming. Our sanctification is not yet completed, and it won't be until we break through this mortal shell to become perfectly and eternally united with God. In the meantime our citizenship is in God's kingdom, and we are here to advance that kingdom throughout our sorry world.

I thank You, my Lord, that even though the journey before me is fraught with darkness and danger, I need not be afraid, for You are with me and will grant me the courage and strength to press on. Amen.

What a Savior We Have!

We see Jesus . . . who was made lower than the angels . . . so that
by the grace of God He might taste death for every one. v. 9

God, through Jesus Christ, has come to us—assuming a status
and a position that was inferior to the very angels that were His
subordinates—becoming mortal, taking upon Himself our very
nature, being born of a human mother, dying at the hands of His
own creatures, all in order that we might live forever as His sons
and daughters. And He continues to dwell with us—through His
Spirit who inhabits our lives, reveals His purposes, and provides His
grace for joyful and meaningful living and serving.

What a Savior we have! We are no longer strangers to God,
aliens to His love and holiness, traitors to His purposes. Jesus
actually became, in spiritual terms, our Brother. He participated in
our humanity in order that we might become God's children. He
identified with our sufferings, shared in our weaknesses, and called
us His brothers and sisters.

We can't fathom this amazing truth; but we can become, with
Christ, God's sons and daughters by becoming identified with this
Christ and His revelations of the Father. Through Christ we now
have the same Father; with Christ we become His beloved children.
It happens the very moment we by faith, claim and lay hold of and
submit to what God through Christ has done on our behalf.

O Christ, You are indeed so full of wonder and splendor!
You have called me Your brother and redeemed and reconciled me to Your heavenly Father. You have assigned to
me the fantastic responsibility of carrying on Your purposes
in this world. What a Savior You are, my Lord! Amen.

Can I Forgive Others?

Take heed to yourselves; if your brother sins . . . forgive him. v. 3a

Can I forgive others? a spouse who cannot respond to some of my childish needs? a son who shuns the moral values in which he and I have been brought up? a friend who turns his back when I need him? a husband who leaves his family without any support? a reckless driver who runs down a child? What about infidelity, addiction, cruelty? Can I—should I—forgive the perpetrators of such atrocities?

I can, and according to the words of our Lord, I must. This is what Jesus did and what He commanded His disciples in His earthly ministry. His love-your-enemy, do-not-resist, turn-the-other-cheek, go-the-second-mile style of life appears to be rather impractical, if not a little ridiculous, in our kind of world. It was His style of life, nonetheless, and His injunction to those whom He invited to follow Him.

This does not mean that we are to condone the failures and distortions of others any more than we are expected to condone our own. We may have to tolerate the weaknesses that others have not yet learned to transform into strength, or the liabilities they have not yet turned into assets. We need, for our sakes and theirs, to love them as valid, significant, worthwhile people even in the midst of their faults and failures.

Not only must we forgive others; our forgiveness must be genuine. True forgiveness is not a degrading or demoting of the people to whom we are to relate. We are to accept them as our equals, our brothers and sisters in Christ. We can, with God's enabling grace, forgive others—and we must.

You have accepted me as a sinner, O God, and You have forgiven me. Now, as Your child and servant, enable me to lovingly accept my fellow beings irrespective of their failures and faults. Amen.

Lest We Be Ashamed

Do not be ashamed then of testifying to our Lord. v. 8a

Some of us, in our timidity or our foolish feelings of inadequacy, almost give the appearance of being ashamed of our faith. Perhaps we are threatened by today's intellectuals or frightened by the hypotheses of our scientists or the theories of humanists and agnostics that appear to contradict the blessed truths of God's Word as we have been taught and have experienced them. We may have earned the scorn of secular scholars by our childish clutch upon the traditional symbols or the ancient explanations of our faith, but our belief in the one true God as revealed by Jesus Christ is something of which we never need to be ashamed.

God is our Creator, our Redeemer, and the Source of all the grace and power we need to live happy, contributive lives. We can proclaim and demonstrate the grace and power of this great God by claiming our freedom from the fears and anxieties, the temporal and materialistic bondages of this world, to love and serve our fellow beings in joy. We know, not by the fallible tests and explorations of scientists but by personal experience, that we are the sons and daughters of God and that we have been commissioned to be the ministers of His saving love to all who will listen and respond.

We have, in Christ, the answer to the aches and needs of people in our world. Let us proclaim and communicate it with boldness.

Though there have been and will continue to be things in my life of which I am ashamed, I claim Your forgiveness and pray for the courage to joyfully proclaim Your life and salvation, my Lord. Amen.

Learning How to Wait

O Lord, how long shall I cry for help? v. 2a

"If it seems slow, wait for it . . ."

"I waited patiently for the Lord; He inclined to me and heard my cry" (Psalm 40:1).

The Israelites waited thousands of years for the kingdom that God through His prophets promised them. Not recognizing the revealing of that kingdom in the Messiah, Jesus Christ, many of them are still waiting. Christians have been waiting for the last two thousand years for Christ's second coming to fully reveal God's kingdom among the inhabitants of this planet—and they are still waiting, expecting that great Day to break in upon us at every turn in the road. We are learning that "faith is the assurance of things hoped for, the conviction of things not seen" (Hebrews 11:1).

The waiting goes on. Men and women have visions, real or imaginary, and because they are slow in becoming realities, they "wait for it" or abandon it. We become impatient in waiting for the visible return of Jesus to draw together God's eternal kingdom and enthrone Himself as King, so impatient that some of us are conned into latching on to the date-setting antics of self-styled prophets.

Unfortunately, most of us haven't learned how to wait gracefully. The life of faith is, in essence, a life of waiting and hoping, reaching out for the fulfillment that will not be completed or consummated until we leave this dimension to be totally and eternally with God.

We are enjoined to wait patiently. It is also possible to wait joyfully, to take each day as a gift from God and to serve Him by serving others about us—even while we wait for the response of God to some great need, some future direction for our lives, or the final revelation of His kingdom.

Our Lord and Savior, while we joyfully anticipate Your return to assume Your kingship over this planet, bless our endeavors to proclaim and manifest Your saving grace to those who still do not belong to Your kingdom. Amen.

Come to God's Party

Go therefore to the thoroughfares, and invite . . . as many as you find. v. 9

Only those who accept the invitation will enjoy the party. There is no limit to the number who are invited to this ongoing event—the experience of eternal joy that God has prepared. Nor are there qualifications or standards to measure up to in order to attend. There is, however, no room for procrastinators.

It appears that most of the invitees are apparently involved in parties of their own. Or they are so busy about mundane matters that they have no time to embrace and celebrate the love and joy of God. They make all sorts of excuses: a family to rear, a paycheck to earn, a prize to win, a goal to attain, a life to live—even some religious exercise to perform. God's party can wait until some more convenient time, or after the other parties have proven dull and unsatisfying. God is indeed patient, but the opportunities to come to Him are not unlimited. And there are others who will respond to His invitation; they are the ones He will seek out and receive to Himself. They shall feast at God's banquet table forever.

We are invited. There is one requirement that must be met. Not only must we truly desire to come, we must come as we are—with no strings attached. It is not a costume ball. It is a celebration, a recognition of who we are and what we have become by the grace of God. Those who come under the disguise of their personal merits will find little joy at God's party. They will have little to celebrate, for they are incapable of receiving what the Host so graciously offers.

We have accepted the invitation. Let us rejoice! This is God's party.

I have accepted Your invitation, my loving Host. I will celebrate for all eternity Your gift of righteousness. I will give thanks unto You, for Your love endures forever. Amen.

Let Us Be Happy

Rejoice in the Lord always; again I will say, rejoice. v. 4

Let us be happy. It is not expected that we be constantly ecstatic or continually exuberent, but happy, full of joy, that deep-down inner contentment that persists even in the midst of trials and tribulations and difficult circumstances. As the very children of God, we really don't have a thing to worry about. Whatever our real needs, we know that God will fulfill them in His own time and in accordance with His will. We can well afford to celebrate, to live in thankfulness, and to allow the incomprehensible peace of God to mend the frayed edges of our troubled lives and make us serene and secure in our relationship to God.

Whether we are rich or poor, in the valley or on the mount, whether there be sorrow or pain, conflict or defeat, this need not threaten our relationship with God. It may not be easy, but worthy of every effort to cast out the troublesome demons that assail us. We don't have to allow these things to come between us and God. We belong to Him, and if we think and act as if we really belong to Him, nothing will alter that glorious relationship. We are His forever, and we can celebrate forever our adoption and our identity as His sons and daughters. He will provide us with the strength and courage that we need to confront and overcome anything that comes our way.

Embrace God's love anew today—and be happy!

I do praise You, O God. As long as I have breath in my body, I will praise You. You are the ultimate fulfillment of my deep-est longings and the focal point of all my joys. Grant that my life be a perpetual offering of thanksgiving and praise. Amen.

God's Cure for One Man's Sickness

For all things are possible with God. v. 27

The man in question was well-heeled, but in need of inner *healing.* He had kept all the rules of his religion, but there was a serious malady in his life that he couldn't account for. It is identical to that which all men and women carry about until they allow Christ to have His way within them. This rich young fellow was at least wise enough to recognize it and to question Jesus about it.

First came the diagnosis: "You lack one thing," said Jesus. It is the diagnosis that our Lord would write upon every heart that does not harbor Him today. It is the sickness of our society and our world. "You have been weighed in the balances and found wanting," or lacking, said Daniel (5:27) to Belshazzar in interpreting the handwriting on the wall. It is this lack, this spiritual illness, that separates a person from his or her Creator and Redeemer regardless of that person's physical health or material worth.

Then came the prescription: "Go, sell what you have, and give to the poor, and you will have treasure in heaven; and come, follow Me." In this instance, at least, Jesus did not tell him to "believe" or "receive" Him, but came out with a fantastic statement that demanded a drastic alteration in the life of this man. It is a very disturbing statement to us as well, one we cannot accept without dramatically altering our lives. Our Lord's words, nevertheless, are plain, and we ignore them at our peril. While we refuse to take them literally—as a necessary prerequisite for salvation—we may need to take them seriously as some sort of diagnosis and prescription for our inner sicknesses. The wealth of this individual who had come to Jesus for the cure to his inner sickness was the very thing that stood in the way of a cure, "and he went away sorrowful."

It is something worth thinking about.

If there is anything that stands in the way of You and Your purposes in my life, O Lord, enable me to see it and surrender it. Amen.

310

The Household of God

We are His house if we hold fast our confidence and pride in our hope. v. 6b

Jesus is truly our Brother, but He is much more. Whereas we love and share as siblings in God's household, we glorify our Brother Jesus as God's beloved Son, our Redeemer and Lord, as one with God in the very creation of our universe, and as far more important to us than any gifted teacher or eloquent preacher of this or any other century. Therefore when we hear His voice, as we have heard and hope to continue hearing it, we had better take notice. Our salvation is dependent upon a true faith in what Christ has done on our behalf, the kind of faith that expresses itself not only in vocal expression but also in loving obedience to His proclamations and commands.

We know what happened to our forebears who deliberately or carelessly fell short of God's commandments and standards. God speaks to us through Jesus Christ and His ever-present Spirit in our lives. It is quite possible that we, too, may fail to hear His Word or may foolishly ignore His will for our lives. Our relationship with God, our inclusion in His household, is effected and sustained by faith. That faith is demonstrated in our ever-deepening commitment to God and His purposes.

It is very difficult to go solo in respect to our daily relationship with God. Not only do we continue to rely on God's grace, we need each other's help, and we need to love, share, learn together, rejoice together, and support one another in our walk with God.

O God, we who are Your sons and daughters, and brothers and sisters with Your beloved Son, pray that You will strengthen our faith and our love for one another that we may journey together in joy. Amen.

The Necessity of Gratitude

And he fell on his face at Jesus' feet, giving Him thanks. v. 16

Concerning ungodly people, Paul once wrote: "For although they knew God they did not honor Him as God or give thanks to Him." And then he added, "they became futile in their thinking and their senseless minds were darkened" (Romans 1:21).

What about genuine gratitude? In the first place, it must be *prefaced with penitence.* Someone once prayed: "Forgive us, our great God, for giving nothing more than surpluses toward the fulfillment of human need and accomplishment of divine purposes." Giving that is "left-over" giving may mark us as decent, civilized human beings, but there is hardly anything Christian or commendable about this kind of giving or sharing.

Second, our gratitude must be *manifested by faith.* Gratitude is, in essence, the confidence that, whatever may come our way, God is lovingly and perpetually present. To be grateful, to give thanks, in spite of or in the midst of the tragic things that befall us, is to manifest the healthy conviction that God can bring beauty out of ashes and transform even the very elements designed for our destruction into the agents of our salvation.

Third, our gratitude must be *expressed in worship.* It is recognizing God for what He is worth, seeing something of His splendor and glory, His love and grace, His rich provision for us in our needs.

Finally, it must be *demonstrated through love.* Having been made eternally rich through Christ, we are now enjoined to offer our sacrifices of gratitude on the altar of humanity's needs— particularly the needs of our fellow persons all about us.

O Lord, may my gratitude and thanksgiving be so genuine that it will result in the sharing of my life and means with my brothers and sisters about me. Amen.

Expect to Suffer

If we endure, we shall also reign with Him. v. 12a

Suffering is to be expected in the course of Christian living and ministering. It is, in fact, an integral part of any course of life in our world. Laborers, professional people, dedicated artists—all must endure times of suffering and hardship if they are truly dedicated to their respective callings. Even the ordinary but highly important task of rearing a family involves suffering. Is it so unusual or unthinkable that the ministers of God be expected to endure suffering as they serve among suffering people in a suffering world?

We are to be reminded of Jesus Christ and what He suffered on our behalf. We are also to remember His promise that, as we suffer and endure for His sake, we shall discover the joy of living, that out of the ashes of our suffering and dying comes the beauty of life everlasting. We have nothing to lose but everything to gain as we suffer in our walk with God and in our service to humanity. God will grant to us the grace to endure and even to grow and mature through our suffering.

We are engaged in the grandest vocation granted to God's creatures—that of serving Him through our loving service to our fellow creatures. It is worth everything we have to give to it. Even the sufferings, the conflicts, the crucible experiences that prepare us to be God's ministers of love, are worth enduring if they better equip us for His assignment for us. We need not pray that God remove our painful experiences, but that He transform them into cleansing fires that renew and refresh us for His purposes, and that we always remain faithful to Him.

I pray, O Lord, that Your Word speak to me, and Your promises reassure me, and Your Spirit grant me courage and hope that I may remain faithful to You in times of distress. Amen.

The Matter of Loyalties

Render therefore to Caesar the things that are Caesar's, and to God the things that are God's. v. 21

Men and women willingly or unwilling "render . . . to Caesar the things that are Caesar's." They toil and sweat, risk and sacrifice, to keep on good terms with the visible world about them. They make their primary investments in this brief earthbound interlude. It is hardly surprising that people encounter disorder and disharmony in their lives. They have their wires crossed; they are living in a wrong relationship with creation about them; they give their foremost allegiance to the wrong values and forces.

Jesus emphatically underscores the matter of our responsibility to another world, another loyalty: "Render . . . to God the things that are God's." He does not deny or ignore the existence of the physical and temporal world nor the dues humanity must pay to it. Jesus full well recognizes our humanness. He endured it; He understands it. But never does He for one minute lose sight of the eternal and ultimate world of the spiritual and the divine. And never does He cease to exhort His disciples as to the necessity of making this their primary and foremost loyalty.

We live in this world; there are certain dues we must render to it. If we are to find genuine meaning and purpose for our lives, however, our primary focus must be upon the eternal world which is ours through faith in Jesus Christ, the Savior sent by God the Father. As did the coin that bore the imprint of Caesar thus belong to Caesar, so every man, woman, and child created by God, redeemed through Jesus Christ, and infilled by the Holy Spirit bears in his or her very nature and upon his or her immortal soul the stamp of God's ownership. We owe our lives, and all that may include, first and foremost to God.

I am blessed and grateful, my God, that above all that is earthly and temporal is the glorious truth that You are my Creator and Redeemer, my Savior and King, forever. Amen.

For Those on the Front Lines

We give thanks to God always for you all. v. 2

We are grateful for the family of God, the followers of Christ who are laboring faithfully within His purposes. Our gratitude and concern are especially directed toward those who are on the front lines in positions of great risk to health and life. Many of them have endured torture and imprisonment as a consequence of their faith and arduous service. Some have joined the martyrs of ancient times in their efforts to advance the kingdom of God. Thousands of our colleagues are enduring suffering and material loss because they persist in proclaiming and witnessing to Christ in difficult places.

We are, of course, grateful for those who are quietly and profoundly pursuing God's objectives in places and in ways unknown to us. We applaud our brothers and sisters and pray that God will grant them much joy and fill them with His power as they faithfully witness in word and deed to people about them.

It is important that we commend one another, and that we encourage and support our co-laborers in whatever ways we can. The task is difficult, the road is rough at times. We all need the feeling of strong, undergirding arms to enable us to bear the burdens of our respective ministries.

May God grant to each of us the sensitivity to comprehend something of what others are going through, those known to us as well as those unknown, and the urgency to hold one another up before God in prayer.

Our gracious heavenly Father, we pray for Your great family throughout our world, especially those who live and work in difficult and dangerous places on this day before us. Amen.

How to Become Great

Whoever would be great among you must be your servant. v. 43

It is probable that most of us, at some time in our lives, aspire to greatness, or at least to some prominence or preeminence in life. It is this top-of-the-pile compulsion that dominates so many of the frenzied and bizarre activities that characterize our religious, social, entertainment, and political activities today.

The disciples of Jesus were no exception. They had listened to Jesus talk about the kingdom of God that was to come. It was probably out of love for the Christ that they made their request of Jesus. They were fond of their Lord and wanted to stay close to Him. It was also, in part, self-concern. They were looking for positions of prominence and responsibility in this new kingdom that was about to emerge. "Grant us," they requested of Jesus, "to sit, one at Your right hand and one at Your left, in Your glory."

Jesus didn't put them down, but He put them off for the time being. They would soon enough learn the price of greatness. Our Lord set before His disciples and before the world the example of true greatness in suffering for the sins of all humanity. "Though He was in the form of God . . . [He] emptied Himself, taking the form of a servant . . ., He humbled Himself and became obedient unto death . . . on a cross" (Philippians 2:6–8). It doesn't make any sense to the world, but in the eyes of God, this is how to become great. "Whoever would be great among you must be your servant," He said to His disciples. It is this that puts us all within the range of greatness. It is a call not to personal esteem or worldly acclaim, but to servanthood.

You and I are candidates for this kind of greatness.

My loving God, may the crucible of this life purge me of my lust for self-esteem and render me effective as Your child and servant. I need no longer to be a winner or to be king-of-the-hill; I need only Your grace to be what You want me to be. Amen.

Serenity in the Midst of Struggle

Let us then with confidence draw near to the throne of grace, that we may receive mercy and find grace to help in time of need.
v. 16

Those who, by faith, enter into the life and grace granted by God are introduced to a life of joy and peace and rest. They can cease their fruitless struggles to please or win the favor of their Creator and rest in what God through Christ has already done for them. There are other kinds of struggles and conflicts for the redeemed children of God, but they never need to grapple for God's love and grace, or wrestle with guilt feelings, or deliberate over doubts as to their status and identity as God's children.

They enter, as well, a whole new vocation for their lives, for while they rest in God's loving-kindness, they begin to labor in a new dimension as children and servants of God to introduce others to the life of eternal joy and rest that is available to them through Jesus Christ.

We need to renew, to charge our faith from time to time, to make sure we keep the faith, lest we regress in our relationship with God and fall once more into that fruitless struggle to exist apart from Him. Nevertheless, we have in our Lord, Jesus Christ, not only a Savior but a Keeper, a Guardian over our souls, One who knows well our failings and hang-ups, who understands the trials and conflicts that come our way, and who will grant us the grace to come through them unscathed. There will be wounds, even scars to remind us of those wounds, but victory is assured if we stay close to that One who is the dispenser of divine grace.

O God, the vacuum, the bitterness, the sorrow, and the pain sometimes flattens us in despair. We pray that You will fill the vaccum, resolve the bitterness, and enable us to endure the pain. Grant to us the serenity and peace of knowing that You are always with us. Amen.

Thoughts about Prayer

And will not God vindicate His elect, who cry to Him day and night?
v. 7

The privilege of prayer: Because Jesus Christ has entered through the veil into the Holy of Holies before us, we through faith have direct access to the very mercy seat of God. "Let us then with confidence draw near to the throne of grace," writes the author of the Letter to the Hebrews, "that we may receive mercy and find grace to help in time of need" (4:16).

The purpose of prayer: Prayer is not simply petition and repetition, feeling and sentiment; nor is it a sanctified form of begging, or convincing God of something He already knows and thereby compelling Him to some sort of action. It is primarily an act of devotion whereby Christians dedicate, submit, consecrate themselves to God and can be brought to the place where God through them can accomplish the very things for which they have prayed.

The power of prayer: It lies not in its particular method or exercise, nor in the number of hours spent in that exercise. It lies in God. To pray in power means to pray in faith, to pray Spirit-guided prayers.

The persistency of prayer: If an unjust judge, who has regard for neither God nor man, would yield to the persistency of an unknown widow because he was afraid that she would annoy him by her repetitious requests, how much more will a just and merciful God respond to and reward the persevering petitions of His own loved ones who cry to Him and relate to Him.

Let us pray . . .

Almighty and everlasting God, may our confessions and pe-titions, our intercessions and praises, whether or not we move our lips, be a continuous relationship to You on our day-by-day journey of faith. Amen.

Preach the Word—Be the Word

Be steady, endure suffering, do the work of an evangelist, fulfil your ministry. v. 5

"Preach the Word . . .," Paul exhorted Timothy.

"Go therefore and make disciples of all nations," Jesus commanded His disciples.

This is our commission and our responsibility as 20th century disciples of Jesus Christ. We are to preach, to verbalize, to proclaim. But we are to do more than that; we are to be the Word of God. In a very real sense, God is incarnate in us. His loving Spirit indwells us. We are not only channels or conduits of His life and salvation, of the saving, redeeming, liberating grace of God, we are preaching and communicating that which is a part of ourselves. We are to be the sacrament of the glorious message of salvation, broken bread and poured-out wine among the lost, lonely, broken, sin-bound inhabitants of this planet. Pentecost has made us the incarnation of what we preach. There are times when verbal proclamation is secondary; the first requirement is to be what God has empowered us to be—loving, concerned, caring, Spirit-filled servants of God. Then we may be inspired to verbalize what we are by God's grace and to make our words the living Word of God to heart-hungry people about us.

Most of the people we relate to have heard the words of the Gospel before. Some of us are especially called and trained to proclaim that Gospel—to put it into words that can be heard and understood. All of us are responsible for living that Word, fleshing out the proclaimed Word, and thereby communicating God's liberating grace to those around us.

Merciful God, You have come to me through Jesus Christ as He has been proclaimed and manifested through the proclaimed Word and the Word as demonstrated in the lives of Your children about me. I thank You, my God, for those who have brought the Word to me. Amen.

319

Wrestling with God

Your name shall no more be called Jacob, but Israel, for you have striven with God . . . and have prevailed. v. 28

"For I have seen God . . . and yet my life is preserved." It appears to be ridiculous—and of questionable value, but people have wrestled with God from the beginning of time. Most wrestle in rebellion, seeking (all too often successfully) to keep Him from occupying and controlling their lives. It may appear to be paradoxical, but one aspect of God's graciousness and loving-kindness is His willingness to wrestle with us. He refuses to step over the threshold of a person's rebel will. No one is forced to submit to the purposes of the Creator. Yet God continues to wrestle with His stubborn, recalcitrant creatures. Some of them will appear to win—only to lose forever their battle with God, nevermore to experience the love and joy of His blessed will and purposes for their lives. Only those who "lose" their battle with God, submitting to His will and purposes, discover the joy and beauty for which they were created.

Yet we continue to wrestle with God even as we grow in wisdom and understanding of who He is and what He proposes to do in and through us. Sometimes it has to do with guilt and doubt, at other times with our sin-stained will that continues to offer resistance to our Creator and Redeemer as long as we are shackled by the mortality of this existence. God will always, we pray and confidently hope, be the ultimate winner in these frequent conflicts that envelop us. We need to submit to that divine love that can overpower our self-centeredness and live victoriously in and through us. God does not deny us the wrestling of doubt, or guilt, or self-will. Even if it results in a painful limp, He willingly and lovingly draws us into submission to His blessed will and makes our feet strong again to carry out our commission as His beloved servants.

I give thanks to You, O Lord, for Your steadfast love endures forever! Amen.

What Do You Think of Christ?

What do you think of the Christ? v. 42a

We know what the Pharisees thought of Christ. We understand something of the disciples' early comprehension of their Master, the Lord Jesus. The question that Jesus put to the Pharisees is fully as pertinent today: "What do you think of the Christ?"

Some people look upon Him as a mere historic figure and profess no faith whatsoever in Him. There are others who regard Him and even worship Him as He was often presented in their past experiences, a sort of meek, mild, gentle, comforting, problem-solving Christ to whom they can turn when the road gets rough. There are those who see Him today as a radical, revolutionary figure who hacked at the establishment of His day and gave validity to the sinner and the slave, the poor and the outcast of society. Many in our generation attempt to find in Him a refuge or escape from all that afflicts our world today; others use Him strictly as a means for personal gain or pleasure. Then there are those, of course, who discover in Him and His teachings meaning for life and purpose for living.

God's Word and our doctrines based on that Word define Him as Son of God and Son of man, human and divine, Savior and Lord. But what do we think of Him? He is not truly real to so many people, but just a picture on the wall, a lovely memory from the past, a symbol or a name to pray to when they are desperate enough to pray. What is He to us?

It is when we accept Him as He is, our Savior and Lord, and all that He wants and intends to be in us and through us, that our lives are total and complete.

Grant, O Lord, that we may grow in our comprehension of You and Your purposes for our lives and that we become ever more deeply committed to You and Your will for us in our world today. Amen.

When Our Witness Bears Fruit

For our gospel came to you not only in word, but also in power and in the Holy Spirit. v. 5a

"For you received the Word in much affliction, with joy inspired by the Holy Spirit . . . you became an example to all believers . . . your faith in God has gone forth everywhere . . ."

The letter of Paul to the church at Thessalonica begins on the high note of joy and enthusiasm. His arduous ministry, which often took him through towns where he was stoned for his preaching and driven out, was finally beginning to pay off. According to Luke's narrative in the book of Acts, the church in Thessalonica began amidst much affliction. Paul began by preaching in the synagogues of the Jews and won a few converts, but a larger number of Greeks were attracted to Paul's preaching and converted to Paul's Christ, which resulted in a riot, and Paul had to flee the city. Now the church that was established there had grown and the Christians welcomed this contact with Paul with whom it all began, and Paul was overjoyed at what had transpired among the the the Thessalonian Christians.

It is a beautiful example of what happens when the seed that is sown finally takes root, blossoms forth, and eventually bears fruit. The church of Jesus Christ is not totally dependent upon Paul or any single person to keep it going and growing. The Spirit of God through dedicated people will work the wonders of God in the most difficult situations. Affliction there will be, but there is likewise "joy inspired by the Holy Spirit," and the wonders that God works through His children make the church live, not only at Thessalonica, but everywhere.

We praise You, our almighty God, that sometimes because of us, often in spite of us, You can bring forth fruit from the seed which we as Your servants have sown. We pray that we may continue to be the kind of Christians through whom Your Spirit can inspire and bless others in our congregation. Amen.

Serving People Where They Are

What do you want Me to do for you? v. 51a

I remember that sermons on this particular gospel portion usually turned this episode in the life of Jesus into a sort of analogy to point up our Lord's ability and purpose in healing spiritual blindness. Other interpreters look upon this incident as indicative of Christ's power to perform miracles, thereby revealing His divine origins and ultimate objectives.

Both of these interpretations are valid, but perhaps we would do well to take this healing-the-blind incident at face value. It may give us some direction in respect to the ministry of the church today. Implied and demonstrated is the real meaning of Christian discipleship and servanthood. The time is past when we can simply hold forth with weekly preaching services and center our activities around the sacred few who gather regularly in our sanctuaries. We may have gotten by with a modified concept of discipleship in years past that all but ignored the needy—the blind and the lame, the hungry and the unsheltered, the dispossessed and disinherited multitudes throughout our world. We left this task, for most part, to secular agencies or governmental policies and pacified our consciences by supporting our denominational efforts to build a few schools, hospitals, and homes for the aged.

Jesus did not preach to the blind man. He healed him, enabling him to see again, and thus enabling him to be a whole man again. This is, as far as we know, all that He did at this time. He met and lovingly dealt with this man at the point of his obvious and immediate need. The net result, as told in Luke's version of this incident, was that this man glorified God for the restoration of his sight and subsequently became a follower of Jesus Christ.

It is important, O Lord, that I proclaim and witness to Your message of eternal salvation. May I also be a conveyer of Your love and compassion to those who are in need of mental, physical, and material aid. Amen.

Growing Up as God's Children

Although He was a Son, He learned obedience through what He suffered. v. 8

In the days of old, high priests were appointed to stand between a sinful people and a holy God, to act on behalf of the people. These priests were themselves sinners and could therefore understand the frailties and weaknesses of the children of Israel for whom, through sacrifices and ceremonies, they sought God's forgiveness.

In Christ we honor the Priest of priests, who has been assigned by God Himself to present the Sacrifice of sacrifices, His own body on the cross, as sufficient to atone for all the sins of all people in all the world. Knowing our weaknesses without succumbing to weakness, tempted without yielding to temptation, Jesus is our worthy Advocate in reconciling sinners with a forgiving God.

And yet some of us act at times as if the price Jesus paid is insufficient to cover our guilt. If we as God's children are assigned to be the ministers of God, how dare we be content with the pablum of works-righteousness, or the sweet honey of subjective ecstasy, the milk of cloud-hopping experiences, when we ought by now to be feeding on the solid meat of Christ's radical, risk-fraught, joy-giving teachings and activities?

God help us to grow up in the Christian life, to mature, to develop some sensitivity to the needs of people and some skill in terms of applying the life and doctrines of Christ to those needs. We are God's ministers; may He make us worthy of our appointment.

I pray, O God, for a deeper sensitivity, a warm compassion, a greater concern, that I may become more like You and enabled to emulate You in respect to the hurts and needs of my fellow persons. Amen.

King of the Hill

Every one who exalts himself will be humbled, but he who humbles himself will be exalted. v. 14b

There is one vice of which no person is free. It is one which we loathe when we see it in someone else and yet are reluctant to admit it ourselves. We know of those who are bad-tempered or are weak when it comes to sex or drink or money, but hardly do we ever hear anyone accusing himself or herself of this vice. It is the vice of pride, the temptation and endeavor to be "king of the hill." This is the central and basic evil within a person's nature. It was through pride that the devil became the devil. It is pride that leads to every other vice.

It is represented and presented in today's Gospel portion in the character of the Pharisee in the temple. Here is a picture of a man who was satisfied with himself and, as such, could never meet God. He was decent, law-abiding, religious—and he knew it. He was self-confident and sufficient unto himself, a sort of "king of the hill," a winner in the game of life. He had prestige, ample wealth, and some power. What else could he want? And he was thankful to God for what he was—or so his prayer seems to indicate.

Our text draws another picture, a picture of a loser. He was one who had little thought about anybody else at this moment, no criticism of others, but was utterly dissatisfied with himself. He couldn't even lift his eyes, but in his sorrow over his sins, his failures and flaws, with despair in his soul, smote his breast and prayed: "God, be merciful to me a sinner."

Two men came to church that day, but only one met God. At the risk of making some ecstatic, positive-thinking, king-of-the-hill Christians very nervous, it is noted that it was the one who came in humility, seeing nobody's failures but his own, with no axes to grind, and his only desire was to get right in his own heart with God. According to Jesus, he did. He "went down to his house justified."

I cannot, O Lord, glory in Your resurrection unless I come by way of the cross. "Lord, be merciful to me a sinner." Amen.

Testimony and Challenge

I have fought the good fight . . . I have kept the faith. v. 7

"I am already on the point of being sacrificed," said Paul. In another version it reads: ". . . my life is being poured out on the altar" (NEB).

I suspect that few of us can identify with Paul as to the content and depth of his commitment. We find it difficult to believe that Jesus expects this of any of us. Yet He did of His original disciples. "The cup that I drink you will drink," He once said to them (Mark 10:39).

The truth is, however, He is expecting and getting this kind of response from many of His disciples throughout our world today. Christians are risking their lives to be "little Christs" in the most difficult situations in which they find themselves. They are not seeking martyrdom any more than we are, but they are compelled by the love of God to risk their lives and whatever they possess to bring the love of God into the lives of people about them. "Present your bodies as a living sacrifice," wrote Paul to the Christians at Rome (12:1). Paul followed his own injunction and exemplified the kind of response Christians ought to be making to their God.

A good question to ponder today: "Am I ready to be offered?" God may not expect us to measure up to the intensity and courage of Paul's life and witness. He may, however, be looking for our willingness to be "poured out" in our love for others and in the accomplishment of His purposes. Would He really be our loving God if He expected anything else?

My gracious heavenly Father, I do not know if I am yet willing to be "poured out on the altar." While You may not demand such, I know that this ought to be my response to Your great love. May it be so, dear Lord, may it be so. Enable me to be willing and ready to be offered, to "present my body as a living sacrifice." Amen.

A Song of Hope

Proclaim, give praise, and say, "The Lord has saved His people."
v. 7b

We are likely to remember Jeremiah for his lamentations over the infidelities of Israel. In this Old Testament portion we hear a new song, a song of God's love for His children. It is not the words of judgment, but the music of hope that we hear through the lips of the great prophet: "The Lord has saved His people, the remnant of Israel . . . With weeping they shall come, and with consolations I will lead them back . . . Proclaim, give praise, and say, 'The Lord has saved His people . . .'" And with hope there comes joy: "Sing aloud with gladness for Jacob."

It was hope indeed—kept alive in the hearts of a remnant until the time that God sent forth His Son to make that promise valid not only for the Jews, but for all people on this planet. The promise has been fulfilled in the coming of Christ. With His coming, God came to His people, His creatures upon this earth. With His sacrifice on the cross, His resurrection from the dead, God's judgment upon sin was overturned and His love poured out upon all who believe. Gathered from "the farthest parts of the earth," we have come to know our great God as a God of love who came to us and who now abides within us through His Spirit.

The new kingdom has still not been fully revealed, but Christ has strengthened our hope with the assurance that the great Day will soon break in upon us and that we are the children of God forever.

O God, hopelessness and despair haunt the hearts of so many men and women. And I am impatient as I seek clear signs or Your presence. Forgive me, my God, and help me to know You are here and to feel Your presence. Strengthen my faith that I may walk my journey in joy. Amen.

While We Sleep

Watch therefore, for you know neither the day nor the hour. v. 13

Our Lord is not entertaining children with fairy tales; He is forewarning and forearming His faithful followers for a future event of tremendous significance. It is an event so dazzling in its importance that it outshines every other event the world has ever known.

It has to do with our Lord's final advent to our world. This final advent of our Lord, whenever it happens, will take men and women by surprise. This was true about Christ's first advent. Though our Lord's final advent must ultimately be accepted, it is not really expected by the masses of our world.

The final advent of Jesus Christ will find many within the institutional church and the average congregation who are not ready for His coming. All of the maidens had burning lamps; five of those lamps burned out. Some of us may be holding lamps which are burning very low, a faith about to burn out. This lack or defect did not divide the wise maidens from the foolish until it was too late to do anything about it. Could this happen to us.?

The final advent of Christ will be a time of rich reward for those who have surrendered their lives to Him and have labored faithfully in His vineyard. This has been promised and is awaiting those who truly "keep the faith" and are constantly working and watching in view of the final advent.

"Watch therefore, for you know neither the day nor the hour," said Jesus. We are called and empowered by God's Spirit to be loving, serving, devoted children in our world today. By being such we are thereby hastening the day of His final coming and are ready for that final coming and are ready for that great Day, whenever it may be.

Turn up the flickering flame in my life, dear Lord, that I may be more enthusiastic and intense and conspiciuous in my witness to You and Your kingdom as that great Day approaches. Amen.

It Will All Be Worthwhile

Therefore comfort one another with these words. v. 18

Whereas we need never to strive for our salvation, for God's forgiveness love and acceptance, we need constantly to struggle and strive within the process of Christian growth. It is the struggle to allow God to have His way with us, to cast off the shackles of self-concern, the appendages of fear and worry, our dependence upon the things of this earth, our fleshly desires for material security and recognition, the gnawing need to be successful in this life. It is in the process of doing this that we become open and pliable, loose and flexible, to the Spirit's indwelling and outpouring. If we could truly abide in the Vine, we would grow and bear fruit. Our problem lies in learning how to abide, to let go and let God, to rest in what He has done for us and be totally committed to Him and what He wants to do through us.

It is all worthwhile, for our earthly conflicts will one day be resolved in an eternal life and experience that is more glorious than anything we can imagine. Our dear ones who are no longer with us, who were wrenched from us through suffering and pain, have already entered into that experience. It awaits every one of us who remains faithful to our Lord and to His commission for us in our remaining days upon this earth.

Remember, Jesus died—and rose again. So we shall rise again and, with those who have preceded us, be joined totally and eternally to our God and Christ.

My Lord, I get tired of the hard road, the dusty valley, dirty hands and sore feet, dark nights and smoggy days. Yet it is this to which You have called me. Sometimes, Lord, I need Your special assurance that all this is truly worthwhile. Amen.

Morality—Jesus' Style

Love the Lord your God ... love your neighbor as yourself.
vv. 30, 31

In the first years of the Christian church there were many struggles on the part of those first believers between the Old Testament and New Testament moralities, or between those who were still hung up on the ancient Law and those who had gained some insight into the meaning of the Gospel. Paul was probably the most enlightened and avid interpreter of Jesus' Gospel, and he emphatically declared that Christians are set free from the Law in order to accept God's love as revealed in Christ and His redemption and are enabled by His Spirit to relate in love to their fellow beings. People must go back to the basic absolutes of love-God-love your-neighbor, which can be understood and fulfilled only as a consequence of faith in and obedience to Jesus Christ and His teachings.

According to New Testament morality, when we accept Jesus Christ as Savior and crown Him Lord of life and living, we will recognize and confess our utter inability to please God by way of rules and regulations and accept that One sent by God who kept the Law in our stead and who sets us free from its demands and judgments to receive God's forgiving love and to relate in divinely impelled human love to our fellow creatures.

Immorality, then, as we need to understand it, is the failure to love God and our neighbor, even to love others in the measure that Jesus loves us. It is, as well, our failure to stand up against those inhuman institutions and laws that come between us and our love for God and our love for our fellow beings—that divide races, perpetuate bigotry, favor the rich over against the poor, or that promote wars of violence and destroy the souls, if not the bodies, of our fellow citizens.

Help us, our loving God, to recognize our immoralities, and by Your grace, seek to overcome them. And may we truly love You with our hearts, minds, and bodies, and our fellow persons even as we love ourselves. Amen.

Jesus Christ, the One and Only

He is able for all time to save those who draw near to God through Him. v. 25a

The ancient Israelites needed priests to meditate between them and God. Jesus Christ is the one and only High Priest who broke through every barrier between human beings and God and revealed His God and Father as a forgiving, loving, grace-giving God. We need no longer lean on symbols or rely on priests to make God real and available to us. He has been revealed through Jesus Christ. The act of reconciliation has been effected through His sacrificial death and supernatural resurrection on our behalf. God continues to reveal Himself through His Spirit and through the activities and proclamations of those who follow Christ.

Jesus did what no mortal priest or religious leader can ever do, He obliterated the darkness, the uncertainty, and the inscrutability that once existed between God and His creatures, and restored us forever to an intimate relationship with Him. Everything that happened before Christ was but a shadow of what was to come, even the ancient worship that prepared the way for the coming of Christ. Christ is the Truth that has come, and He is here with us to draw men and women to the Truth. He is the Way to God—directly and eternally. He is the Life that sustains us and compels us to dedicate our lives to broadcasting this Truth to those who are still in darkness. He is the Fulfillment of our deepest longings, the Answer to our most complex problems. He is Christ, our Lord, our God, and our Way to God.

"Jesus, Lord and precious Savior, all my comfort and my joy, graciously extend Thy favor, let Thy word my soul employ. Jesus, come, abide with me, let me ever be with Thee." Amen.

When Conversion Is Genuine

For the Son of man came to seek and to save the lost. v. 10

Our gospel reading is an excellent portrayal of the *significance of circumstances* and the part that such circumstances about us, be they joyful or tragic, ordinary or extraordinary, have to play in the process of bringing us to God. In the manner that hunting dogs "tree" a racoon, so a self-centered and self-sufficient person often has to be "chased up a tree" before he or she is somewhat prepared for God's message of eternal life and hope.

The incident before us also presents a beautiful picture of the *outflow of divine grace.* The character of Zaccheus was less than remarkable. He was, as a tax collector, very unpopular, and unscrupulous as well. And yet this was the individual who was about to become the object of divine grace and, as a result of such grace, to undergo a remarkable transformation. Whatever Zacchaeus may have understood about himself, Jesus saw a man who was "up a tree" in his life, a need for the divine grace that He had come to grant to humanity. "Zacchaeus, make haste and come down; for I must stay at your house today," said Jesus.

The final picture emerging from this lesson is that of the *necessary response.* Zacchaeus, our reading informs us, "made haste and came down, and received Him joyfully." Then he said to this Jesus, as the grace of God took hold of his life: "Behold, Lord, the half of my goods I give to the poor; and if I have defrauded anyone of anything, I restore it fourfold." There was hard-core, agonizing reality in that little speech, but it was a necessary response for Zacchaeus, and our Lord regarded graciously his confession and commitment: "Today salvation has come to this house."

This is what God needs from us—our glad and unlimited response. Only then can He translate and transform us as His beloved children. May our response be genuine.

I thank You, my Lord, for the various circumstances in my life that have drawn me to You. I pledge anew my life and goods to the accomplishment of Your purposes. Amen.

The Extent of Servanthood

We were ready to share with you not only the gospel of God but also our own selves. v. 8

Paul's initial and primary task in promoting the God-movement and advancing the new kingdom was proclamation. It is probable, however, that he and his co-workers would have had little success with the church at Thessalonica if their responsibility had been limited to proclamation alone. Paul was successful in his leadership role, because he came to serve these people, to share himself with them. A successful pastor is one who serves, who shares himself, gives of himself to his co-ministers, the members of his congregation. And that congregation will be successful only inasmuch as its members share themselves with others in the community.

The Christians who are most effective in their person-to-person attempts at soul-winning are not necessarily those who go door-to-door in their efforts to spread the Gospel and win converts. God can use such methods even if they are confined to handing out tracts or Bible portions, but the most effective witness is generally over a long period of time, during which loving, caring, and sharing are involved. Such loving involves a measure of pain, self-denial and cross-bearing on behalf of others. This is what servanthood is all about. It is difficult to see how one can channel the love of God without being a loving person. Proclamation is essential; it needs to be accompanied by and usually preceded by loving and sharing.

"Make love your aim," Paul once said (1 Corinthians 14:1). That is the crux of and motivation for servanthood.

As I rejoice in your eternal love, O Lord, may I zealously and joyfully share that love with my brothers and sisters in the human family about me. Amen.

Let Justice Roll

Let justice roll down like waters, and righteousness like an ever-flowing stream. v. 24

The words of Amos, or the words of God through Amos, are a severe indictment against the worship activities of the Israelites. We wouldn't expect such an indictment over our beautiful and impressive worship services. They are Word-centered, faith-strengthening celebrations that turn us on and send us out into our Monday-through-Saturday world with joy and enthusiasm. Yet God may have something to say about our religious celebrations as well. It may go something like this: "Your robed choirs and great organs may stimulate congregations, but such is not always music to My heart. Your proper liturgies and impressive pageantry will probably make people feel devout and religious without doing much to extend My kingdom or accomplish my purposes. Even the Word that is preached, the sacraments administered, may be little more than hollow mockery if they do not proceed from and result in hearts and lives that are committed to My Word and My will as revealed through My Son. If the people who gather to make their confessions and sing My praises do not feel lovingly compelled to carry out My objectives, to stand with the oppressed against their oppressors, to work for the dignity of every human being, to share their goods and gifts with those who are deprived, to accept and love their fellow persons even as they accept and love themselves, and to proclaim the love of God to those who will listen, then their worship is farcical and their relationship to Me very much in question."

God would never speak words like these to us—or would He?

We thank You, O God, for our worship services where we can lift our hearts and our voices in thanksgivings and praises to You. We thank You for each and every day where we can put our faith and commitment to work by carrying out Your objectives among our fellow persons. Amen.

The Case of the Missing Talents

For to every one who has will more be given, and he will have abundance. v. 29a

Many in our generation have some misgivings about the church. Membership is lagging. Young people laugh at the church as irrelevant. Philosophers and even theologians announce the death of God. Even where there appears to be an upsurge in religious interest and activity, it is not necessarily in spiritual vitality and validity. Hungry people still view the church as uncaring. Politicians scoff at the church as incompetent. Businessmen spurn the church as unrealistic. The church is peripheral when it should be central. It is on the edge when it should be at the heart. It is silent when it should speak. It dallies when it should act. And Malcolm Muggeridge, a devout Christian, boldly announces or predicts "the end of Christendom."

Maybe it adds up to a case of missing talents. Our great God has through His Spirit equipped His redeemed children with all that is needed to make the church a powerful, effective instrument in a power-mad but powerless world today. God is always out to do the impossible: to bring order into disorder, purpose into purposelessness, fullness into emptiness, healing into sickness, and to restore aching, hungry hearts to Himself. He can do this, however, only through His faithful children as individuals and as members of the institutional church. It seems, however, that the church has not discovered or recovered all the missing talents, or has invested God's gifts to His children in ways and matters that serve its institutional programs and purposes rather than human need in the world about it.

Is it possible that we, by our neglect to lovingly invest our talents and gifts in the needs of people, are contributing to "the end of Christendom?"

O Lord, instead of finding answers to the problems of this world, we have too often been a part of the problem. Enable us, our Lord, to fulfill our servanthood by using Your talents and gifts to us to communicate Your love and grace to people in need. Amen.

Are We Ready?

So let us not sleep, as others do, but let us keep awake and be sober.
v. 6

Over against those far-fetched attempts by self-appointed prophets to predict the time of the visible return of our Lord are our Lord's own words informing us that His return or reappearance will be sudden and unexpected. And yet the final coming of Christ, whenever it happens, should be no surprise to His faithful disciples. We ought to be ready to meet our Lord whatever the appointed day or hour. It really makes little difference whether we are alive or have already passed on to life everlasting, when He comes we shall see Him and with Him judge the world.

While we live upon this planet, we should live as if He were already here. Indeed, He is here! His disappearance after His resurrection was followed by Pentecost. And Pentecost marked, by a wonderful event, His return to invisibly infill and indwell the hearts of His disciples. The way in which we can always be ready for the final and ultimate reappearance of Christ is not to gather on some hill in pious meditation. It is to recognize and rely upon the Spirit of God within us and to extend His kingdom through witnessing to and serving humanity about us. We are to walk in faith, to serve in joy, and to praise God whatever the circumstances that surround us. God grant that we remain totally dedicated to Him and His purposes. Then we are ever ready for His visible reappearance.

It truly appears, our Lord, that You really are about to return to this planet. While we joyously anticipate Your soon appearance, grant to us Your grace and strength to reach out to others with the Good News of Your love and salvation. Amen.

Empty Hands

He . . . watched the multitude putting money into the treasury.
v. 41

A verse out of the book of Deuteronomy (16:16–17) pictures the manner in which the Old Testament worshipers were to come to God: "They shall not appear before the Lord empty-handed; every man shall give as he is able, according to the blessing of the Lord your God which He has given you."

All of us, as we come to God, come with "dirty hands." They have been soiled with the deeds of self-centered living. We come, however, sincerely and in faith believing that in Christ there is cleansing and atonement. Something that continues to cause sorrow to the heart of our Lord is that so many who have found cleansing and forgiveness at the Divine Fountainhead are still coming to God with "empty hands," or with fists clenched tightly in miserliness and selfishness. They fail to bring with them the sacrificial offerings of love and gratitude, of praise and thanksgiving. They know not the experience of Luther who said: "I have had many things in my hands, and I have lost them all; but whatever I have placed in God's hands, that I still possess."

Jesus noted in an act of temple worship people's real attitudes toward their Creator God. He first saw the kind of giving we might call *surplus giving:* "Many rich people put in large sums." He did not scorn their gifts and made no comment whatsoever concerning their actions, except to say, "Many rich people put in large sums." The second thing our Lord noted was an example of *sacrificial giving:* a little figure of a woman making her cautious, timid, almost ashamed approach to the temple treasury to deposit her two copper coins. Listen to His evaluation: "This poor widow has put in more than all those who are contributing to the treasure . . . her whole living."

We pray, O Lord, that Your love for each of us be so overwhelmingly obvious that we will gladly and sacrificially commit ourselves and our possessions to spreading the Gospel and helping others about us. Amen.

In Our Stead—On Our Behalf

[Christ] appeared once for all . . . to put away sin by the sacrifice of Himself. v. 26b

Jesus, our great High Priest, entered the Holy of Holies, the inner sanctum of God, to make the one-for-all and once-for-all sacrifice, giving His life as the one, sufficient, perfect sacrifice to end all sacrifices, in order to make men and women holy, righteous, and totally acceptable to His heavenly Father. What the ancient Law and religion could not do, and what we cannot do for ourselves, God did on our behalf through His Son, Jesus Christ. The forgiveness of God is complete, canceling out the necessity of any future offerings or sacrifices.

It is for this reason, because of what Christ has done for us, that we have the assurance and confidence we need in order to boldly approach our loving God. We can come before God with untroubled consciences, knowing that our past sins will no longer be held against us. We are now truly the people of God, His children and servants forever.

How important it is that we who have by faith entered with Christ into the Holy of Holies keep that faith and allow nothing to deter us in our walk of faith and obedience! It is worth whatever cost we may have to pay—loss of jobs, reputations, material possessions, even the sacrifice of our lives—to hold fast our salvation and follow closely behind our Lord.

This we will do with the help of God.

I claim, O God, Your forgiveness for the failings and faults of my earthbound nature. I seek, O God, the grace and courage to begin again. May I remember always Your victory over sin and death. May I see some reflection of that victory in my daily circumstances. Amen.

After This—Then What?

[God] is not God of the dead, but of the living; for all live to Him.
v. 38

An Indian chief named Crowfoot is reported to have said, "A little while and I will be gone from among you, whither I cannot tell. From nowhere we come, into nowhere we go. What is life? It is a flash of a firefly in the night. It is a breath of buffalo in the wintertime. It is a little shadow that runs across the grass and loses itself in the sunset." "It is appointed for men to die once," the Scriptures declare (Hebrews 9:27). "What man can live and never see death?" queried the psalmist (89:48).

Despite the exquisite and dignified words of the Indian chief, or even the words of Scripture, we cannot entirely reduce the ugliness or minimize the horror of death. We cannot forget our first childhood contact with it, nor the shock and pain of its brutal invasion of our family circle. We cannot completely rid ourselves of its insidious threat to our being. As surely as comes the end of summer, the yellow grass and the fallen leaves, so surely must we face up to the fact of death, its parting of the ways, its incomprehensible darkness.

But faith does have an answer for this ultimate anxiety. Our Christ not only faced it, bluntly and biologically; He was victorious over it. He transformed it from an enemy bent on our destruction into a friend that promises to usher us into eternal glory. The Christian faith says that we bear the mark of the eternal. Thus death is *not* final; it does *not* have the last word. It is a necessary incident in the journey of faith to our full enjoyment of life everlasting.

Our concern, O Lord, is not that we shall die, but that we live the days still remaining to us on this planet within Your life and purposes and for the benefit of our brothers and sisters about us. Amen.

While We Wait

The Lord is faithful; He will strengthen you and guard you from evil.
v. 3

It is not surprising, in the darkness of this world's chaotic struggles, that we hope intensely for the very special intervention of God through the promised return of our Lord Jesus Christ. We feel at times so unnerved, frightened, bowled over with frustration and despair, that we look desperately for some sign in the sky, some miracle out of heaven, and even wish for the final day of this dispensation, the culmination of God's purposes upon this world that will put an end to the misery that abounds about us. Nor is it surprising that some of us will grab at any straw in the wind, latch on to any strange happening that may suggest the possibility of this taking place in our lifetime. Christians have been doing this for centuries, and yet time marches on, and with it the sorrows and joys of this world's inhabitants.

Maybe God is telling us to mind our own business, to tend to those matters which He would have us be concerned about, to leave these cosmic, still unknown and unrevealed things in His hands. While we accept and anticipate His promises concerning the great Day of our deliverance, when we shall blissfully go to be with Him for all eternity, He would have us occupy ourselves with the task at hand—that of laboring within our suffering world to reveal and communicate His love to all His human creatures.

Let us remember that the Lord is faithful, even when our faith falters. He will sustain us and watch over us whatever the difficult times or the circumstances that press in upon us.

While I wait, help me, my gracious God, to wait patiently and serve faithfully within the purposes and objectives of Your plan for my life and for Your kingdom in respect to this planet. Help me to effectively use the time allowed to me to prepare others for that great Day that Your children so joyously anticipate. Amen.

The Incomparable Love of God

I led them with cords of compassion, with the bands of love . . .
v. 4a

Should God speak to us through Hosea today, it might go like this: "How profoundly I love My children whom I have created. I continue to reveal to them My compassion; I help to bear their burdens and accompany them through the adversities that afflict them; I heal many of their sicknesses and demonstrate My loving concern in the midst of their deep sorrows and excruciating sufferings; I hold out to them My salvation and invite them to partake of My saving and redeeming grace. Yet they turn from Me to pursue their own objectives. They expend their energy upon the fleeting things about them. Even those who honor Me with their lips persist in investing their lives in the foolishness of their world.

"What more can I do for My beloved children than I am already doing? It is even as I love them and because I love them that I must allow them to go their own way, to satisfy their desires upon the husks of their temporary existence, to fill their emptiness with things that rust and decay and will pass away. When they refuse to follow Me, I will follow them—even into the dark, cold caves of nothingness or the pits of despair—seeking always to draw them back to My redeeming love, to restore them to My will for their lives. How much I love My children whom I have created!"

Return, you who have strayed from God's blessed will for your life; return to that One who created you, who loves you, and who patiently waits for you to come back to Him!

And so it is, my loving God, that I return day by day to Your will and purposes for my life. Forgive me for so often straying off the narrow, well-beaten path. Continue, gracious Father, to draw me and hold me close to Your loving heart. Amen.

Every Christian a Leader

He who is greatest among you shall be your servant. v. 11

It is well to remember that those who are led by the Spirit of God will often be considered "losers" by the world-at-large. This is because they follow Jesus Christ, and His leadership is synonymous with servanthood. It is because they, rather than resolving the conflicts and problems of the world, point to the new kingdom and to their God who alone can resolve the conflicts and struggles of humanity. Rather than promoting themselves and their own glory, they lead people in glorifying God. Instead of promising people success, they challenge them to make sacrifices; instead of comforting them in their self-centeredness and apathy, they provoke them into accepting responsibility for the poor and the less fortunate about them. Instead of being leaders of people, they take the lead in being servants to people, seeking to lead them into spiritual fulfillment, as well as responding to their physical needs. This is because they are lovers of people rather than masters over people, and they dedicate themselves to communicating and demonstrating, in word and deed, God's saving love and grace to His creatures about them.

All this refers not only to leaders, but to every one of us, for we are all called to be servants of our heavenly Father and of our fellow beings among whom we live and work. In a very real sense we are all leaders of one sort or another, at least in the measure that we seek to "lead' others to Christ. We can't drive people to the Lord; we must lead them. We can do this only through servanthood, not through domination or mastery.

I thank You, my Lord, for the many who have influenced my life and living and for those who have led me to the Living Waters of your love and grace. I thank You for those who continue to provoke and challenge me as I walk in Your ways and commit myself to Your purposes in seeking to lead others to Your saving grace. Amen.

Thanksgiving and Giving

We always pray for you . . . that our God may make you worthy of His call . . . v. 11a

While we thank our God for His loving patience in the face of our reluctance to grow, our slowness in maturing and developing into the kind of instruments that would be useful to Him, and praise Him for the comfort and security we find in Him even in the midst of this world's conflicts and calamities, we are disturbed by the cries of pain, the sounds of suffering, that break through into our hallowed little circles.

There are some people we cannot help at this moment—and we prayerfully commit them to the loving-kindness of God. There are others that we can aid and support. If we neglect to do all that we can to hold them up or share in their suffering, we ourselves may be subject to God's judgment.

Our thanksgiving must be thanks accompanied by giving—the giving of ourselves to others in need—or it may be little more than mockery. It is relatively easy to condemn our world's oppressors and relegate them to whatever hell God may have prepared for them. It is more difficult, and far more important, that we lovingly and sacrificially identify with the oppressed, that we share their afflictions and stand with them against the monsters who use and abuse them, and that we discover together the joy and freedom of living for God. We are, thanks be to God, His servants.

I do offer my thanksgivings to You, O God, and yet I see how so much of my giving is simply surplus-giving, giving after my desires and needs have been met. May my love for You grow and mature that I be willing to joyfully give of myself, as well as my gifts and possessions to those who are in need. Amen.

343

A Matter of Endurance

Take heed that no one leads you astray. v. 5

"He who endures to the end will be saved."

It's not the sort of thing we enjoy preaching or hearing sermons about, but Christ's ominous warnings of what might happen to His followers were anything but encouraging. If we were actually exposed to what Jesus and His original disciples had to face, it is probable that few of us would be very enthusiastic or aggressive about the Christian faith. It is, nevertheless, the same Lord and the same faith that we are celebrating today and, in several areas of our world, God's children are experiencing these very things that Jesus talks about in this Gospel portion.

It is possible that something of this sort—call it persecution or cross-bearing or whatever—could happen to us before our course in life runs out. It is rather noble of us to say, as said Peter to the Lord, "I will lay down my life for you" (John 13:37). What would we say or do if we actually faced up to that necessity?

Cheer up! It may never happen—to us, that is. And if it does happen somewhere along life's journey, God will give us the courage and grace to cope with it. The point is, if some "Christ" or self-styled prophet or apostle peddles a primrose-path kind of gospel that excludes the cost and pain of discipleship, hold that person suspect. He or she is not telling the whole truth.

"He who endures to the end will be saved," said our Lord. We are not saved by enduring, but by the grace of our loving God as revealed in Jesus Christ. The faith that accepts and appropriates that forgiving and sustaining grace must, however, endure to the end— and this by the grace of God.

We praise You, our heavenly Father, for You have promised and do offer to us the grace both to cope and to endure along our journey of faith. We claim that grace as we continue our journey in joy. Amen.

Again, We Are Forgiven!

I will remember their sins and their misdeeds no more. v. 17

"Christ . . . offered for all time a single sacrifice for sins . . . By a single offering He has perfected for all time those who are sanctified."

We are forgiven all our sin, past, present, and future, because "Christ . . . offered for all time a single sacrifice for sins," because He died on the cross on our behalf. The proclamation of the Word, the administration of the sacraments, confession and absolution—these repeatedly bring us back to the center and core of our faith, our recognition of and commitment to this blessed gift, this grace, that draws us, cleansed, redeemed, and perfected, into the very heart of God.

We are forgiven! Even as we sin, we are forgiven. We need not seek forgiveness, we *are* forgiven. Yet with profound grief and sorrow we come daily to the cross to unload our grievous burdens and claim anew this superlative gift, this release from sin's guilt. We don't offer sacrifices, but we offer our gratitude. This will, if we are truly sincere and understanding of the meaning of forgiveness, result in sacrifices of another sort—our lives and all that we are and have in loving service to God and to our fellow beings.

Praise be to God who "remembers [our] sins and [our] misdeeds no more."

"I acknowledged my sin to Thee, and I did not hide my iniquity; I said, 'I will confess my transgressions to the Lord'; then Thou didst forgive the guilt of my sin" (Psalm 32:5). I praise You, O God, from whom all blessings flow! Amen.

Hang in There; the End Is Near

This will be time for you to bear testimony. v. 13

Jesus is telling His disciples just how it is in this world, and what it will be like as we near the end of this dispensation. When His followers pressed upon Him for some sign that would indicate that the end is near, His response was, "Take heed that you are not led astray" and that we should "not go after" those who confuse people with their foolhardy, premature predictions. The time of this dialog with the disciples was some two thousand years ago. Our modern prophets are correct in announcing that "the time is at hand." And it has always been "at hand" from the day of Pentecost until this very day. "But the end will not be at once," said Jesus. It is possible that the end is still many years into the future. Meanwhile, we still exist in the midst of all these things that "must first take place."

It is not a pleasant scene that Jesus portrays as a prelude to that final event. Whereas we may not yet be personally involved in these horrendous happenings, we are through the media alerted to the fact that these very things are taking place throughout our world. Our Lord's injunction to us is not to run and hide, or to thumb-twiddle on some mountaintop waiting for His coming, but to endure, to keep the faith, to be His loyal servants in the midst of these things.

The word of comfort He passes on to us is, "not a hair of your head will perish." It is a figurative statement indicating God's loving concern for His children and promises that if we endure, and this by His grace, the wisdom and strength that He provides, then, in the words of Paul, "the sufferings of this present time are not worth comparing with the glory that is to be revealed to us" (Romans 8:18).

Come quickly, my Lord. And while I wait, grant to me the grace to hold on, to keep the faith, and to walk patiently and joyfully the journey of faith. Amen.

For Such Times as These

Do not be weary in well-doing. v. 13

We ought to be thankful that He saved, appointed, and commissioned us for just such a time as this. This world at this moment is exactly where He wants us to be. He has entrusted us with the commission to represent Him and reveal Him to this kind of world. He is the only hope for humankind, and we are the harbingers of that hope. He is, and this is beyond our comprehension, dependent upon His redeemed children to prepare this world for the Day of His appearing. We obviously have not completed that important assignment. Let us be about it—and leave those things that need not be our ultimate concern up to Him.

The conditions of our world, the apostasy, the corruption, the utter disregard for God and His will, the atrocities and tragedies, and our failures in attempting to change the course of our world's mad rush to destruction, drive us back to our God to be renewed and recharged, to be reassured and encouraged. This is good; but God forbid that we crawl into some dark cave or become engrossed in some self-concocted ecstasy that numbs us to the world about us while we wait for His appearing. If we do, we may be caught short, for He would thrust us out, again and again, into the frightful tempests of our world to earn our living with the talents He has given us and to bring His light and love and salvation to the impoverished souls of fear-stricken men and women.

While we wait for the great Day of Your final appearance, our Lord, we continue to celebrate Your first coming to save us and make us the children of God. We do praise You for appointing us to be Your servants and for choosing and em-powering us to carry out Your objectives in precisely this kind of world in which we live today. Amen.

Something That Is Secure

When you see these things taking place, you know that He is near, at the very gates. v. 29

"Heaven and earth will pass away, but my words will not pass away."

The judgment of God falls not only upon His creatures who inhabit this world, but upon the institutions they create. Every nation upon this planet will be judged. All authorities, bureaucracies, ideologies, governing bodies, traditions, institutions shall be called to account before the judgment seat of God. Whatever their motives for existence, whatever their contributions to humanity's existence and benefit, they bear the stamp of depravity. They become, for the most part, the very enemies of God's kingdom. While many of them are necessary to our present existence and have been useful in furthering God's purposes, they will never become a part of His kingdom in that great Day when His kingdom shall be fully revealed.

Yet over against the wickedness of Babylon is the righteousness of Jerusalem—the remnant, redeemed by Jesus Christ, who persist, even within the institutions that seek to control them, to follow and serve their Redeemer and King. God knows who they are, this remnant, and while the institutions which men create fall under His judgment and are destined to "pass away," there shall come out of these institutions those who bear upon them the brand of God's redeeming grace, and they shall live forever as the citizens of His eternal kingdom.

In an unstable and insecure world, my God, I thank You for the eternal certainty and security of the Word who is Christ, and the very words of Christ as they comfort and assure and challenge and give purpose and guidance to my life. Amen.

We Are Equipped

Now may the God of peace . . . equip you with everything good that you may do His will. v. 21a

Peter once wrote: "God's divine power has given us everything we need to live a truly religious life through our knowledge of the One who called us to share in His own glory and goodness" (2 Peter 1:3 TEV).

We are assigned to live and serve in these end-times. We cannot run and hide as the world crumbles about us; we can stand up and be counted. We are equipped for this very thing. We need to acknowledge and learn how to use our equipment. The New Testament writers wrote to people who had suffered much and who expected to suffer much more in the world they encountered. Now it is our world; the end-times are upon us. We are to expect suffering; we are also expected to serve in the midst of suffering.

We, of course, seriously question our capabilities in respect to our assignment in these end-times. In a world of computers and space shuttles and laser beams, of atheistic ideologies and totalitarian political philosophies, a world that could be destroyed instantly by a push-button war or gradually become extinct through the continued misuse and abuse of its natural resources, a world that appears to be on the brink of great and violent conflict, our first inclination may be to burrow into some deep, dark hole and pull it in after us. Our natural faculties simply do not enable us to face this kind of world. But we are credentialed, appointed, and commissioned for just such a time as this. "God's divine power has given us everything we need . . ." It is now time to go about accepting it, laying claim to it, and making it work in and through our lives.

Our almighty, all powerful, ever-loving God, we belong to You. We are not only Your children, we are Your servants equipped by You to serve You on this planet. Grant to us the assurance of Your presence and Your power to do just that— in scorn of the consequences to our lives and living. Amen.

We Are Motivated

Be steadfast, immovable, always abounding in the work of the
Lord . . . v. 58a

There are some people who can discover motivation for good works apart from the commands and promises of the Christian faith. For most of us it is the fact that death in this world is followed by everlasting life in the next that gives us the courage to go on—even to the point of risking our lives on behalf of others.

We shall indeed be raised from the dead. Our God has not given to us the explanation of just how it shall be done. Our three-dimensional insights would not be capable of comprehending it even if He had. But this we know: The perishable shall become imperishable, and the mortal will become immortal on that great Day. And this is really all we need to know; it provides all the motivation we need to labor committedly and sacrificially in the purposes of our Lord.

Let us be awake and aware—always! Even as we rest in what God has done on our behalf, let us be on the tiptoe of expectancy, working, serving, giving, loving, keeping the faith and demonstrating that faith to the world of men and women about us. The time will come soon enough when we shall experience together the eternal wonders of the next dimension. As for now, let us praise God for the assurance of our salvation, our citizenship in His kingdom about to be revealed, and the glorious truth that our death in this world will be followed by our resurrection into the next. Let us hold on to one another in love and dedicate ourselves in loving service to God and humanity.

You have, O God, not only redeemed me, but You have chosen and equipped and empowered me through Your Spirit to proclaim Your work of redemption. Help me not only to realize my identity as Your child but my responsibility as Your servant. Amen.

We Are Blessed!

In that day [you] shall know that it is I who speak; here am I. v. 6

How blessed are those who are chosen to be the servants of God! What a message they have to proclaim concerning God's love for the human family! Not only do they speak of God's judgment, but imbued with His Spirit and authorized and empowered by His saving grace, they are to make known His salvation, to spread the glad tidings of His redeeming and reconciling love to all who will listen to His gracious Word. As it says in poetic language in the verses following today's reading, they are "beautiful!"

It is true that God will judge and condemn to eternal darkness all who persist in opposing Him and His purposes. It is equally true that those who deserve nothing less, who have rebelled against their Creator-God and broken His Law and have worshiped and lived for the things of this world—that they can be redeemed from the pits of darkness and be reconciled God. We who are now God's children and servants were once the children of darkness and disobedience. God sought us, found us, and took us back to Himself. Now we are enjoined and assigned to live out and proclaim boldly the redeeming, reconciling love of our God to our fallen, lost, suffering brothers and sisters throughout this planet.

It's a joyous task, a tremendous responsibility, an exciting adventure, a difficult and pain-filled struggle.

We plunge ahead with confidence—and with the assurance that our great God has circumscribed us with His love and care, and that we are His precious vessels, His children and servants forever.

We are indeed blessed!

I am blessed, my Lord, and can approach this day as Your child and servant without doubt or fear, knowing that whatever happens, my relationship to You is never in jeopardy. Now may I go forth to bring Your love and joy into the difficult circumstances that confront me. Amen.

The Lord Is Our Righteousness

The Lord is our righteousness. v. 6b

What a glorious song with which to end the church year! Sing it again; sing it often: "The Lord is our righteousness." Only the righteous can be citizens of God's kingdom. No one else need apply. Only those who recognize their bankruptcy, their utter inability to do anything to please God, who realize that there is nothing righteous within them, that they are among the lost, will be eligible for citizenship in the kingdom and prepared to receive as a divine gift the righteousness of God. It is only because Jesus, the Righteous One, has become our righteousness that we can account ourselves among the accepted and redeemed children of God. There is no other way to enter the kingdom—to regard Jesus as our King rather than our Judge—than to approach the kingdom as undeserving sinners who through faith in Jesus are accepting that One who took God's judgment upon Himself and covered us with His own righteousness.

The Lord continues to be our righteousness. No matter how devoted and successful we are in our service assignments, or how defeated and failure-fraught we may feel in the depressing hours of our lives, "The Lord is our righteousness." Nothing else matters—success or failures—in respect to our relationship to God. Nothing changes in respect to God's regard for us. We are righteous in His eyes and eternally His sons and daughters.

And so we begin the new church year with the song. Continue through the year singing the song. Take heart, rejoice, for "The Lord is our righteousness!"

"Lord God, heavenly king, almighty God and Father: We worship You, we give You thanks, we praise You for Your glory. Lord Jesus Christ, only Son of the Father, Lord God, Lamb of God: You take away the sin of the world; have mercy on us." Amen.

Later Than You Think

Therefore you also must be ready; for the Son of man is coming at an hour you do not expect. v. 44

"Heaven and earth will pass away . . .," announced Jesus in a verse just before this Gospel portion. And all the rioting, flag-waving, dissenting, and politicizing in the world will not stop this predicted and unprecedented event which guarantees that life as we know it, the pleasures that pamper, the comforts that coddle, the toys we tinker with, will not be ours forever.

Jesus refers to Noah and the flood to get His point across: "For as in those days before the flood they were eating and drinking, marrying and giving in marriage, until the day when Noah entered the ark." There is no mention of wife-swapping, drug addiction, nudie bars, or sexploitation films. As unsavory and degenerate as these things are, they were not the things that brought on world destruction. What provoked God's anger in Noah's day was not the various outer symptoms of sin that disturb us today, but the self-centeredness which is really unbelief, of people who felt they didn't need God or anybody else outside of their selfish circles. God apparently could take their egotism and arrogance no longer. He simply turned on the water.

Whether or not it is the wickedness of God's children that will bring on the end of the world as we know it, Jesus uses the Old Testament event to illustrate the suddenness and unexpectedness of His final appearance. Irrespective of the numerous would-be prophets and their predictions, "the Son of man is coming at an hour you do not expect." Escape from that judgment is possible only by faith in Him who stayed the hand of God from utterly destroying the rebellious world.

Almighty God, while my relationship to You is a joyful and fulfilling day-by-day experience, it is accompanied by solemnity and concern as I consider the uncountable millions who know You not. Have mercy upon them, my Lord. Amen.

Time to Get Up

It is full time now for you to wake from sleep. v. 11

It is time to get up and "put on the Lord Jesus Christ." "The night is far gone, the day is at hand," wrote Paul, and that is as close as he comes to making any predictions in respect to Christ's coming and the final gathering together of God's children into His eternal kingdom. While Paul warned against date-setting and even reprimanded some of his readers for giving up their jobs and daily duties to ready themselves for Christ's promised return, he was filled with anticipation and expectation concerning that great and ultimate event.

There is, nonetheless, something we can do as we anticipate that incomprehensible happening. It is to "put on the Lord Jesus Christ," to emulate Jesus, to walk with God as He has been revealed through Christ. This most certainly means a daily "dying" to those things within our natures and our world that come between us and God—and between us and our fellow beings. It means, as well, that we work as servants and ministers of the kingdom to which we already belong. As God came to us through Christ, so Christ seeks to reach our brothers and sisters in the human family through us.

We are to live and act as if the kingdom has already been revealed, the sun already risen, for even while there is much darkness about us, Christ *has* come, the kingdom of God *is* here. We are to "cast off the works of darkness" and live and love, minister and serve, as God's sons and daughters are destined to do. It is as we do this that the coming dawn dispels all fear and fills our beings with joy and exaltation.

I pray, O Lord, that You forgive me for all the foolish things that clutter up my life and render me less than effective as Your servant in these end-time days of this dispensation. Amen.

Amazing Grace

I give thanks to God . . . because of the grace of God which was given you in Christ Jesus. v. 4

It is the very grace of God that makes us capable of being and doing what He would have us to be and do. By His grace we were received into God's family through Christ's redeeming love. By His grace we are made guiltless and will be sustained and kept to and beyond the end of this world. Because of His grace we are gifted—enriched with all the provision and power needed to carry out His plans for us in this life and within this world. Paul insists that we are "not lacking in any spiritual gift" as we work and wait "for the revealing of our Lord Jesus Christ."

This is amazing, astounding—almost unbelievable! Yet it is true. We need not bemoan our inadequacies nor envy our colleagues who appear to be better endowed than we. We are redeemed, forgiven, ordained for service in God's kingdom, and empowered to carry out our assignment as God's messengers and ministers.

Something we must do, however, as the dawn of the new kingdom turns into the full light of day, is to act on our assignment, to utilize God's gracious gifts for the benefit of others. We must renew our commitment to God and His purposes and yield our bodies and beings to His control. God is faithful; we must walk in faith and serve in loving obedience as His responsible servants within His eternal kingdom.

Help us, our God, to sense Your loving presence and to lay hold of Your grace which You have assured us is sufficient to keep us steady and faithful whatever the storms that beat upon us. We rejoice and praise You because of Your amazing grace! Amen.

Living in the Shadows

*Take heed to yourselves lest . . . that day come upon you suddenly
like a snare.* v. 34

Thomas Campbell, a poet of the last century, once penned
these words: "'Tis the sunset of life gives mystical lore, and coming
events cast their shadows before." We are living in the shadows.
The gaiety, the buying and selling activity, the sensuality and
superficiality about us do not succeed in obliterating these shadows.

There are shadows flitting across our paths that are both
ominous and exhilarating. We may not see much happening "in sun
and moon and stars," but the things that transpire about us, the wild
commotions and calamities that engulf the nations of the earth, the
fears and forebodings that afflict the hearts of men and women, may
indeed indicate that our "redemption is drawing near." While
people wonder what the world is coming to, we are wondering
what is coming to our world. Whatever the event these shadows
portend, it is time that we "take heed" to ourselves, to make
preparations, not in fear of the things to come, but by faith in the
God who has come, who is here, and who at any moment may
consummate His purposes for this planet on which we live.

It is time that we cease shadow-boxing with God, get off the
fence, and begin making some genuine decisions in respect to our
relationship with Him. It is time that we who claim to follow Christ
begin to act like the Christ we follow. It is time that we desist from
our competitive, profit-and-gain aspirations, recognize the human
family as our family, and dedicate our lives and means to God and
His purposes and share our abundance with our brothers and sisters
throughout the world. It is time that we who are God's children
begin to recognize who we are and demonstrate the joy of that
relationship to our fellow beings about us. It is time that we wake
up and look up, for "the kingdom of God is near."

Aware of the times in which I live and of Your purposes for
my life, I sincerely renew my commitment to You and pray
that You will have Your way with me. Amen.

Ready for His Coming

May the Lord make you increase and abound in love to one another.
v. 12

As we contemplate "the coming of our Lord Jesus with all His saints," we are lovingly concerned about our dear friends, our brothers and sisters in the Lord, who are faithfully laboring and serving in the various arenas in which God through call or circumstance has placed them.

We are grateful for them. They are our colleagues in kingdom service and, whether their station be high or low, out front or behind the scenes, their contributions are vital to the purposes of our Father.

We must remember them in our prayers—these brothers and sisters of ours. We sincerely hope they remember us in their meditations before God.

God grant that our love for one another is increased and enriched as we work within His kingdom and anticipate the coming of our Lord Jesus Christ to consummate our labors upon this earth. It is such love, our love for another, through which our God strengthens and sustains us in those difficult hours when our efforts appear to bear so little fruit.

Of this we can be sure: As we individually and mutually lay claim to God's righteousness as revealed and made available through Jesus Christ and abound in our love for one another and thereby become effective vehicles of His love to others about us, our hearts will be "unblamable in holiness before our God and Father at the coming of our Lord Jesus with all His saints."

As we embrace You, O Christ, as our Lord and Savior, we are ready for Your coming, whenever that may be. We pray that those we know and love may also be ready. We pray especially for our colleagues who are faithfully laboring in Your vineyard. Grant them comfort and joy as they carry out their duties even while they look forward to Your approaching kingdom. Amen.

Promises, Promises

Behold, the days are coming when I will fulfill the promise I made . . . v. 14a

The pages of the Old Testament—along with its portrayal of many conflicts and struggles—are permeated with bright flashes of divine light. They revealed, through inspired prophets such as Jeremiah, the plan of God to execute righteousness amidst this world's darkness.

We live in the day of promise-fulfillment. God has visited this planet. This is what Christmas is all about. Through Jesus Christ, God-incarnate, His righteousness has been manifested and made available to this world's inhabitants, and the Judah and Jerusalem that Jeremiah referred to becomes the church that embraces the blessed recipients of this divinely-imparted righteousness.

Inherent in Jeremiah's prophecy is the great event that is still to come—the final revelation and gathering together of God's kingdom of righteousness that will become the new and eternal Judah and Jerusalem. It is a part of Jeremiah's prophecy; it is an integral part of what is even now being fulfilled. We are citizens of that promised kingdom. We are servants of God who are working by His grace and indwelling Spirit towards its fulfillment. We look forward with anticipation and joy to its consummation.

Promises, promises. We live even now among fulfilled promises. The ultimate fulfillment is not yet, but when it happens we will be a part of it even as we are now observers and participants in the prophet's proclamations and promises.

As Your ancient promises concerning Your first coming to us was surely fulfilled in the coming of Christ, so will Your promise of Your final coming to gather us together into Your ultimate kingdom. We believe, our Lord, and we shall love and serve You forever. Amen.

The Need for a Changed Heart

Prepare the way of the Lord, make His paths straight. v. 3b

"Repent, for the kingdom of heaven is at hand," was John the Baptist's message to those who gathered to hear him in the Judean wilderness. He was preparing the way for Jesus' entrance into His public ministry. "You must change your hearts," John cried, "for God's kingdom has arrived."

It means that we must tear down, by the grace God grants, those obstructions that stand between us and our God—the deceit, the hypocrisy, the pride and self-sufficiency, the inordinate affection for the things of this world. They must be stripped from us as if they were plague-infested garments, for they come between us and the Christ of Christmas, between us and Christmas joy, between us and eternal life.

John the Baptist didn't stop there—though we often do. "Bear fruit that befits repentance," he challenged. "Go and do something to show that your hearts are really changed," he says in essence. It is this second half of the Gospel that we tend to ignore. John said it and Jesus reiterated it, that the tree, or the life, "that does not bear good fruit is cut down and thrown into the fire." We cherish Christ's invitation to "come" unto Him; God grant that we hear and obey His command to "go" with Him—into the dark places of this world to channel His life and power into the hearts and lives of hungry, oppressed, unregenerate people.

I praise and thank You, my Lord, for the grace that saves us and Your gift of righteousness that covers us, and the power that infills and works out Your purposes through us. I pray that my life will in some way reveal Your love for Your creatures and bear fruit and will draw people into Your saving grace. Amen.

Abounding Hope

May the God of hope fill you with all joy and peace in believing.

We would like to begin each day with a smattering of ecstasy—rising to our feet with happiness in our hearts and hallelujahs on our lips. There are those days, however, when we have to settle for hope. Spiritual ecstasies may be few and far between, but hope abounds forever. Even the dark days of our lives are pregnant with hope. Behind the heavy clouds that threaten is the sun that will eventually burn them away and flood dull lives with light and joy. Thus there is hope; always there is hope.

The Scriptures encourage us and give us hope—as do the lives of those suffering saints before us. God loves us; Christ has come to declare and demonstrate that love. We may not always *feel* this to be true, but it is true nonetheless, and this is the source of the everlasting joy that overcomes our bouts with depression and undergirds our lives with that incomprehensible peace that is not obliterated by the tempests of this daily existence.

We can begin each day with praises on our lips—no matter how heavy the heart. Indeed, as we praise God for the facts concerning our redemption and adoption as His children, for His eternal and unchanging love as our heavenly Father, the heart's burdens are lifted, the sun breaks through the clouds, and we continue, by the power of the Holy Spirit, to "abound in hope."

Help me, dear Lord, to be faithful and obedient to Your hope before me and to the voice of Your Spirit within me, and allow my praises to continue throughout this day, reflecting Your love and glory in all my relationships and activities. Amen.

This Is It!

The beginning of the gospel of Jesus Christ, the Son of God. v. 1

Advent is the beginning of the Church Year. We begin all over again to read and rejoice in God's story. The first Gospel that was ever written was probably the Gospel according to Mark. He was a realist. He doesn't take the time to philosophize or conjecture. His Gospel is the shortest of all the Gospels—and the bluntest—a sort of these-are-the-facts approach to the story of God and the presentation of Christ as God's fullest revelation of Himself and His purposes for His created world.

"Here begins the Gospel of Jesus Christ, the Son of God." What Mark is saying, in effect, is that "this is it!" This is what God has been preparing His creatures for throughout the centuries; this is what the prophets were dimly predicting as their minds slowly opened to God's eternal truth. "This is it." This One, Jesus Christ, God's Son, is the answer to the aching longings of men and women throughout the ages, the healing and the cure for the twisted and distorted lives of God's human creatures, the canceling out of the debt of sin that has impregnated the lives of all people since the beginning of time, the way back to God's order and orbit, wherein alone there is peace and joy even in the midst of this life's fractures and failures.

"This is it," the purpose for our lives, the reason for our existence—and it is this that will restore us to that purpose and objective. This is the One who has come, who is here, and who confronts us today with the promise, as we embrace Him as our Savior and Lord, to enthrone Himself in our hearts through His Spirit and to make us His children and servants forever.

"Praise God from whom all blessings flow; praise Him all creatures here below!" When we could not come to You, You came to us. You are here; You are in our hearts and lives. We will love and serve You forever. Amen.

Waiting—Patiently and Faithfully

With the Lord one day is as a thousand years, and a thousand years as one day. v. 8

While scoffers treat the promise of Christ's return as sheer nonsense, the children of God are often impatiently awaiting that great event. They ought to regard the fact that He is "slow about His promise with joy," suggested Peter. His immediate return would indeed deliver us from a multitude of trials and temptations that frustrate us and from atrocities that frighten and threaten to destroy us, but might also seal the fate of scores of our friends and relatives—our brothers and sisters in the human family—who have not as yet surrendered to His redeeming love and salvation. God is still waiting for His created children to separate themselves from the degradation of this planet and return to His plan and orbit for their lives. The desire of His loving heart is that they, too, will be ready to greet the Christ when He returns.

In the meantime, we are to wait patiently and serve faithfully. We do not know the day or the hour, not even the year or the century, of His coming. We only know that we belong to Him, and as long as we continue committedly and joyfully to labor within His purposes, we are ready for the fulfillment of His promised return.

In obediently and lovingly serving Him and our fellow beings, we may even bring closer that Day of His final and ultimate revelation.

O Lord, I confess my impatience with the world that is falling apart, and with families that are coming apart, and with the insurmountable problems that cannot be solved, with racism and violence and corruption in high places. I wait desperately for Your final return to our world. Grant to me the grace to wait patiently and serve faithfully. Amen.

Getting Ready for God

Prepare the way of the Lord. v. 4

As John the Baptist was sent by the Spirit to ready the people for God-revealed-through-Christ's ministry, so we must prepare the way for Christ's entrance into and ministry through our lives. Christ's initial coming was demonstrated in the Christmas event and the manger scene. His coming into His public ministry was signaled by John the Baptist. As with Isaiah's picture of the preparation necessary to make possible the journey of an ancient monarch, so the Spirit of God must make possible God's march and manifestation through us.

The Spirit of Christ has to *fill up the valleys in our lives.* This refers to the elimination of those gaping holes that become monumental evidences of our vain efforts and endeavors to find meaning and purpose in life apart from Christ. "Every valley shall be filled," wrote Isaiah, and this is what happens when Christ has His way in and through us.

God's Spirit must *tear down the mountains and hills,* the obstructions and obstacles that stand in His way. The smallest molehill may be the greatest mountain as long as it stands between us and God.

The Spirit of God must *straighten out the crooked paths and make the rough ways smooth.* It means that all irregularities, hindrances, distortions, all that is shady and sinful, must be brought out of the dark corners of our inner beings and submitted to the judgment and forgiveness of a loving God.

Christ will carry out His mission through us as long as we permit Him to fill the emptiness, tear down the obstacles, straighten the crooked paths, and through us reach out to touch others around us with His saving grace.

I pray, O God, that You will uproot and tear out anything and everything in my life that stands in the way of Your love and purposes in and through me. Amen.

Keep on Loving

He who began a good work in you will bring it to completion at the day of Jesus Christ. v. 6

In view of Christ's eventual second advent to this planet, it is Paul's prayer that the love of his Christian brothers and sisters will continue to increase and to abound—along with the gifts of knowledge and discernment. And this in order that they may be "filled with the fruits of righteousness which come through Jesus Christ."

Paul's injunction is to keep on loving—loving God and loving one another. We need, in these precarious days, not only the everflowing grace of God which comes to us through His Spirit by way of Word and Sacrament, but the strength and encouragement that comes through loving relationships with one another.

We can be as certain as was Paul that God, who adopted us as His children and gifted us with His Spirit, will complete this great thing He has done for us "at the Day of Jesus Christ." Let us pray as Paul prayed that we may be "filled with the fruits of righteousness which come through Jesus Christ" and that our lives today and always may be lived "to the glory and praise of God."

Thus, whatever the difficulties this day and this life hold for us, we must keep on loving. Whether or not others reciprocate and respond to our love, we must keep on loving—our family, friends, adversaries, especially our fellow laborers within the kingdom of God. This is God's role for us in our world today.

God help us to keep on loving!

Gracious heavenly Father, You have sent Your Son to reveal Your love for me and all Your creatures in our world. May that love impel me to risk loving and thereby relate the knowledge and experience of Your love to others about me. Amen.

364

A Comforting God

He will feed His flock like a shepherd, He will gather the lambs in His arms. v. 11a

The Old Testament seems, at times, to be overweighted with frightening visions and prophecies of God as the One who would enforce justice upon this world—a sort of warring God who would lead heavenly armies against the enemies of righteousness and destroy idol-worshipers and wicked rulers and all those people and things that stand between Him and His purposes for this world and its creatures. Every now and then, however, prophets and poets saw or envisioned something of the Almighty's loving concern for His created children. They beheld Him not only as a God of justice and righteousness, but as One who seeks to comfort His children within an unjust, atrocity-ridden world.

"He will feed His flock like a shepherd," announces Isaiah. "The Lord is my shepherd, I shall not want," said the psalmist. God will come—indeed He has come—not only to judge, to rule, and ultimately to destroy all that stands in the way of His kingdom, but to comfort His people, to "gather the lambs in His arms" and "carry them in His bosom."

It is this facet of God that is revealed through God-incarnate, Jesus Christ. Now we know that God loves us, cares about us, and comforts us as we strive to serve Him in our kind of world. And this is the Good News we are assigned to share with our suffering, struggling colleagues on this planet. This makes each day a joyful and significant one.

I praise You, my Lord, for Your words of comfort and challenge through the prophets and apostles and the uncountable saints that have gone before me, and for the gift of Your Spirit within me. These will sustain me, loving God, whatever I must face on my journey. Amen.

John's Question—Christ's Response

Are you He who is to come, or shall we look for another? v. 3

John the Baptist's blunt and courageous tongue soon talked him into jail and execution, but not before he baptized a plain, simple son-of-a-carpenter called Jesus and received a sign from God that this man was God's Son who was sent to establish and build His Father's kingdom. While marking time in Herod's prison, John was anticipating and assuming that this Jesus, whom he had announced and introduced to the crowds that followed him, would be uniting Israel to resist Herod and Rome and reign over a rebellious world as God's chosen people. This obviously was not happening, and so John asked his comrades to go out and see what Jesus was doing— to find out if this man was truly the Christ, the Messiah, who was to come. "Are you He who is to come, or shall we look for another?" they asked Him.

Jesus, who dearly loved and deeply respected John, did not respond directly to their inquiry. He simply stated: "Go and tell John what you hear and see: the blind receive their sight and the lame walk, lepers are cleansed and the deaf hear, and the dead are raised up, and the poor have good news preached to them."

Salvation is by faith, not works. While it is essential to proclaim this, our salvation ought to be dramatized by going where Jesus goes, doing what He does—out there in the world—relating to God's creatures in love, drawing them to God's eternal love and grace through acts of sacrificial service, healing, helping, sharing, communicating God's divine power to humanity about us. This is what it means to be, in Luther's words, "a little Christ" in our world today.

Help me to understand, dear Lord, that faith is not simply a leisurely abiding in what you have done for me, but is also striving and sometimes struggling to lay hold of Your gifts in order to serve others. Amen.

God Will Intervene

Establish your hearts, for the coming of the Lord is at hand. v. 8b

Whereas we may not be riddled by fear in the midst of the ugly, atrocious things that transpire in the world about us, we are often uneasy, frustrated, and sometimes very angry. Almost every newscast violates our sensibilities, and we inwardly call out for divine intervention in this planet's sad state of affairs. The world is well on its way to self-annihilation, and the children of God are apparently helpless and incapable of arresting its mad rush to destruction. We sometimes wish the world would stop and let us get off—sincerely feeling that we cannot put up with it any longer.

Neither James nor any other of the apostles held any high hopes for the world as such. Their hopes and their faith were in the promises and purposes of God as revealed through Jesus Christ. God will intervene; the Lord will come, they insisted. Their message was needed in their day; it is needed as much or more in our day. "Be patient"—as were the ancient prophets—shore up your failing hearts; "the coming of the Lord is at hand."

We will not accomplish anything for God by fretting about this world's conditions or focusing all our energies on praying for His immediate return. It is important that we recognize the Christ who came at Christmas, who sent His Spirit at Pentecost, and who is here even now indwelling His redeemed brothers and sisters, the sons and daughters of God, and that we dedicate our lives to carrying on toward fulfillment the objectives of our heavenly Father.

He will come; "the coming of the Lord is at hand." We must be patient, obedient, and faithful.

God of all creation, King of all the universe, remind our restless hearts of Your great intervention at Christmas, and Your promise to unite us totally with Yourself and Your kingdom at Your next and final great intervention. Amen.

One Whom You Do Not Know

I am the voice of one crying in the wilderness. v. 23a

John may not have realized the full significance of his classic statement to the priests and Levites, but it has characterized humankind in its relationship to God from the very beginning of history. "Among you stands One whom you do not know." It was true of the ancient Jews during the period of the judges, the fall of the kingdom of Israel, the Babylonian Exile. Even as multitudes were being converted under John the Baptist's fiery preaching and were baptized at the Jordan River, "among them stood One whom they did not know."

Even to this day when the birthday of Christ is celebrated throughout the world and honored throughout the churches where the Gospel is repeatedly proclaimed, men and women still do not know Him and the masses give only slight acknowledgment of Him.

How can Christmas mean what it is designed to mean to us this year? John gives the answer: "Behold, the Lamb of God, who takes away the sin of the world!" There is no other way to discover the true meaning of Christmas. God has come to this planet; God has made Himself known, available, revealing Himself in such a way that His creatures might know and love and worship and serve Him. It is when we are willing to accept and follow Jesus Christ as our Savior, Lord, and King, that we will truly know the Christ who came at Christmas.

"Joy to the world! the Lord has come; let earth receive her King." I thank You, my Lord, for all Your prophets and apostles and priests and ministers throughout the ages, who have made You known and reachable to me and my brothers and sisters in the human family. Amen.

In All Circumstances—Give Thanks

For this is the will of God in Christ Jesus for you. v. 18b

"Rejoice always, pray constantly, give thanks in all circumstances." Paul sounds like a fanatic. In view of the pain and misery that circumvent this world, how can one rejoice at all? In the midst of the fast-paced living and the innumerable, unreasonable demands that plague us today, how is it possible to be continuously engaged in prayer? And to "give thanks in all circumstances?" It sounds like a person who is possessed or obsessed; it is utterly unrealistic. Yet Paul defines this as "the will of God" for His children.

Paul did not have rocks in his head—he had Christ in his heart—and he found that it was possible to be joyful and thankful even in the face of the dire circumstances that afflict this planet and its inhabitants.

Paradoxical as it may appear, it is only when a person does find joy and peace—acknowledged with gratitude—in a redeeming and reconciling relationship with God that he or she can stand firm amidst this world's tempests and effectively relate to people in the midst of its distortions and dissipations. Whereas God's children cannot be grateful for the ugly things that happen to them or about them, they can be joyful and grateful in the assurance that God is not the author of such things and is indeed pained by them and promises to keep His own spiritually secure irrespective of the horrendous things that afflict this earth.

"God's will" for His children is not the ugly circumstances they confront; it is the kind of abiding in Him and relationship of love and trust to Him that is demonstrated in rejoicing, prayer, and thanksgiving despite the conditions and circumstances of the world around them.

There are indeed reasons for rejoicing, my Lord, and this despite the difficult and sometimes tragic circumstances that befall most members of this human family. I praise and rejoice in You, O Christ. Amen.

Sharing One's Shirts

Bear fruits that befit repentance . . . v. 8a

We may have difficulty in accepting John the Baptist as the forerunner or introducer of Christ, as the one who was to bring down mountains and smooth out rough roads for that One who was to follow him. It certainly was not a very popular ministry, though by his strange appearance and fiery proclamations he brought back nostalgic and nervous memories to the crowds gathered to hear him speak. He looked and sounded like a prophet out of the ancient past. He spoke a language they could understand and to which they could respond. But it was a far cry from the let-Jesus-come-into-your-hearts injunctions we have been subjected to throughout our lives. He came on like a bulldozer, blasting away the foolish facades that people hide behind, driving his listeners to their knees in recognition of the spiritual poverty and the emptiness of their lives.

"What then shall we do?" they cried. John's reply was simple and to the point: "The man with two shirts must share with him who has none" (NEB).

We are tempted to relegate the do-or-die message of John the Baptist to the realm of Old Testament obscurity. We like the words of Jesus better—those words, at least, that appear to carry little threat to our awesome indifference to the needs of the masses about us or our apathy in the face of the inhumanity perpetrated upon those masses. We have "let Jesus come into our hearts." We make regular visits to our religious shrines. We assume that this puts us in solid with God. But every now and then we are brought up short with the possibility that this "shirt-sharing" demand is as relevant to our theology as is the Apostles' Creed.

Is it possible, my Lord, that the number of shirts in my closet, my middle-class prosperity over against the multitudes of de-prived, may point up a serious flaw in my relationship to You? O Lord, have mercy. Amen.

Rejoice Always?

Have no anxiety about anything . . . v. 6

A letter from my English authoress friend jolted me out of my mid-winter malaise: "Paul encouraged the Philippians to 'rejoice in the Lord always,' and he himself exemplified an inner state of permanent happiness," she wrote. "It was as if joy were completely independent of or able to transcend the situation in which he and his fellow believers found themselves. 'That's all very well,' we may say. 'Life is far more complicated now. How can modern Christians possibly rejoice always in this corrupt society?' We can if we open ourselves to the same Spirit of the Christ that filled the early church. That has not changed nor ever will."

Paul then follows with another fantastic injunction: "Have no anxiety about anything . . ." We might understand if he had written this letter after a huge lottery winning, but he probably wrote it in some Roman jail. Yet he who experienced both sorrow and anxiety in his day of persecution was able to charge his readers in Philippi to "rejoice in the Lord always" and "have no anxiety about anything."

As long as we are on this planet there will be both sorrows and anxieties to contend with. Some of them are a very necessary part of our experience—and may even contribute to our development as God's children and servants. Most of our bouts with depression and anxiety are unnecessary and possibly destructive to our health and our attempts to serve God and fellow beings. My friend in England is right; we should be enabled to rid ourselves of these debilitating periods of doubt, fear, worry, and despair "if we open ourselves to the same Spirit of the Christ that filled the early church."

"Spirit of the living God, fall afresh on me. Melt me. Mold me. Fill me. Use me. Spirit of the living God, fall afresh on me." Amen.

Christ for Everyone

[God] has anointed me to bring good tidings to the afflicted . . . bind up the broken-hearted . . . proclaim liberty to the captives . . . v. 1a

One reason this Scripture portion out of the Old Testament has become a most important and memorable piece of literature is because it was the lesson Jesus read and commented on in what may have been the first sermon He ever preached. The scene of His "baptism of fire" in respect to His preaching ministry was His hometown, Nazareth, where He lived in His youth. His listeners thought well of His choice of Scripture and were quite impressed by His interpretation and application of these words of Isaiah.

Not for long, however. When Jesus attempted to place before His listeners the real challenge of Isaiah's words—what they really meant or ought to mean to these synagogue-goers, they became very provoked and proceeded to evict Him from their place of worship and their city.

Jesus obviously saw elements of truth behind Isaiah's prophecy that those worshipers were not able or willing to embrace and which Isaiah himself may not have fully understood. Isaiah, whether he realized it or not, was proclaiming the positive message that God's love is for the world and all men and women, Jew or Gentile, white or black, and was revealing God's plan to minister such love and grace to the physical hurts as well as the spiritual needs of every human being.

Isaiah is saying, in effect, that the challenge of social service, the plea for human justice and dignity, the endeavor to lovingly and sacrificially reach out to our debased, oppressed, disenfranchised brothers and sisters about us, is a necessary fruit of the same Gospel that offers the forgiveness and acceptance and grace and love of God. This is God's commission to every one of us—what He empowers us for and expects us to do.

All-loving God, may my acceptance of Your great love be reflected in and demonstrated by my love for all Your creatures about me. Amen.

A Significant Happening

Behold, a virgin shall conceive and bear a son, and His name shall be called Emmanuel. v. 23

The Bible reports and interprets significant happenings. Whereas all of them may be significant, the most important to our faith are those which relate to Jesus Christ, God-incarnate. They are not abstractions or theories or pantheistic generalities, but concrete, actual events localized in time and space. Long before Christmas, even with creation itself, God revealed Himself in omnipotent action. At Christmas, through the Christ of Christmas, He became visible before humankind and began to relate to people in redeeming love.

"Faith in Jesus Christ," wrote Emil Brunner, "is not an interpretation of the world, but it is participation in an event, in something which has happened, and which is going to happen." In other words, either in Christ, God the Creator and Redeemer came right into human life or else the Gospels are the record of some conspired fallacy. Either God was born in a manger, God ascended the cross, God bore our sins on our behalf and arose from the dead, or else Christmas—and Easter—are a gigantic farce.

This is the central miracle of Christianity—the Incarnation. Every other true miracle prepares for this, or exhibits this, or results from this. It was toward this, the Incarnation, that everything moved until its accomplishment, finding therein fulfillment and explanation. It is from this, the Incarnation, that all subsequent movements have proceeded, depending upon it for direction and dynamic.

As Christians we believe, by the grace of God, that these happenings are more significant than anything else in life.

"Love caused Thine incarnation, love brought Thee down to me; Thy thirst for my salvation procured my liberty. O love beyond all telling that led Thee to embrace, in love all love excelling, our lost and fallen race." Amen.

God Is with Us!

The child to be born will be called holy, the Son of God. v. 35b

It is true! God has visited our planet! He broke through into our dimension of existence. We may never comprehend just how or why, but God, Eternal, All-Glorious, Infinite Spirit, has come to us— as a baby!

As incredible as it is, it was to a young Jewish girl, very poor, who held no position or prominence among her peers, that God sent the angel Gabriel with the earthshaking announcement that she was chosen by God to be the mother of the Messiah, the Lord Jesus Christ. Thus it happened as it was announced, and this poor, insignificant girl was destined to become the most significant and heralded woman in the civilized world.

Her significance is, of course, because of the magnificence of Christ, to whom she gave birth. Jesus Christ was the One about whom the prophets had spoken and whom the children of Israel had anticipated throughout the centuries. It was this One, God-incarnate, the Word made flesh, who would draw God's human creatures back into His loving orbit for their lives and bring joy and peace and significance back into the lives of the poor, the oppressed, the despairing inhabitants of this distorted world.

It is God's act through the virgin Mary and God's coming to us through the birth of Jesus that makes not only that Jewish teenager, but every one of us, significant as God's children and as His servants and disciples.

"Here am I," said Mary to the angel. "I am the Lord's servant; as you have spoken, so be it" (NEB). It is this that ought to be our prayer to God who is now with us.

"Come, Jesus, glorious heavenly guest, keep Thine own Christmas in our breast." I pray that the Mass of Christmas may be a daily event in my life and living. Amen.

Blessed Are Those Who Believe

Blessed are you among women, and blessed is the fruit of your womb! v. 42

"With God nothing will be impossible," said the angel to Mary. Mary indeed discovered this to be true. Not only was it declared by a heavenly creature that she would give birth to the Son of God, but her kinswoman, Elizabeth, who was old and considered to be barren, conceived, and upon hearing Mary's greeting felt her baby move within her. Elizabeth's real joy, however, was in the touch of God's Spirit upon her, revealing that Mary was chosen by God to give birth to the Christ. It was probably this visit with Elizabeth—and what transpired there—that fully assured Mary that all that was said to her by the angel was true. She was really to be the mother of God's Son, to give birth to the Messiah, the Christ. Her heart rises in gratitude as her lips form the words of praise, the beautiful Magnificat.

Some things are untouchable and ought not be subjected to critical interpretation. One of them might well be the response of Mary to God's choice of her to give birth to His Son. It is an ecstatic song, flooded with praises to God and full of confidence in God's promise to accomplish His purposes through this humble handmaiden of the Lord. Yet it is a song that we, too, can sing. As it was with Mary and her very special appointment and subsequent contribution as God's servant, so all of us are redeemed, adopted, and appointed to be God's children and servants in this world He has created. In an amazing way God is also born in us and through His Spirit reaches out through us to accomplish His purposes in the world around us.

"Our souls magnify the Lord and our spirits rejoice in God our Savior . . . For He who is mighty has done great things for us, and holy is His name." Lo, we, too, are here, O Lord. And we truly want to believe and to do Your will for our lives. Amen.

Christmas—It Really Happened!

To you is born this day . . . a Savior who is Christ the Lord. v. 11

Christmas—it really happened! God has visited our planet! He broke through into our dimension of existence. We may never comprehend how or even why, but the fact is He came by way of the Bethlehem manger. This great One who astounded the masses with His out-of-this-world feats and amazed people with His out-of this-world teachings, whom no one is really able to ignore, who drew men's thoughts to Himself with a mysterious power, who rises in stature above all even as He was nailed on a cross by those who hated Him, and who conquered over death itself as He arose from the grave—He came to us by way of the manger!

It's a true story! The people around this incredible event are real: Caesar Augustus, Cyrenius, Mary, Joseph, and the Christ Child. It is a story that needs to be told again and again. Catching the world with its head in the emptiness of outer space or the dumps of existential despair, Christmas proclaims what our world desperately needs to hear and to take to heart. Christmas really happened; God has visited our planet. Perhaps this manger-happening is the only way God could come to us. We could never approach the Holy and All Righteous God, anymore than we can draw near to the sun that blazes in our sky. Thus God condescended to come to us—by way of the manger. Christmas really happened, and because it happened we are assured of God's love for and acceptance of us. We are loved and accepted not simply as a part of humanity's masses but as individual entities and personalities. And it is this that gives meaning and purpose to our lives.

"O holy Child of Bethlehem, descend to us, we pray. Cast out our sin, and enter in, be born in us today. We hear the Christmas angels the great glad tidings tell. O come to us, abide with us, our Lord Immanuel!" Amen.

The Purpose of Christmas

By [God's] will we have been sanctified through the offering of the body of Jesus Christ once for all. v. 10

"Lo, I have come to do Thy will, O God." These were the very words of Christ according to the author of the Letter to the Hebrews. This was the purpose of His coming, of His first Advent, which we celebrate this Christmas—to carry out the purposes and objectives of His Father. The day of sacrifices and burnt offerings had passed. The Law of God as revealed through the Old Testament was incapable of reconciling men and women to God. It had, nonetheless, prepared the way for the next order of events, whereby God Himself would come to His human creatures through Jesus Christ and through the single sacrifice of His Son make it possible for the inhabitants of this world to be redeemed and reconciled to their Creator.

This would happen—and did happen—because Jesus, God-incarnate, came to this planet and carried out God's will even to the point of offering up His own body on the cross as the one, single sacrifice sufficient to atone for all the sins of the human family.

Now God's redeemed creatures are drawn into the blessed, loving will of God. They are, in a sense, Christ-incarnate, appointed and destined to offer up their lives in the course of carrying out the Father's purposes in this world. They present their bodies and beings as living sacrifices—offered up to God on the altar of their neighbor's need.

While Jesus presented the all-sufficient sacrifice on our behalf, there is a sacrifice for us to offer, a cross for us to carry, not to secure our salvation, but to proclaim and demonstrate the Good News of God's saving love to our fellow-beings.

"Lo, we are here to do Your will, O God." Grant to us the courage and wisdom to give our lives back to You by presenting our bodies as living sacrifices on the altar of our neighbor's need. Amen.

Debts and Obligations

Through whom we have received grace . . . to bring about obedience to the faith for the sake of His name among all nations. v. 5

The apostle Paul introduces himself to the church at Rome as one who is set apart for God and His purposes. He thus speaks on behalf of all God's children and servants. The Good News was first promised and proclaimed through the prophets in the ancient Scriptures and has now been revealed through God-incarnate, the resurrection Christ, God's Son and our Lord and Master. It is through Christ that we have been commissioned and empowered to communicate and convey this Gospel, the Good News of God's saving love, to the human family throughout the world.

This is something to really celebrate. The blessed Word of God has been enfleshed in us. And while we celebrate, we need, as well, to continually remind one another of this splendid truth and encourage one another to be faithful to our adoption as God's children and our appointment as His servants.

Paul goes on to say that because of our great deliverance, we are obligated and indebted to every man, woman, and child. Our assignment is to love them into God's kingdom, to demonstrate in our lives and living, to proclaim in our speaking and writing, to reflect in our concern and caring our great God's love for His human creatures.

We could not come to You, our loving God, so You have through the Christ of Christmas sought us out. You have made Yourself known to our world through Your Son. And You continue to come into the hearts of all those who are open to You and Your will for their lives. May Your coming give us strength and throw light on our dark paths and make us the vehicles and messengers of Your gifts of grace to the hearts and lives of others. Amen.

He Is Able

That . . . kept secret for long ages [is now] disclosed and through the prophetic writings is made known to all nations . . . v. 26

"To Him who is able to strengthen you," wrote Paul in the final paragraph of his letter to the church at Rome, "according to my Gospel and the preaching of Jesus Christ, according to the revelation of the mystery which was kept secret for long ages but is now disclosed and through the prophetic writings is made known . . . according to the command of the eternal God . . ."

It means that we have a lot going for us—we who are, through faith in Christ's manger birth and atoning death, the adopted and redeemed sons and daughters of God and who work and serve in the "obedience of faith." We have a God who came to us. This is what we celebrate at Christmas—and every day of the year. We have a God who goes with us into busy streets and high-pressure jobs, through difficult days and dark, lonely nights, and crises and conflicts, depression and despair. Christmas means that we need not face any of these things alone. God is with us—and He is able to strengthen and secure us whatever the consternations and circumstances that come our way.

It is no wonder that Paul concludes his remarkable letter to the persecuted church of Rome with praise: "to the only wise God be glory for evermore through Jesus Christ! Amen."

You came to us, our Lord, by way of the stable and the manger and the womb of a woman. And You came to be our Savior and our King. You have broken through the distortions and darkness of sin to prepare a way of salvation for every human creature. Enable us now, O God, to follow that One You have sent and to discover the joys of Your love and grace. Amen.

Crown Him as King

Jesus, remember me when You come into Your kingdom. v. 42

"He saved others; let Him save Himself," scoffed the rulers of the people. "If You are the King of the Jews, save Yourself," the soldiers mocked.

It was precisely because He did come to save others that He could not save Himself. It was necessary that He die for the sins of the people. It is not surprising that the religious leaders of His day could not understand all this and had to revert to mocking and scoffing. We cannot fully understand it. Yet this was the manner in which the kingdom of God was initiated among God's creatures. "Therefore," said the writer of the Letter to the Hebrews, "let us be grateful for receiving a kingdom that cannot be shaken . . ." (12:28). And Luther wrote in his famous hymn: "The Word they still shall let remain nor any thanks have for it; He's by our side upon the plain with his good gifts and Spirit. And take they our life, goods, fame, child, and wife. Though these all be gone, our victory has been won; the Kingdom ours remaineth." This is the certainty that encompasses the true followers of Jesus Christ, to whom He said: "Fear not, little flock, for it is your Father's good pleasure to give you the Kingdom" (Luke 12:32).

We crown Jesus as King; but if we crown Him King at all, we must crown Him King of all. He is with us today, leading us to high adventure, self-denial, danger, sacrifice, for nothing is too great to risk or to lose for the sake of the kingdom. He will be with us through all eternity in the kingdom of God, where He truly will be King of all and over all forevermore.

O Christ, who came by way of the manger; who died on the cross; who arose from the grave victorious over sin and death; You truly are my King, and I praise You, applaud You, and surrender my life to Your service throughout this life and for all eternity. Amen.

Our King Is Coming

I am the Alpha and the Omega . . . who is and who was and who is to come, the Almighty. v. 8

"Behold, He is coming with the clouds, and every eye shall see Him, everyone who pierced Him; and all the tribes of the earth will wail on account of Him."

One can perceive an excited writer in these words of John. It is almost as if he had just received a message from the great beyond and could hardly wait to pass it on to the suffering, persecuted Christians throughout the then-known world. There are, no doubt, some staid, lethargic, apathetic Christians who need to be awakened and shaken up from time to time, but for most of Christendom the message is being proclaimed loudly today: "He is coming; our King is coming!"

Unfortunately, the concentration of many Christians on the coming King does not appear to inspire and motivate them for loving service to this world's inhabitants on behalf of their King. Rather it seems to numb them to the suffering about them and to their responsibility in the midst of it all.

May Christ the King be the king of our lives even now as He shall be forever in that kingdom to be revealed, and may the truth of His kingship spur us on to living our lives for Him and for our fellow human beings.

We have recognized You as our Savior, our Lord, and continue to praise and glorify You for accepting us just the way we are, for forgiving our sins and making us the children of God. Now we need to accept You as King, our Lord and Master, and to crown You in our lives and activities and surrender ourselves to You and Your purposes. This we want to do, O Christ, our King. Amen.

This Is Christ—Let Him Love You

For in Him all the fullness of God was pleased to dwell, and through Him to reconcile to Himself all things. vv. 19, 20

"[God] has delivered us from the dominion of darkness and transferred us to the kingdom of His beloved Son, in whom we have redemption, the forgiveness of sins."

Jesus did not make Himself King. He did what no king is ever expected to do. "[He] emptied Himself, taking the form of a servant, being born in the likeness of men . . . He humbled Himself and became obedient unto death, even death on a cross" (Philippians 2:7–8). It was God, His Father, who made Him King. And what a King we have! How gracious is our loving God to place us in His hands and under His domain! "Image of . . . God . . . first-born of all creation . . . In [Him] all the fullness of God was pleased to dwell, and through [Him] to reconcile to Himself all things . . . making peace by the blood of His cross." This is the Christ whom millions of people refuse to accept as the King of their lives, whom men and women scorn or ignore or crucify afresh in their unbelief and rebelliousness, whom many of us often hold back from or fail to trust and obey.

It is He who is our King. Do we dare to do any less than crown Him Lord of all? How can we ever withhold our love, our loyalty, our lives, and all we possess from the King of kings?

This is the end of the calendar year. Tomorrow we start over again. May we do so by adoring and celebrating the Christ of Christmas and the Christ of the Gospel, the Son of God, that One who has come to save us from our sins and who will come again to gather us into His kingdom. This is the Christ; let Him love us, comfort us, reign over us, sustain us, advance His kingdom on earth through us. This is the Christ, our Savior and Lord and King, and we are His forever.

We thank You, our Savior, Lord, and King, for loving us and keeping us through the year past. We renew our commitment to You and Your purposes for the year ahead and pray that we will be pleasing to You. Amen.